Tales
from the
Toolbox

**A collection of
behind-the-scenes
tales from Grand Prix
mechanics**

A selection of other great Veloce titles –

Those Were The Days ... Series
Alpine Trials & Rallies 1910-1973 (Pfundner)
American 'Independent' Automakers – AMC to Willys 1945 to 1960 (Mort)
American Station Wagons – The Golden Era 1950-1975 (Mort)
American Trucks of the 1950s (Mort)
American Trucks of the 1960s (Mort)
American Woodies 1928-1953 (Mort)
Anglo-American Cars from the 1930s to the 1970s (Mort)
Austerity Motoring (Bobbitt)
Austins, The last real (Peck)
Brighton National Speed Trials (Gardiner)
British Lorries of the 1950s (Bobbitt)
British Lorries of the 1960s (Bobbitt)
British Touring Car Racing (Collins)
British Police Cars (Walker)
British Woodies (Peck)
Café Racer Phenomenon, The (Walker)
Dune Buggy Phenomenon (Hale)
Dune Buggy Phenomenon Volume 2 (Hale)
Endurance Racing at Silverstone in the 1970s & 1980s (Parker)
Hot Rod & Stock Car Racing in Britain in the 1980s (Neil)
Last Real Austins, The, 1946-1959 (Peck)
MG's Abingdon Factory (Moylan)
Motor Racing at Brands Hatch in the Seventies (Parker)
Motor Racing at Brands Hatch in the Eighties (Parker)
Motor Racing at Crystal Palace (Collins)
Motor Racing at Goodwood in the Sixties (Gardiner)
Motor Racing at Nassau in the 1950s & 1960s (O'Neil)
Motor Racing at Oulton Park in the 1960s (McFadyen)
Motor Racing at Oulton Park in the 1970s (McFadyen)

Superprix (Page & Collins)
Three Wheelers (Bobbitt)

General
1½-litre GP Racing 1961-1965 (Whitelock)
AC Two-litre Saloons & Buckland Sportscars (Archibald)
Alfa Tipo 33 (McDonough & Collins)
André Lefebvre, and the cars he created at Voisin and Citroën (Beck)
Armstrong-Siddeley (Smith)
Art Deco and British Car Design (Down)
Autodrome (Collins & Ireland)
Autodrome 2 (Collins & Ireland)
Automotive Mascots (Kay & Springate)
Bahamas Speed Weeks, The (O'Neil)
Bentley Continental, Corniche and Azure (Bennett)
Bentley MkVI, Rolls-Royce Silver Wraith, Dawn & Cloud/Bentley R & S-Series (Nutland)
British Cars, The Complete Catalogue of, 1895-1975 (Culshaw & Horrobin)
BRM – A Mechanic's Tale (Salmon)
Bugatti Type 40 (Price)
Bugatti 46/50 Updated Edition (Price & Arbey)
Bugatti T44 & T49 (Price & Arbey)
Bugatti 57 2nd Edition (Price)
Cliff Allison, The Official Biography of – From the Fells to Ferrari (Gauld)
Edward Turner: The Man Behind the Motorcycles (Clew)
Fast Ladies – Female Racing Drivers 1888 to 1970 (Bouzanquet)
Ford Model Y (Roberts)
Jack Sears, The Official Biography of – Gentleman Jack (Gauld)
Jaguar, The Rise of (Price)
John Chatham – 'Mr Big Healey' – The Official Biography (Burr)
Lea-Francis Story, The (Price)
Lola – The Illustrated History

1957-1977) (Starkey)
Lola – All the Sports Racing & Single-seater Racing Cars 1978-1997 (Starkey)
Lola T70 – The Racing History & Individual Chassis Record 4th Edition (Starkey)
Lotus 49 (Oliver))
Monthléry, The Story of the Paris Autodrome (Boddy)
Motor Racing – Reflections of a Lost Era (Carter)
Motorcycle Apprentice (Cakebread)
Motorsport In colour, 1950s (Wainwright)
Peking to Paris 2007 (Young)
Rolls-Royce Silver Shadow/Bentley T Series Corniche & Camargue Revised & Enlarged Edition (Bobbitt)
Rolls-Royce Silver Spirit, Silver Spur & Bentley Mulsanne 2nd Edition (Bobbitt)
Speedway – Auto racing's ghost tracks (Collins & Ireland)
Toleman Story, The (Hilton)

From Veloce Publishing's new imprints:

Battle Cry!
Soviet General & field rank officer uniforms: 1955 to 1991 (Streather)

Hubble & Hattie
My dog is blind – but lives life to the full! (Horsky)
Smellorama – nose games for your dog (Theby)
Waggy Tails & Wheelchairs (Epp)
Winston ... the dog who changed my life (Klute)

www.veloce.co.uk

First published in November 2009 by Veloce Publishing Limited, 33 Trinity Street, Dorchester DT1 1TT, England.
Fax 01305 268864/e-mail info@veloce.co.uk or www.velocebooks.com.
ISBN: 978-1-84584-199-7 UPC: 6-36847-04199-1
Readers with ideas for automotive books, or books on other transport or related hobby subjects, are invited to write to the editorial director of Veloce Publishing at the above address.
British Library Cataloguing in Publication Data – A catalogue record for this book is available from the British Library. Typesetting, design and page make-up all by Veloce Publishing Ltd on Apple Mac. Printed in India by Replika Press.

Contents

Acknowledgements

This book would not have been possible without the wholehearted co-operation of the Grand Prix Mechanics Charitable Trust over a period of several years. Specifically, I would like to thank Trust Administrator Ann Wood, who went to great lengths to encourage, persuade and cajole mechanics on the register to make themselves available to me.

I would also like to thank Trust Chairman Sir Jackie Stewart OBE, who was enthusiastic about the project right from when it was first mooted, and has shown his support by providing the Foreword.

It is worth considering for a moment that, without the efforts of Sir Jackie, the Trust wouldn't exist today and all the good work that it does would not be possible. Since it was founded in 1987, Jackie has campaigned tirelessly on behalf of those he calls "the real professionals in the Formula 1 pitlane." However, as teams have grown considerably in size in recent decades, the need to draw on the Trust's reserves in the future may increase; therefore, it is vital that it continues to actively raise funds.

If you have bought this book you have already helped, because the Grand Prix Mechanics Charitable Trust receives 40 per cent of the royalties from every copy sold. If you are reading a borrowed copy, or one from a library, I ask you, please, to consider making a donation to the Trust at www.gpmechanicstrust.com, or on 01896 820263.

Of course, this book – indeed, the sport we love – would not have been possible without the mechanics themselves. Membership of the Trust runs into the hundreds: I didn't manage to interview them all but am very grateful to the following for generously giving up their time to speak to me:

Hughie Absalom, Mike Barney, Roger Barsby, Arthur Birchall, Peter Bracewell, Pat Carvath, Ben Casey, Alan Challis, Tony Cleverley, Stan Collier, Bill Cowe, Bob Dance, Neil Davis, Denis Daviss, Maurice Edwards, Eamon Fullalove, Ralph Gilbert, Peter Hennessy, Roger Hill, Gerry Hones, Keith Leighton, Mike Lowman, Roland Moate, Jim Pickles, Tony Reeson, Tony Robinson, Ray Rowe, Dick Salmon, Dick Scammell, Cedric Selzer, Bob Sparshott, Roy Topp, Peter Turland, Ray Wardell, Richard Watson, Derek Wootton and Mike Young.

In addition, I drew on material gathered during the course of writing my previous books about Lotus, as well as features, and am grateful for contributions from:

Herbie Blash, Eddie Dennis, Dougie Garner, Gordon Huckle, Steve May, Allan McCall and Derek Mower.

I am also extremely appreciative of the assistance that mechanics have given me in sourcing photographs for this book, a large number of which have come from their personal archives, including private photo albums and scrap books. I would also like to thank Ford Motor Company, Tim Wright of LAT, Mary Ellen Loscar of the Indianapolis Motor Speedway, and Gary Critcher of the Supercharged Collection photographic archive for their help with images. Every effort has been made to identify and contact copyright holders of photographs used in this book. If anyone feels I have used one of their photographs without providing appropriate credit or acknowledgement, please contact me and I will be happy to put this right in any subsequent edition. Thanks are also due to cartoonist Jim Bamber, a long-time supporter of the Trust, for the cartoon that graces the book's cover.

This entire project would not have been possible without the support, encouragement and help of my family and friends, in particular my wife, Gill, who put her considerable experience of editing and proof-reading to good use on my manuscript, while she has also had to deal with being virtually a lone parent for the duration of time it has taken me to research and write this. My father Robert has been a valuable 'sounding board,' reading first drafts and providing feedback, as did my mother, Helen, while Dad also acted as the 'virtual motor sport librarian,' looking up things in his extensive library when I could not answer questions from my own resources. Finally, my two boys, Matt and Dom, who have put up with my prolonged absence from family activities with gracious stoicism and understanding, and to whom, when they ask "Is your book written yet, Dad?" I can now reply, at last, "Yes!"

Foreword
by Sir Jackie Stewart OBE

I have always said that the only real professionals in motorsport are the mechanics. The role of a Grand Prix mechanic has, however, changed dramatically; even since the days when I was driving for BRM and Ken Tyrrell.

Mechanics, in those days, were part and parcel of machining and manufacturing many parts of a Formula 1 car, as well as assembling it, taking it to races, being the mechanics, working hideous hours when things went wrong, and producing a race car that someone like myself could slip into with total confidence, because of the trust that I had in the people who worked for the team and, in a large way, for me.

The versatility of many of the people mentioned in this book is the hallmark of the incredible skills that Grand Prix mechanics had in those days, which in no way minimises the skills and talents of all those who make up a Grand Prix team today. Many times the people who worked as mechanics on the cars also transported them to racetracks all over Europe, and this was certainly true of Formula 3, Formula 2 and Formula 1, when I was racing.

The humour and character of the motor racing fraternity in garages around the world is fantastic. Almost everyone has a 'nickname' which can either be flattering or embarrassing, and the camaraderie amongst mechanics, which still exists today, is a pleasure to witness.

Much of my professional life was spent driving for Ken Tyrrell, perhaps the best example of a team leader, who fully appreciated and looked after his mechanics and all who worked with him. I have often said that people like Roger Hill, Roy Topp, Max Rutherford, and many more who worked on my cars were artists; better at what they did than I ever was at what I did.

The work and dedication, the loyalty, the thoroughness and the integrity of the mechanics that I was able to work with as a driver was of the very highest standard, and it was for this reason that I founded

Sir Jackie Stewart OBE, Formula 1 World Champion driver 1969, 1971 and 1973, and founder of the Grand Prix Mechanics Chartiable Trust. (Roy Topp)

the Grand Prix Mechanics Charitable Trust more than twenty years ago. The Trust endeavours to help and assist mechanics and their families in times of hardship, ill-health, or need.

This book will break new ground, allowing its readers to fully understand and appreciate what those very special people who are called 'mechanics' are capable of which permits us prima donna racing drivers to achieve success. Without them; not only would we perhaps not be anything like as successful, we might also not be alive ...

I lift my glass to toast all of those who have played a part in allowing *Tales from the Toolbox* to be brought to what I hope will be many enthusiastic and appreciative readers.

Sir Jackie Stewart OBE

Introduction

In today's era of flying to races, staying in the best hotels, working in spotless pit garages and enjoying hospitality in luxurious paddock superstructures, it is hard to imagine or appreciate the life of a racing mechanic back in the 1950s, 60s and 70s. Not only did they build the entire car, they also loaded it onto a transporter or trailer, drove by road to the event, worked on it all through the race weekend, drove home again – and then prepared it for the next race! All of which took place on an archaic European road network, staying in shabby bed and breakfasts, and working in dusty paddocks or the corner of a local garage. But, boy, did they enjoy themselves ...

With so many drivers from that era no longer with us, these mechanics provide a vital historic link with that period. I have lost count of the number of times I have found myself turning to a mechanic for a first-hand account of something that happened all those years ago. They really are the unsung heroes of motor sport – without them to bolt the cars together and rebuild them when they broke or were damaged, the show wouldn't have happened, and none of the history that I have gained so much pleasure from writing about over the past decade or so would have been established. What is more, their stories remain largely untold.

When I discovered the existence of the Grand Prix Mechanics Charitable Trust, which does such a marvellous job of looking after their interests, the germ of an idea was planted in my mind, and I resolved to try and do something which would highlight their contribution, whilst at the same time helping to raise the profile of, and funds for, the Trust. This book is the result.

I hope you enjoy reading this book as much as I have enjoyed talking to the mechanics during the course of my research. My only regret is that I haven't been able to include all of the stories that have been recounted to me, because of both space constraints and the fact that some of them could still probably land the protagonists in a lot of trouble if they came out today, even all these years later ...

1
Getting there: travel trials and tribulations

It seems incredible now, but forty or fifty years ago, travelling to races around Europe was a hugely difficult and time-consuming undertaking. Aside from the hassle of crossing various borders between countries, there simply wasn't the road network that there is today, particularly in terms of motorways, where a steady average speed could be maintained. Transferring from France, Switzerland or Austria into Italy often necessitated crossing the Alps via one of the passes, which meant that journeys to races were not measured in hours but days, with the longest trips taking almost a week to complete.

During the mid-1950s, when Tony Robinson worked for drivers such as Stirling Moss and Bruce Halford, who ran Maserati 250Fs, the journey down to the factory at Modena was a well-worn route, as Tony recalls: "When the season started, in early April you had to head for Modena, going over the Alpine passes, because there were no tunnels at that time. We used to go over the Mont Cenis pass from Lyon up to St Jean de Maurienne, and come down into the Turin area. The passes were usually snowed in and we had an old front-wheel drive, three-tonne truck that we inherited from Prince Bira when I was working for Halford. The snowplough would be in front and the snow was as high as the roof of the vehicle; you couldn't see left or right, you just put your foot down and drove it like a rally car."

In fact, the passes – and in particular Mont Cenis – seemed to be responsible for a significant proportion of the grief experienced by racing mechanics when travelling from A to B. BRM mechanic Ben Casey remembers one such occasion. "In the old Leyland Tiger, one year when we were running in the Marlboro colours, we lost first gear. We couldn't get up Mont Cenis and were stuck. We were 'umming and ahhing' about what to do when Denis Jenkinson [*MotorSport* journalist] came along in an open-topped E-type and stopped to see if he could help.

"We concluded that the Dunlop wagon couldn't be too far in front of us. Because they had an articulated vehicle, it was possible that, if we could catch them up, they'd come back down and tow us up the hill. I got lumbered with the job of going with Jenks in his E-type. I'll swear blind we were never actually pointing anywhere near where we were supposed to be heading, the back end was hanging out around all those hairpin bends – there were no barriers in those days – but we caught them up. They'd stopped at the café at the top, so they turned around and came and towed us up."

The mountain passes were particularly hard on transporters, with transmissions

Track record   Tony Robinson

❝ *When I came out of the RAF in about 1949, I was employed as a mechanic to look after the cars and commercial vehicles of D W Price, at the time the biggest glass merchant in London. He was also into rallying and trials, so I became involved in looking after and building his trials cars. I saw an advert in* Autocar *and went for an interview for a job with Ray Martin Motors. Alf Francis, who was manager of Ray's garage, interviewed me. This was in winter 1952 and my first job was to help with the build of the Ray Martin-designed Cooper-Alta Formula 2 car for Stirling Moss. The car suffered from handling problems and Alf and Ray Martin parted company. I stayed with Alf and, for the rest of the 1953 season, we worked for Stirling Moss Ltd, operating from Cooper's in Surbiton, where we built a second Cooper-Alta for Moss using a standard Cooper chassis, and as many bits as we could salvage from the original car.*❞

In 1954, Tony and Alf ran a Maserati 250F for Moss, which they also entered in some races in 1955 when Stirling wasn't driving in Grands Prix for Mercedes. In 1956 and 57, Tony spannered on Bruce Halford's 250F, then, between 1958 and 1965, he worked for the British Racing Partnership (BRP), initially as chief mechanic overseeing work, but later as technical director and team manager, designing Formula 1 and Indy BRP challengers. After the demise of BRP in spring 1965, he enjoyed several spells working with Cooper on the 3-litre, Maserati-engined Formula 1 cars until the company closed its doors at the end of 1968. After spells working in the ice cream business, running a drinking club and owning a garage, he went into property. Tony is now aged 80 and retired, but still as keen as ever on the sport.

Tony Robinson, seen here with Innes Ireland, started as assistant to legendary racing mechanic Alf Francis, working on Stirling Moss' cars, then ran Bruce Halford's Maserati 250F. He later went on to be chief mechanic then technical director/ team manager for BRP. (Stan Collier)

taking a beating on the upward leg, and the brakes a hammering on the way down the other side. Former British Racing Partnership (BRP), Parnell Racing and Rob Walker Racing Team mechanic Stan Collier, recalls one particular epic which required a spot of improvisation to get them moving again. "We were coming back from Monza, over Mont Cenis, with the Parnell truck when the clutch went. We coasted downhill and, as it was a Saturday night, parked up. On Sunday I found a local garage owner who said 'Nothing doing today, but what's the problem?' I told him the clutch had gone and he agreed to take a look. So me, this guy, and Pat Carvath from BRM, dropped the gearbox down on the Bedford, took the clutch out and saw it had all flown to pieces. The garage bloke said to Pat: 'There's a scrapyard along the road, if you bring the bits, we'll have a

Track record   Stan Collier

"I first met Ken Gregory, the advertising manager for Austin-Healey, when I
worked for Donald Healey in London. Then, in 1959, I joined him at the British
Racing Partnership. That was a good team; there was me, Tony Robinson and Bruce
McIntosh as mechanics. Bruce was only 15 then, he had just left school. They were
running Formula 2 cars for Ivor Bueb and Chris Bristow. Ivor had a shunt at Clermont-
Ferrand and died in hospital. I don't know how they did it but they did a deal with
BRM to get a car for Stirling, so we split the team: I ran the Formula 2 cars and
Tony Robinson ran the Formula 1 car, just until the end of the season. We did alright
– Stirling finished second and we won the Formula 2 race, both at Aintree. Towards
the end of the season, the Samengo-Turner brothers [owners of the Yeoman Credit
finance firm] phoned Ken Gregory and asked if he would run a Formula 2 team
for them; they'd pay if Ken got some cars and ran them under the Yeoman Credit
name [an early instance of commercial sponsorship], and that was when we got the
Coopers and started running them. We packed up the Formula 2 and I went on to the
Formula 1 cars."

For 1961, the team attracted the backing of another financial sponsor and became
UDT-Laystall Racing, reverting to the BRP moniker for 1963 and 1964, when it became
a constructor in its own right. When the team folded at the end of 1964, Stan moved
to Reg Parnell Racing, where he stayed until 1968, then joining
Rob Walker Racing to work on Jo Siffert's Lotus 49. For 1970,
he remained with Walker, which was running Graham Hill
in the now ageing 49. After a period working for Malaya
Garages on a Formula 5000 Leda for Trevor Taylor, Collier
became involved in a small business manufacturing Formula
SuperVees, but this came to grief during the oil crisis of the
mid-70s and he joined Brabham in 1975, where he worked
with drivers such as Carlos Pace, Carlos Reutemann, Niki
Lauda, John Watson and Nelson Piquet, leaving the team (and
motor racing) in 1981.

*Stan Collier enjoyed a
varied career lasting
more than 20 years,
with teams such as
BRP, Reg Parnell
Racing, Rob Walker
Racing Team, and
Brabham.
(Stan Collier)*

look.' We found a clutch the same but the spline was different.
So I had to take the spline out of the old one and put it in the
new one. We messed about and wasted a day, but we got away
the next morning."

Collier had another eventful journey with the same Parnell
Racing truck, returning from Sicily. "Me and another chap
decided to come down through Switzerland and the bloody
camshaft broke on the Bedford. We coasted down the hill to
the nearest hotel where I phoned Tim [Parnell] and told him
the camshaft had gone and he said he'd fly one out to us. While
I was stripping the engine, the other bloke with me had to
hitchhike to Lausanne to pick up the camshaft. By the time he got back I was all ready
to put the new one in and start back on the road."

Many of the problems with driving to, and from, races occurred because teams were not using purpose-built transporters, but old lorries or converted coaches which simply weren't up to the job. One of Tony Robinson's many eventful journeys took place in a former Royal Blue AEC coach. Royal Blue was a famous English brand and the vehicle had been gutted internally and a pair of doors fitted on the rear so that Bruce Halford's Maserati 250F could be loaded through them. "Bruce was racing in Caen, in Normandy, and I had left Modena and reached another mountain next door to Mont Cenis, called Mont Geneve, which is a little bit lower.

"I got to the top of this mountain and the big end bearings went. I made sure I reached the top because then I could coast down the other side, to a place called Briançon. But coasting down I realized that, without the engine running, I didn't have any brakes. Every now and again I'd switch the engine on to get a bit of air pressure and eventually reached Briançon with this AEC coach with the bloody big-ends gone, a 250F in the back, and about 48 hours to get to Caen.

"I had a good night's sleep and, in the morning, started looking around for alternative transport. Eventually I found a local builder who had a big old Berliet tipper truck, and talked him and his son into loading the 250F onto the back of the tipper and driving from Briançon to Caen. I told him we would pay him when we reached Caen. Bruce was there waiting for the car and Jenks was with him. Of course, they had all been worried when the car didn't arrive. Eventually, I phoned and told him what was happening.

"We kept going all through the night. The builder bloke drove like a lunatic. Imagine an old Berliet with about a turn-and-a-half of free play in the steering wheel. On the other hand, the son he had with him was doing only about 20mph. When he was driving, I thought 'We'll never get there' and with the old builder bloke it was 'He's going to write us off.' Eventually, I went onto the back of the tipper under the tarpaulin with a bottle of wine and just slept until we got to Caen.

"When we arrived, we unloaded the Maserati off the old tipper, Bruce did the race and finished third, qualifying for some prize money. The builder bloke and his son were supposed to go home after being paid, but Jenks and Bruce talked him into taking us to the Nürburgring. Unfortunately, his paperwork didn't permit him to leave the country, so he drove us up to Saarland, Saarbrucken, where the border was. He unloaded the 250F on the side of the road and off he went.

"I pushed the Maserati with a toolbox over the border and got talking to the guard there who had a mate in Saarbrucken, He came and gave us a tow into town and found an old railway yard which had a bit of a platform, where we could load it up onto another lorry, then we drove it to the Nürburgring, unloaded it and did the race, I can't remember where Bruce finished.

"Afterwards, I rented a car, drove back to Briançon, took the AEC engine to pieces, cleaned the crankshaft, drove into Lyon with the battered con-rod heavy-duty bearing, found a bearing that was somewhere near, fitted it all up, put the engine back, drove back to the Nürburgring, picked the Maserati up, then drove back to the works [in Modena] and carried on from there.

"I think somewhere in-between I had a nervous breakdown. Eventually, when I finished with Bruce at the end of 1957 the transporter quietly gave up the ghost in Stuttgart somewhere and that was the last I heard of it. It was only a 32-seater coach with a maximum speed of 38mph, designed for running around the Devon and Cornwall lanes."

Usually, the longest journeys were the toughest for the mechanics. Rob Walker's mechanic Tony Cleverley recalls a trip to the 1958 Moroccan Grand Prix as being particularly bad. "Casablanca was one of the worst journeys because it was in an old Commer truck with cart-leaf springs, and it was quite a trek down there in those days. We went right the way down from Calais, through Spain to Bilbao. There were four of us in the truck and you were lucky if it was a two-seater vehicle in those days. I squeezed up in the right-hand corner with the driver. We had things hopping in through the windows and everybody was bailing out, but it was quite good fun, really."

However, the journey that probably caused more anguish and heartache than any other was the trip to Sicily to visit either the Enna-Pergusa or Syracuse circuits. Not content with making it just about the furthest journey possible from the UK, the sadists who set the motor sport calendar in those days managed to schedule races in Karlskoga in Sweden, up near Stockholm one weekend, and in Enna in Sicily the next. Given that it was generally considered wise to allow six or seven days for the journey from the UK, and that the transporters leaving Karlskoga on Sunday night needed to be in Sicily for first practice on Friday, the enormity of the challenge can be appreciated ...

Former Tyrrell mechanic Neil Davis remembers one such journey with the Formula 2 team in 1967, which, at the time, was running the French-built Matras. "We left Karlskoga on Sunday night and drove non-stop to Naples, then boarded a boat to Palermo and drove to Enna. There were no motorways in Sicily in those days and it was a very twisty road; to do 25 miles took about an hour-and-a-half. There were three of us and we drove non-stop. There were autostradas in Italy, so when we got into Italy, that was fine, you could bomb along and obviously in Germany it was OK. We came from Sweden to north Germany and then drove right the way down through Germany into Austria and Italy.

"We had our Leyland, which was part of a shipment of buses bound for Cuba that sank

Tyrrell's transport (1): A Matra Formula 2 car waits to be loaded onto the team's transporter in the Tyrrell Racing Organisation's yard, with Ken's modest Morris 1100 parked outside his modest former timber yard's office. (Neil Davis)

Tyrrell's transport (2): This transporter was built by Tiverton on a coach chassis salvaged from the River Thames after a shipment bound for Cuba sank. (Neil Davis)

Track record
Neil Davis

❝*I was an apprentice at Coombs of Guildford. Alan Brown and another guy ran a pair of 1500cc, FPF Climax-engined Formula 2 Coopers out of there. Alan knew I was interested in racing and asked if I'd like to go up in the evenings to help his mechanic Alan Stait, on an unpaid basis. This was in 1958 and then in 1959 they asked me to go and work for them full-time. In 1960, Ken Tyrrell started his Formula Junior team and asked Alan [Stait] and I to come and work for him.*

"We ended up doing Formula Junior and Formula Two, and then moving into Formula 1 in 1968. In 1971, I began looking after the guys back in the factory, then became factory manager. The operation slowly expanded and, at one point, we had 160 people working for us. I stayed with Ken until he sold the company in 1998, so was with him for 38 years."

Neil Davis, on the left here with fellow Tyrrell mechanics Les Sheppard (centre) and Rex Hart: 'the day they made Ken Tyrrell they broke the mould.' Jacky Ickx, sat in his Matra Formula 2 car, is just visible bottom left. (Neil Davis)

in the Thames. We bought one and turned it into a transporter. It was a very nice vehicle actually. We had bunks behind the driver and aircraft seats in the front, and could actually change drivers without stopping. We used to do two hours on and four off. It was quite an incredible journey. There were no tunnels in those days – we went over the top of the Alps.

"We got jammed between the Austrian and German customs stations because there was a bank holiday. The Germans let us out of Germany but the Austrians wouldn't let us into Austria until midnight the following day. So we decided we would get the cars out and change the ratios in the Hewland gearboxes. We did this with big crowds around us, looking at these cars, it was fantastic. Jackie [Stewart] won in both Karlskoga and Enna, so that was a worthwhile trip."

Bob Sparshott, who worked for Team Lotus in the 1960s before going on to establish his own BS Fabrications team, also remembers a journey down to Sicily with Lotus which was equally eventful. "We had a race in Karlskoga in Sweden one Sunday and the following Sunday we were at Enna. We had to drive all the way down, so literally as soon as the race ended in Sweden, we packed everything in the truck and set straight off because there were a series of ferries in those days rather than bridges, and we worked out that we had to make Naples by Thursday to catch the ferry across to Palermo. We were halfway through Germany when the exhauster pump on the diesel engine on the Bedford went. So we had to take a load of it apart and fix it, much to the amusement of the Germans, who couldn't work out what we were doing.

"There was one other odd thing about that trip: on the night we left Karlskoga, we were driving down past this long lake, everyone was tired, and I suddenly heard this weird knocking noise from the front of the lorry, so I pulled over and saw our wheel nuts were undone. We've never understood it because they don't come loose but, fortunately, we picked it up early because the wheel started moving about and we were able to stop and tighten them. We made the Palermo ferry but when we reached Sicily the hotel couldn't find the booking. That's all you need after that sort of journey, isn't it?"

Stan Collier also cited Sicily as one of the toughest but enjoyable trips he made. "The driving around was quite fantastic. With BRP we used to do a lot of Formula 1 races that weren't Championship and we did Karlskoga, then Roskilde, down to Modena, then to Monza. Another time we went down to Monza, then Sicily.

"I did one trip with BRP where we left for Sicily, in 1959 or 1960, and it took six days to drive down there. Everybody thinks of motorways these days but there were none then. It took us a day-and-a-half to get out of France. It was winter, so we had to go right round Monaco to get into Italy because all the passes were closed, and then drive the whole length of the country to Sicily, through the mountains and all that sort of thing. But I used to like it because I enjoy driving. And those sorts of trips were what made life interesting. When it became that you flew to a meeting on a Thursday and then flew back Sunday night, that's when I started to lose interest."

Former Rob Walker Racing Team mechanic Tony Cleverley recalls one trip to Sicily with the Rob Walker team which had an extra element, that of competition. "We took a Porsche down there and prepared the car in Stuttgart. The factory team was going as well and they looked at our little old Commer, which was a one-car truck, and said 'That'll never make it, it's crap.' We set off from Stuttgart and were chasing their Opel trucks, which were quite new and posh, and I thought 'There's only one way to treat these guys and that's to bloody pass them with our little old Commer truck.' So when we got to a long downhill bit, we knocked it out of gear and flew by them. Which shut them up completely for the rest of the trip."

Ralph Gilbert, who used to mechanic for Bob Gerard Racing, also has 'fond' memories of the trek to Sicily. "The journey that was always a disaster was the one to Enna. Bob's transporter was a converted AEC coach. On those long journeys, you were almost falling asleep at the wheel, it was so tiring. The coach had enormous fuel tanks so

when we turned up at an Italian filling station and asked the pump attendant to fill it up, we knew we had time to go for a shower. We came back to find the bloke crawling under it to try and find out where his diesel was going, as it could take 150 gallons.

"There was also the time we ran out of air brakes in the Alps. The drums heat-checked and became like files and machined

The Rob Walker Commer stops en route to a race. John Chisman is the mechanic leaning out of the cab. (Tony Cleverley)

off the brake linings, so we had to drive it home on the handbrake. Then, on another trip, coming up to Rome, it ran out of fan belts. We rang AEC, and Bob and Joan Gerard went to Fiumicino airport and shipped out new belts. We fitted them and then went to a hotel for the night. The following morning, all the staff came out to wave us off. Unfortunately, we'd parked the truck close to a wall and when we turned sharp right, the back end of the coach came round, hit the wall and demolished it.

"There were no credit cards in those days. We always had to have French francs, Swiss francs and Italian lira with us when we were travelling. That was a pain. We were running on a Shell carnet [customs document] so at least all our fuel costs were charged back to the UK. Also, they used to pay the start and prize money in cash on the Monday morning after the race, with the prize-giving on the Sunday evening. When we went down to Pergusa we got paid one million lira so we had a safe built into the floor of the transporter."

But it wasn't just travelling down to Sicily that presented challenges, it was coming back off the island as well. By the 1970s, mechanics used to forgo the prize-giving in order to make an early start for home, as Ray Wardell recollects: "Normally, one boat would leave about six or seven o'clock in the evening from Palermo so there would be this almighty race to load your car and equipment, get out of the track and to Palermo. If you didn't make that boat, you finished up having to drive all the way from Sicily up the coast of Italy, whereas you could get that boat from Palermo to Naples and it cut a big chunk off the journey.

"One year I was with the Surtees truck and another mechanic, who drove the truck, and nobody could have moved it quicker than him. We got to the dock and they tried to stop us to check our tickets. We knew we were very, very late and could see the boat, so he literally drove the truck onto the ramp and blocked it so they couldn't put the ramp up and walked back with the tickets. I got into the driver's seat and, of course, once they'd seen the ticket, they waved me onto the boat. What he hadn't told me is that, by now, we had no brakes. I got to the bottom of the ramp, tried to brake, and nothing happened. I hit the first truck in line. Later, I found out that we hadn't had brakes for a long time …"

A trip to Sicily for Bernard White's Team Chamaco-Collect was Roland Moate's first assignment as a Formula 1 mechanic. If it hadn't been for a fortuitous delay to the start, it would have turned out to be a wasted journey. "When I went down to Syracuse to do the Formula 1 race, I drove the transporter to Sicily and we called at Monte Carlo coming back. I lost a stone-and-a-half in weight on that trip. I'd never been away from home in my life but I got on this ferry at Hull and off at Rotterdam, and because we had only a few days to get down there, we had to drive day and night. We nearly missed the race but Jack Brabham had been racing at Oulton Park and was late getting to Sicily, so they put it back a few hours, meaning we were in."

It was while searching for the ferry terminal in Naples that Ken Tyrrell's team fell victim to a couple of young opportunists, as former chief mechanic Roger Hill explains: "We were lost, couldn't find the dock where the ferry left. There were a couple of lads of about 17 or 18 on the side of the road, so we stopped to ask them where the ferry was. They said it was just down the road and they would show us. One spoke a wee bit of English, so we thought that was alright; they jumped in and off we went down the road. About 20 minutes later they said 'It's just around the corner, we want to get out here.'

It turned out that all they wanted was a ride home, so we'd been 'done' by some Italian lads. They'd led us up the bloody path. It took us hours to find it after that."

Occasionally, in their haste to get from A to B, mechanics would overstep the mark and find themselves in trouble. During one trip home from Sicily, Tony Cleverley encountered some 'problems with the locals' that landed him in jail. "I got arrested once in Italy. I couldn't get by a Fiat and, in the end, I did pull alongside it, but he persisted, on a long straight, in keeping me out there. It was all getting a bit tight towards the end and I had to pull in a little bit. I don't know whether I touched him or what, but suddenly he was spinning on his roof. A couple of villages later, a crowd was out in the middle of the road to stop us. They had us banged up in the prison for a day."

On one relatively rare occasion in 1961, as former Cooper, Parnell and Brabham mechanic Gerry Hones recounts, the teams clubbed together and flew their cars and drivers down, at the suggestion of Yeoman Credit team manager Reg Parnell. "We had a race at Aintree on the Saturday [the BARC '200'] and another on the Tuesday, in Syracuse, Sicily [the Gran Premio Siracusa], both with the Cooper Formula 1s. Reg thought he'd better get it organised so we rang round all the other teams that were going down and through Webbair we chartered two aircraft. One was a Bristol airfreighter, which they put scaffold down the centre of, so we'd got a top and bottom and could fit in six or eight cars. The other was an Elizabethan or something similar, like a Fokker Friendship with the high wing on it.

"We got our cars ready, went to Aintree and did the race. There was Reg Parnell, Jill Harris, Jimmy Potton and myself. Immediately afterwards, we left for Gatwick and the transporter followed. We booked straight into a motel and they reached there a couple of hours after us. We unloaded the cars and helped load them onto the Bristol airfreighter, which took off very early on the Sunday morning. We got up and met everybody else at the airport. There was Jack [Brabham] and his mechanic, [Roy] Salvadori, John Surtees, Innes Ireland and Jimmy Clark. All with their mechanics so it was a full plane.

Track record   Tony Cleverley
❝I worked for Pippbrook Garage, which was Rob Walker's. My father got me the job by going and seeing Rob after I left school. He told him I wanted to go on the racing team, which I really didn't know anything about. I started there and got involved with the racing team, going away at weekends and working of an evening with them, and it progressed from there. That was in 1955 when I first worked on a Connaught for Jack Fairman."
   Tony remained a loyal employee of Rob Walker for 17 years, working with drivers such as Moss, Bonnier, Trintignant, Siffert and Graham Hill, until the team merged with Team Surtees in 1971.

Rob Walker mechanic Tony Cleverley, shown here on the right with Malcolm Simpson (centre) and Erik Carlsson, who married Pat Moss. (Tony Cleverley)

"We flew direct to Catania airport. The Bristol landed in Nice, got a puncture and was late, so, instead of arriving before us, got there after. Packed lunches came round in boxes and somebody threw a bread roll and that started it. There was bloody murder on the plane – bananas and food flying everywhere and stewardesses being grabbed and laid across the drivers' laps, and all that sort of thing, which the crew thought was blooming wonderful. When we got to Catania, there were some big flat-back trucks waiting for us, but these blokes didn't have any ramps or ropes, so we had about a dozen blokes round each Formula 1 car, lifting them up onto these flat-back trucks. Then they didn't have anything to fix them down, so from Catania airport into Syracuse – which was a fair few miles – the mechanics had to sit in the cars and hold the brakes on.

"The first day of practice there was a brick wall all the way around this circuit, so they decided to use the hire cars. Needless to say, when we took the hire cars back there wasn't a piece of tread on any of the tyres. Anyway, the race went off quite well. Then we went through the same procedure returning the cars out to Catania, sitting in them again. As soon as we took off from Catania we passed over the Mount Etna volcano, so the pilot took us down in to have a look at the opening. Most of the drivers had a pilot's licence so, a bit later, Innes Ireland went up front to fly the plane. Jack Brabham stood up and said 'When I give the word, all rush to the front, so everybody rushed to the front and the nose went down and then lifted back up again. Then Jack said 'When I give the word, everybody rush to one side,' at which, everybody rushed to one side and held on to the luggage racks. Then the loudspeaker opened and we heard all these obscenities coming from the pilot's seat. But a good time was had by all." There is some question about whether it was Brabham flying the plane and Ireland directing the passengers, though Hones is adamant that it was Innes at the controls …

Former Team Lotus mechanic Arthur Birchall finds it difficult to pick just one trip, and points out that these journeys were another reason why mechanics got so tired. "Most were eventful. I think probably the quickest journey I did was from Hethel to Silverstone on race morning with Graham Hill's car that he had virtually written off going into Woodcote when a suspension part broke. We gathered it all up and brought it back to the factory and worked through the night. I was told to go home at four o'clock and get some sleep and be back at six when I drove the truck to Silverstone in record time.

"It wasn't unusual to not get home from an event until seven or eight o'clock the following evening, having driven across the Continent, and to go to bed on Monday evening and not wake up until Wednesday morning. The body needed it. It was always a very hectic life, motor racing, because of the vast distances travelled between the circuits. Also, there were no test teams in those days – if you did go testing you took a race car."

One disadvantage of not having a purpose-built transporter was that it was hard for some teams to transport all their cars and spares, and they often resorted to towing a trailer to give them extra capacity. Former Cooper, McLaren, Williams and Brabham mechanic Mike Barney tells the story of one particular expedition where things nearly went disastrously wrong for the Cooper Formula 1 team. "We were coming back from the Monaco Grand Prix and had been driving for God knows how long. It was the second day – we'd left Monaco on the Sunday night and kept driving until we reached

Calais. Somewhere along the way – I can't remember where – I was driving and the sun was low, with shadows showing across the field, so you could see the shadow of the truck. Some time previously, I had idly looked, sort of half-asleep and noticed the shadow of the trailer.

"Then, all of a sudden, I realised I couldn't see the shadow any more. So I told Noddy (Michael Grohmann), I thought the trailer had come off and he replied not to be a twit. But by this point, I'd realised that I couldn't feel it either, so we stopped and got out to find … no trailer. We turned the truck around and tore back down the road – at all of 30mph because that was about as quick as it would go – and found it parked in a

---

Track record   Ray Wardell

❝I was doing an apprenticeship as a mechanic in a regular car dealership when a friend – who was also the parts truck driver – came back from a delivery and said to me almost jokingly 'I was at a place called Pagham delivering parts and they've got a couple of race cars. Next time I'm there, I'll see if there are any jobs going.' About two weeks later, he came back in and said 'I mentioned it to them and they said to come and see them.'

"He explained where this place was so I turned up there and met Derek Bell. I didn't land a job as a racing mechanic because Derek was trying to make a bit of money on the side tuning Minis to pay for the racing and I happened to be a bit of a Mini specialist – I'd done a factory course and all that – so he said 'Why don't you work for me in the evenings, doing the Minis and you can come racing with us on the weekends?' I did that for twelve months while I finished my apprenticeship.

"Then I was supposed to go full-time with them and was going to be home-based as he already had one mechanic. It was going to be Derek's first full international year of Formula 3 and a new Lotus 31 turned up, about three or four weeks before the season started. A couple of days later his mechanic vanished off the face of the earth – I've no idea what happened to him – and left me with the whole lot. From that day on, I was Derek's racing mechanic."

Later, Wardell joined March, building the company's very first racing car, the

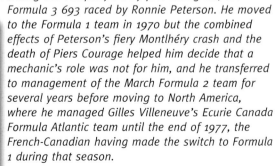

Formula 3 693 raced by Ronnie Peterson. He moved to the Formula 1 team in 1970 but the combined effects of Peterson's fiery Montlhéry crash and the death of Piers Courage helped him decide that a mechanic's role was not for him, and he transferred to management of the March Formula 2 team for several years before moving to North America, where he managed Gilles Villeneuve's Ecurie Canada Formula Atlantic team until the end of 1977, the French-Canadian having made the switch to Formula 1 during that season.

Wardell: Fiery crashes shook him and he switched – very successfully – to management. (Ray Wardell)

hedge across the other side of the road. It was lucky nobody was coming the other way, as it would have wiped them out. More importantly, we would have lost the racing car. The ball-hitch had unscrewed and come out so all we had to do was hook it on and get going again."

Ray Wardell, who worked for Derek Bell, March and Ecurie Canada with Gilles Villeneuve, had another eventful journey towards the end of 1968, as he describes: "When Derek had signed for Ferrari, he was going out to the Tasman series with Chris Amon. He called me one day and said he needed me to go down to Ferrari and pick up the two cars for the Tasman series and bring them back to London for shipping out to New Zealand. At the time we'd only got a transit van and a one-car trailer. So I asked 'How do you think I am going to do that?' He said he'd borrowed a double-deck trailer from somebody, so I set off for Ferrari, taking this empty trailer all the way down there, though when I got to the factory and said I'd come to pick up two cars to send out to New Zealand, the Ferrari people replied: 'Yes, there are two cars but there's an awful lot of equipment going as well.' This poor Transit van, it had engines, gearboxes, everything, crammed into it. It could barely move and then there was this double-deck trailer which, once it was loaded up, was grossly overweight.

"They arranged to clear customs at the factory so that when I got to the border I could just go straight through with it. The customs guys turned up and wanted to seal the cars in the trailer; only problem was, it was an open trailer. So they made us build a wooden frame around the cars so that they could tie this bit of wire and seal it, which was a joke. Then I headed off with this Transit and got 10 miles up the road before the first tyre blew out. I was trying to jack up this Transit van with a little race car hydraulic jack, with the Transit loaded up to the gunnels so it could barely lift it. I finally managed to change that and I suppose it took me two-and-a-half days to get that rig back to London. That was probably the worst drive I ever did. Derek had his E-type Jaguar and was supposedly going to follow me. Well, I never saw him: he wasn't going to drive at that speed all the way back to England, was he?"

Transporters and narrow streets don't mix, so it was with some trepidation that, in the days before the Periphique, crews used to approach the task of crossing Paris, as former Brabham, Anglo American Racers (AAR) and Shadow mechanic Mike Lowman explains. "With the old AAR Eagle truck, we used to share drives and, once on our way back from Monaco, it was my turn. It was night-time and we were coming into Paris. Jo [Ramirez] was navigating and I said 'OK Jo, you're going to have to tell me where the hell we're going here because it's foggy and I have not got a clue.' Somehow, he conspired to get us really, really lost and I ended up driving this rigid coach-chassis thing down this street with cars parked on each side, barely enough room to get through the middle and a T-junction at the end. It must have taken us about ten minutes or more of backwards and forwards, backwards and forwards, shunt, shunt, shunt, to get round. We finally made it out but that was quite interesting."

PMT, and all that ...

As with all-nighters and fuel dramas, some of the most eventful journeys seemed to happen to Team Lotus, as Dick Scammell relates. "The transporters were ones we built ourselves and they weren't very reliable. We had a transporter we called PMT [on

Getting there, Team Lotus-style (1): En route to the tragic 1960 Belgian Grand Prix at Spa-Francorchamps, showing the team's Ford Thames van 903 PMT and double-deck, four-wheel trailer. No wonder the van had problems getting up the hills ... (Dick Scammell)

account of its licence plate, 903 PMT] which was a stretched 1500cwt van with five feet welded in it. It had a Zephyr engine and an Alvis Speed 25 gearbox, and carried the spares inside the rear, with the car on the top. In the front there was a driver's seat and a passenger seat, and then two in the back quarters of the cabin. We used to tow a double-deck trailer with it.

"You knew there were going to be problems getting to Dover because it wouldn't climb the hill between Folkestone and Dover. We used to round the corner at the bottom at breakneck speed, and could just about get up to the first bend before we all had to bail out and start pushing. It is amazing to think about now – I don't know how we had the gall, really – but we used to flag down people in cars and things and persuade them to push us to the top.

"There was a pub up on top of the hill that we were regular visitors to, because we could struggle up there and let it stop boiling. The publican used to give us a drink and a couple of gallons of water, which we could fill the radiator with, and then we used to press on. It did all sorts of funny things like that but we survived them all.

"We broke a steering arm on the Jabbeke Highway, the one from Ostend to Brussels. We were all sitting there and suddenly it veered off to the right, the driver realising he wasn't connected to the front wheels any more. Fortunately, as we went further and

Getting there, Team Lotus-style (2): By the judicious use of scaffolding, Team Lotus managed to produce a three-car transporter based on a Ford Thames Trader flatbed truck. Here, the team's just arrived at its usual base in Eze-sur-Mer, along the coast from Monaco. On the red Thames Trader are the Lotus 18s of Innes Ireland (22), Alan Stacey (24), and John Surtees; in the background, Jim Clark's Formula Junior 18 (114) is just visible on the back of 903 PMT. (Dick Scammell)

Track record   Cedric Selzer

"*I was interested in motor sport in South Africa, where I was born and brought up, and teamed up with some friends who raced. When Stirling Moss came over at the end of 1960, I befriended him and he gave me a letter to BRP, to carry with me to the UK. I went to see Tony Robinson but all positions were taken, so I went to see Reg Parnell at Yeoman Credit, also with no luck.*

"I answered an advertisement in Autosport *that turned out to be a job working for Ian Raby and Chris Andrews on their Formula Junior cars. I went to one race with them in Aspern; the next was going to be in Monaco but we parted company. So I flew down to Nice – my mother happened to be staying there with friends – borrowed a car, and went to the Monaco Grand Prix anyway. I asked around to find where everybody from the race teams drank, and managed to meet Jim Endruweit, Team Lotus chief mechanic. It turned out they were one mechanic short, so I ended up working there. They put me on a month's trial – this was May 1961 and I stayed until 1964."*

After that, Cedric's career included spells working for Ian Walker on his racing Elans, Paul Hawkins and Jackie Epstein (Lola T70 Can-Am), Mike d'Udy and Ulf Norinder (Lola T70 sports cars), and designing the Nerus Silhouette FF100 car. In the 1970s he drifted away from the sport but became involved in historic race car restoration and preparation through a friend, finally retiring for good in 2007.

Cedric Selzer joined Team Lotus after meeting Jim Endruweit in a bar and discovering the team was a mechanic short.
(Tony Cleverly)

further off the road, we spotted a car park. We careered, out of control, through the entrance, touched the guard rail, which straightened up the van, by which time we'd got it stopped. The steering arm had broken off and I think it was amazing that nobody got hurt.

"Many teams were going around in converted Bedfords and this sort of thing. The trouble was in those days, you also had to go over the passes, which was very bad news because though it would go up, coming down the other side was definitely very marginal. You'd have to have the driver straining on the steering wheel and on the footbrake, and his passenger heaving on the handbrake. We were young so thought it was going to be alright, and say 'Cor, that was a bit close, wasn't it?'"

Some Team Lotus trips were so disastrous it was almost comical, and the mechanics could have been forgiven for breaking down and weeping at the side of the road. However, with Colin Chapman leading by example, they were a resourceful bunch, and it was unheard of for them not to make it to a race. However, Dick Scammell remembers one time when they came close. "We were late as usual, so instead of catching the boat, we went over the Channel Airbridge with Bristol Freighters, run by Silver City Airways. The trouble was, the ramp was quite steep and, as we drove into it, the engine tipped over too far and jumped on its mountings, putting the fan blades through the radiator.

"We got it off the other side, and I told Colin, who said: 'Well, don't panic, see if you can get it mended; I'm coming over in any case in my car, so I'll come that way and at least pick up the trailer.' He duly arrived with his Raymond Mays Zephyr and we hitched on this double-deck trailer. This was very early on in my days there and he said 'You and you in the car and bring a tool kit.' I was one of the ones chosen and ended up in the front, which wasn't a good place to be, and we sailed off down the road with this trailer on the back.

"When we came to the first junction, we went straight across and down the escape road, at which Colin said: 'Wait until we get back, I shall sort out those people who are meant to have serviced this trailer.' We backed it up and carried on. He really was flying across France, but the trailer was snaking so badly that people coming the other way were actually moving off the road. In the end, it went very sideways in the road, going quite quickly, and didn't tow too well after that.

"We stopped for fuel and when we got out – it was a four-wheel trailer – there was one wheel missing on the left-hand side of the trailer. Colin said to me 'Pump up the tyre on that side, really hard, and do up the wheel nuts,' which I duly did, all round the trailer. We pressed on again and, as we entered this big long right-hander, carrying on in the same fashion as before, suddenly, the whole lot went sideways and this wheel rolled past us. Colin turned to me and said: 'I told you to bloody well tighten up those wheel nuts, didn't I – what on earth do you think you were doing?' while we were still sliding to a halt.

"I got out and was fortunately redeemed because all the wheel nuts were still on the studs. Colin told us to unload the cars, which we did, got a spare wheel and put it on the trailer. Then he said 'OK, we'll have to drive the cars to Reims,' but we pointed out that, as we couldn't start them, we'd need a push or something. He told us to go and find some French people, which we did in a field, and they duly pushed us off down the road. Of course, all were left lying in the road because anybody who has ever pushed a racing car knows that when it lights up, it really goes. We drove the last 35-40 miles to Reims with the two cars on the road, and Colin could still go quicker than I could. You wouldn't get away with it here but the French policemen were stopping the traffic for us. Here, we would have been locked up."

Cedric Selzer, a mechanic with Team Lotus in the early 1960s, recalls another epic journey with PMT. "Dick Scammell and Ted Woodley took PMT and two cars to a race at Karlskoga. The plan was that they would then drive to Basle in Switzerland. Derek Wild and I would fly from Heathrow with spares and meet them there, and they would use our return tickets and fly home.

"We met Dick and Ted as planned and took over PMT and the trailer. When I started the engine and went to drive off to customs to clear the spares we had brought with us, I realised that the front tyre was flat. We could not believe our fellow mechanics had left us with a puncture, but soon realised why: in order to fit the spare, we needed the jack, which was in the centre locker under the race car. With a lot of effort we got it out without unloading the car.

"Having changed the tyre, we went to head off, only to find that the brake pedal was going to the floor. We checked the master cylinder but it was empty, and there was brake fluid pouring out of the rear wheel cylinders. We jacked up the transporter again and removed a rear wheel and brake drum, to find brake fluid all over the brake shoes. There was only one thing to do: Derek had to go by taxi to the local Ford dealer for wheel cylinder kits. By the time he returned I had taken off the brake shoes, poured petrol on them and set them alight to burn off the brake fluid. We reassembled everything, bled the brakes and were finally off to customs.

"Immediately, we encountered another problem. As there was a ban on racing in Switzerland, customs wanted a deposit of £40,000, refundable when we left the country. I asked Derek how much money he had on him. With our expenses allowance (£2.50 per day) and the company money we had, we managed to scrape together £100. After two hours of wrangling, customs eventually agreed to put seals on the lockers and stamp the carnet.

"At last we were on our way! We worked out that, if we hurried, we could catch the train through the Simplon tunnel. Unfortunately, the transporter began to run hot and consume water. We stopped at a roadside cafe and borrowed a container full of water and pressed on. By this time we had missed the train, with the only option to go over the St Gotthard pass. PMT boiled and boiled until all the water we had in our containers had been used up.

"In pitch darkness, we stopped near the top of the pass. I could hear running water, which we tried to find, but after a couple of falls, due to not being able to see anything, we gave up. Then car headlights appeared, illuminating the mountainside. As cars drove up and down the pass we managed to find the mountain stream we had heard, filled some of our containers and got back on the road. We pressed on till dawn and the customs post. Guess what? They wanted £40,000 from us again!

"They left us to our own devices for an hour-and-a-half. Eventually, the chief customs officer came out, pointed to us and said: 'You British.' He raised his arm in a vertical pumping action, said 'Profumo,' burst out laughing and sent us on our way. It was great to be British and have ambassadors such as Christine Keeler looking after our interests ...

"As we had missed a night's sleep, we decided to treat ourselves to a soft bed and headed for Modena. As we pulled off the autostrada, a car drove up behind us, hooting madly, and we realised it was Alf Francis [the legendary mechanic who worked for Stirling Moss, among others]. He asked where we were off to and we told him we thought we would have a bite to eat and a sleep, in that order. Alf asked if we minded if he joined us at dinner, which was fine, and also if John Surtees could join us, which, naturally, we also welcomed.

"We sat down to dinner and put motor racing to rights. When it came to paying the bill, Alf put his hand in his pocket but John stopped him, saying 'It is these lads' pleasure to take us out.' We were left with no choice but to pick up the tab for the four of us. I asked John recently about this incident but he does not remember anything about it ...

"The following morning we left to continue our journey to Sicily. That day and the next PMT boiled and boiled. Finally, we were 13 kilometres outside Naples when there was a vibration and the centre propshaft bearing gave way. It was driveable if we went at 10 miles per hour on the flat. I phoned Andrew Ferguson back in Cheshunt and told him we could get the cars to Palermo, but would never make it over the mountains to Enna. He said he would meet us in Palermo.

"Andrew flew to Palermo and was there at the docks when we arrived. He had hired a truck and borrowed Carel de Beaufort's big American V8 and trailer as a tow vehicle. Off we climbed into the mountains to Enna and finally arrived 20 hours late for first practice."

The race was a disaster, with Team Lotus driver Trevor Taylor's car ending up severely damaged in a snake-infested lake. Fortunately, someone was able to fish it out for them and the return journey, as Cedric describes, was slightly less eventful. "We loaded up and took the damaged car, Peter's car, and the spares back to Palermo. A garage there had done some repairs to poor old PMT's radiator and it ran cooler after that. Wherever we stopped in Italy we had kids swarming over the wrecked car, pulling bits off.

Getting there, Team Lotus-style (3): By 1961, the team had really arrived, having procured the loan of the former Scarab team transporter, which could comfortably house three cars and copious tools and spares. It is pictured on its way to another fateful race, the 1961 Italian Grand Prix, where Jim Clark (36) would have a collision with Wolfgang von Trips that would lead to the German's death and many years of legal complications for both Clark and the team. (Dick Scammell)

"All went well until we had a puncture in a French town the next day. We had driven non-stop since stepping off the boat at Naples. We found a tyre repairer whose shop happened to be on a corner. Also on the corner was a set of traffic lights. To us, this was unimportant but the local gendarme thought differently and asked us to move on.

"All of a sudden, not one of us could understand a word of French. He got angry and asked us for a driving licence. I gave Derek mine as he was driving and he had left his in England. Very soon a police van arrived and we were taken to the local station and locked in an interview room. We were told we could apply for bail but this could take days. Fortunately, after a couple of hours, the Chief of Police arrived, took pity on us and let us out."

2
Anything to declare?
Customs capers

Now that we live in an era of a borderless mainland Europe, it's hard to imagine, or remember, how extremely complex was the task of moving racing cars between European countries before the UK joined what is now the EU.

The way it worked was that, if you wished to travel outside the UK, customs carnets (special documents relating to the temporary importation of goods) were required for all cars and spares. These were expensive items to obtain and, because chassis and/or serial/part numbers had to be stated on the carnets, this led to a lot of chopping and changing of chassis plates, even when entirely new cars were built, since it was a lot cheaper and less complicated to take a chassis plate from an old car and put it on the new one than to obtain an entirely new carnet. Such practices have made the work of the motor racing chassis historian particularly fraught. When the UK joined the EEC in 1973, for travel within the EEC carnets were no longer necessary though still are for trips outside the EU.

Probably the most frustrating aspect for mechanics was the lack of consistency, not just between customs officers in different countries, but between those in the same country.

Ralph Gilbert, who worked for Bob Gerard Racing in the 1950s and 1960s, remembers a rare occasion when he was able to 'put one over' a customs official. "We were in French customs and they decided they were going to be very efficient. You had to have a carnet for everything, even the spares. One of the items was a 'boit de vitesse' – a gearbox. I wasn't going to unpack the whole transporter to get this out so I pulled out an old chest with some gears in it and they went 'Ah, boit de vitesse – box of gears – yes.'"

Over-zealous officials were a regular problem, remembers former BRM mechanic Peter Bracewell. "Sometimes, you got a customs chap who was a bit too keen and wanted to go all through your carnet list and see what spares you were carrying. Because we ran three cars, we used to carry something like 68 wheel rims, which were all stacked around the cars. Before now, we've had all the back doors down and an irate customs officer wanting to see these wheels. You are trying to show him that there are 68 wheels in there and he doesn't believe you, so you have to take some of them out so that he can count them."

Hughie Absalom recalls similar displays of bureaucracy, but says that very quickly the teams cottoned on to the fact that their passage could be somewhat smoothed by

Track record   Hughie Absalom

"I had served an apprenticeship in a Jaguar garage in Wales and wanted to move into motor racing. When I applied for jobs in Autosport, they all wanted people with experience. I thought there must be another way round this so in January 1965, I got a job at Jack Brabham Motors in Chessington who were doing car conversions on Vauxhalls and Sunbeam Rapiers. While I was there, an opportunity to go on the Formula 1 race team came up and I landed the job, in time for the Monaco Grand Prix in May."

After leaving Brabham at the end of 1966, Hughie (as he was usually known, his real name is Hywel) joined Team Lotus, in their Indy section for 1967 and 1968. A move to the Formula 1 team lasted until March 1969 when, after the Race of Champions, he switched to McLaren to work on its M9A four-wheel-drive car and, in 1970, the M14 with Bruce McLaren and Denny Hulme, as well as the team's Indy effort. At the end of 1970 he moved out of Formula 1 to concentrate on Indy but returned between 1977 and 1980, working with James Hunt, Jochen Mass, John Watson and Patrick Tambay. He came back again briefly in 1987, as part of the Leyton House Formula 1 team, after which he formed his own racing team, Dragon Motorsport, bringing on a host of drivers in the junior Formulae, many of whom made it to Formula One including Mika Häkkinen, Allan McNish and Takuma Sato. Since 1984, he has owned Spot-On Control Cables, which makes control cables for throttles for modern, historic and vintage racing cars, as well as bespoke products for road cars.

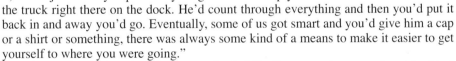

Absalom worked for top teams such as Brabham, Lotus and McLaren during his career. (Bill Cowe)

the provision of 'goodies' for the officials. "Sometimes, when we went to Calais, the customs guy, if he felt like it, would just make you pull everything out. We'd empty the truck right there on the dock. He'd count through everything and then you'd put it back in and away you'd go. Eventually, some of us got smart and you'd give him a cap or a shirt or something, there was always some kind of a means to make it easier to get yourself to where you were going."

Former Anglo American Racers mechanic Mike Lowman also remembers 'freebies' helping them when leaving, but points out that this practice quickly got out of hand as the customs guys wised up to the power they held. "They were fairly good with us. In the early days of commercial involvement in Formula 1, if you gave them a couple of stickers or something like that, they were over the moon. But then, of course, it started to escalate. Guys would be getting into sticky positions and they'd give them hats and things like that and then, unless you gave them a hat, they'd slow you down, it got so it was bigger and bigger items of clothing. In the end, you'd be giving them team shirts and stuff like that."

While giving away goodies was okay, former BRM chief mechanic Alan Challis reckons that there was nothing like hard cash to help you on your way. "The first two or three years we went to Spain you could be held up at the border for two or three days, easily, especially when you went testing. By the time we'd been to a couple of Grands Prix it was organised that there were bonds and things like that put up against the trucks, so you went in and had to sign your name against the bond and get on with it. But you learnt fairly early on that, with all the carnets that you were carrying for all the cars and the engines, and all the bits in the trucks, inside each carnet there'd be something in there for the customs man. Usually stickers and money. You'd always got t-shirts and fags to give away in the truck when you were travelling – especially in France for the Gendarmerie motorbike cops."

Bill Cowe, Graham Hill's mechanic at Team Lotus in 1969, doesn't recall Lotus offering any such incentives at that time, which might go a long way toward explaining some of the niggles and delays they had. "There weren't any goodies in those days, and I'm not aware of any money being innocently left in a carnet or anything like that. Probably that's why we were in so much trouble, because some of the teams did do that and we didn't."

Like Alan Challis, Arthur 'Butty' Birchall, who returned to Team Lotus in the late 1970s, also remembers travelling through France as being a particular issue. Despite Team Lotus having the advantage of sponsorship by a tobacco firm, it was never going to be able to match the appeal of Gauloises, while jingoism was undoubtedly also a factor. "Going into France was always grief. We had the advantage of having packets of cigarettes with us, the John Player Specials. We used to take them with us in the transporter, which we could hand out to the customs people and normally that would see us through fairly easily. There were some of them who were totally anti-British ... I mean the French are a peculiar race anyway but they didn't want us winning on their soil when cars like Matra were running, and when there were French drivers like Lafitte and Pironi, and people like that."

But it is for Spanish customs officials that most mechanics reserve their ire. It seems that, for whatever reason, they were deliberately obstructive, not prepared to accept carnets written in English, and determined to make the passage of Formula 1 cars into their country as difficult as possible.

Stan Collier's story of a visit in 1970 is typical. "When I worked for Rob Walker, me and Tony [Cleverley] went down to Jarama. Going into Spain in those days was terrible and it wasn't only us, it was the same for all the teams. We got stuck at the border, at Irun, for three days. We got in, over the border, and had to go into a compound but we couldn't get out again because the paperwork was wrong, so they said. We had to walk into town and find an agent, who organised it. There were about five teams, all in the same boat. We had to pay Christ knows how much to the agent and to customs, and eventually we got out and arrived on the first day of practice. There used to be a big compound for all the trucks, the cars used to go through a different point. There were trucks that had been there for years, they just never got out because the drivers had got fed up and gone."

Eddie Dennis also remembers that year, which led to the team's mechanics resorting to desperate measures to get their cars built. "That was a tremendous drama because we left with the cars not finished. The plan was to get to Jarama, finish the cars and do some running, but we got stuck at the Spanish customs at Irun and didn't have the correct carnets, so they stuffed us straight into a compound and there we stayed, for about two days. We actually unloaded the cars and were working on them in a loading bay in customs. Ken Tyrrell's son did a lot of the translation with Jo Ramirez who was with Tyrrell at the time. They were a great help in getting us through."

Pat Carvath, a mechanic with BRM, was another who encountered language-based problems, exacerbated by inconsistencies on the part of officials. "We were going to Madrid for testing and reached the Spanish border at Saturday lunchtime with all the carnets written in English. This bloody awkward Spanish bloke said 'Is no good, no good, got to be in Spanish.' We had to rush around and get somebody to translate it for us, which took about four or five hours. When we got back to the post, he'd knocked off and the bloke who'd taken his place had no problem with the English version so that four hours was wasted time."

More dramatic was the experience of another BRM mechanic, Roger Barsby. "I had a gun pulled on me in Spanish customs. We went to Jarama for testing in the old

---

Track record   Pat Carvath

❝I was always interested in engineering and, in a way, I was lucky that BRM was based in Bourne, where I lived. I suppose it helped that my brother-in-law was Tony Rudd [BRM team manager] but I didn't ever try to use that to my advantage. I went along and asked if there were any vacancies and was offered a job. I started off in the engine shop, working on the V16s, when it was still based at Bourne and we used to transport them up to the workshop at Folkingham Aerodrome to do the testing."

Having joined BRM in 1954, Pat did his National Service until 1957, then moved on to the Formula 1 team, working with drivers such as Ron Flockhart, Reg Parnell, Ken Wharton, Jo Bonnier, Graham Hill, Dan Gurney, John Surtees and Jo Siffert before leaving at the end of 1974 when BRM went into administration.

Carvath, shown at the wheel of an H16 BRM, worked for some great drivers, and really rated Graham Hill.
(Pat Carvath)

Leyland transporter. There were three of us in the front, including me driving, and when we got to the border at Irun, we went through the wrong control – where cars rather than lorries go. The French let us through, stamped all the carnets and everything, but when we got to the Spanish bit, in no-man's land, they wouldn't let us through. The guy there reckoned that he couldn't speak English so I said to the guys: 'Right, I'll tell you what we'll do, we'll turn round and go through the proper border crossing.'

"Being semi-automatic, once you'd started the transporter, you couldn't turn the bloody thing off until the air pressure got to 80psi; you had to flick the exhaust brake over and then it cut the engine. I got in to turn it round, started it up and this Guardia Civil bloke came up and kept running his hand across his throat as if to say 'cut the engine,' but I couldn't as there wasn't enough air pressure. So I was revving it to get the air pressure up and he's in front of me putting his hand up to stop me. Just as I got to 80psi on the air pressure, he pulled his bloody gun and was pointing it at me through the cab window. Luckily, the engine cut and stopped. We were at that border for six hours. And the customs guy *could* speak English, the lying sod."

Ray Wardell agrees that Spanish customs were pretty bad but it seems that, in his eyes, the Italian customs people could run them a close second sometimes. "The worst country to get into was Spain. You could spend hours. I don't think we ever bribed anybody, although we got pretty near on occasion, but the Italians could be awkward – you could have all the right papers and they'd still mess you around."

Former Cooper and Honda mechanic Denis Daviss had a close encounter with Italian customs on one of his many trips to the Maserati factory at Modena. "I used to go to Masers quite a lot, picking up and dropping off because there were no truck drivers, and I would leave on time and get back on time. If it meant driving all night, I'd drive all night. Well, this time I took a different route. I was just delivering some stuff so I went through Switzerland and caught the train that goes under the Simplon.

"I arrived at the town on the other side, Domodossola. That was also the Italian border and my papers needed stamping. I went into the little office there and the guy looked at the papers but wouldn't stamp them. Then he just walked out. An hour or so later, another guy walked in who spoke a bit of English and asked me what I was doing. I told him that I needed to get my papers stamped, so he stamped them and off I went.

"About fifty miles down the road, I saw some of these grey Alfa police cars with the blue light on the top coming along and realised they were after me. One of them pulled in front, so I stopped and one of the officers got in my vehicle. They took me back to this office in Domodossola, which had a little room with bars on one side, and I was put in there. One of the previous occupants had left a tin mug in there so I clanged the mug, up and down the bars, until somebody arrived.

"It was the 'good' official again. He asked me what was going on and I told him. Just then the first man arrived and started telling his 'good' colleague all about it. Apparently, he thought I had left the customs post without getting my papers stamped, therefore I was a smuggler. The other guy opened a drawer and pulled out the papers; the other one looked at them, looked at me and just said 'Go!' So off I went again, back to Maserati."

Just to show that not everybody had the same experience, Stan Collier says that he found Italian customs to be okay. "The Italians were very good. If you got all the stickers out and let them have a look at the cars and things like that, you could get through quite reasonably. You never knew how long it was going to take you to get through customs in different countries, though. When we used to go to Spa and places like that, if you went through Aachen, you could be there for hours, so we used to go round the back roads and through a little country crossing, then we were alright.

"In the winter or during bad weather, we used to go over the Mont Cenis into Italy. They were alright; you'd walk in with the papers and they'd all be playing cards in the customs shed and would stamp anything you put in front of them. The Swiss borders were the worst. A lot of people wouldn't go through Switzerland at all because they all had problems."

Different people had their own way of dealing with customs officials. Former Cooper mechanic Richard Watson remembers one particularly novel method adopted by Jack Brabham. "Jack was going to ERSA in Paris to get gearbox parts. I said 'Where's this ERSA place, then?' and he replied 'Oh, somewhere over that way.' Anyhow, there we were with this Ford 10cwt van, with a trailer on the back, so off we trundled.

"Jack had a very good sense of direction and we didn't have to ask anybody, we found the place. We filled this Ford van with these bits. He said 'Don't make it all neat and tidy, throw them all over the place.' 'What for?' I asked, and he replied 'You'll see when we get to customs – throw them all over the place.' The Ford 10 passenger seat sat on a little locker and so we stuffed a lot of the items in there, otherwise we would have had to pay import duty or something. We flew over from Le Touquet to Lydd and landed. By the time we got there, the back of the van was an absolute shambles; there was stuff all over the place. When the customs guy asked if we had anything to declare, Jack told him he could look in the van. The official took one look through the back window and walked away."

So successful was the Brabham team at Reims one year that a van had to be sent from the UK to collect its haul of champagne, which must have taken some explaining at customs, as Gerry Hones recalls. "We went down to Reims to do Formula 2 and Formula 1 and were fastest in practice and got 200 bottles of champagne, won the race and got another 200 bottles of champagne, fastest in Formula 1 practice and won 200 bottles, won the race and got another 200 bottles, making 800 bottles altogether. We had a Holden van back at the works, and they had to send that down to Reims to pick up the champagne."

By the late 1960s, Jack Brabham was a well-known personality, so when he returned to the UK, the customs men, according to Hones, were more interested in how he had fared than what he was bringing back. "When we came back from the continent, we always had to land at Gatwick to clear customs, before flying on to Fairoaks. Jack used to wander in and they'd say 'Hello Jack, how are you doing, did you do any good?' and he'd reply 'Yup, had a first or a second' or whatever, and that was it, that was the customs check."

Unsurprisingly, given the hassle experienced simply moving between countries, it was relatively rare for mechanics to try and bring back any little 'extras,' although, as Bill Cowe relates, there were ways in which this could be done. "It has been known. One of the tricks used was if you bought a watch or something like that, you would put it in the top of the trumpets and, if the customs got a bit close to it, you would just open up the throttle slides and it would drop down underneath the slides. Hopefully, the valve would close and then, when you got back to the works, you'd fish it out again. Not that I've ever done anything like that, of course ..."

Feigning ignorance of a language is another technique that has been successfully adopted many a time by teams in order to clear customs. However, it does require the co-operation of all the people on board the transporter, as Tony Robinson wryly observes. "Once, we were stopped or queried at the border in Aachen. I was giving a lift to Chris Barber, the Jazz man, who was quite fluent in German. We got to the border and I'm playing all dumb and stupid as if I don't understand anything, but, of course, Chris starts chatting away in German, trying to explain things; I had to politely ask him to belt up. My view was that if you didn't speak the language you couldn't get involved, you just pleaded ignorance. Then you couldn't be accused of anything."

As with so many other aspects of Formula 1, the Tyrrell team adopted a different and less hostile approach to the customs issue than most and, as Roger Hill explains, it appears to have paid off. "A lot of times you had a spot of trouble at the borders, with carnets and goodness knows what, getting them stamped, and sometimes you'd get there and their guys wanted to have a look inside, or it was five o'clock and they were going home so you had to wait until tomorrow; things like that. The way we saw it was if you came across some guys who were a wee bit interested, all they wanted was to have a look, stamp everything and let you go. Like most things, if you treated them as people instead of being aggressive ... so we always tried to be sensible and talk to them as people."

On very rare occasions, customs hold-ups could actually be positive for the mechanics; Denis Daviss remembers one such incident. "After Monaco one year, probably 1964, we were planning to go straight to Italy. We left France in the truck at Ventimiglia and went to go through the Italian border, but we didn't have any papers. We couldn't go into Italy so we thought we'd go back into France and round another way. But then the French on the Monaco side wouldn't let us back in either. Now the truck was in-between these two border posts, with nowhere to go. As chief mechanic Gordon Whitehead was the man in charge at the time, he went off to sort this out, whilst we spent a couple of days at the beach, which was quite nice."

3

The all-nighter: par for the course

Formula 1 team owners had two distinct philosophies concerning the practice of their mechanics working through the night. For some – like Team Lotus boss Colin Chapman, it was de rigeur, an accepted part of the job that gave extra hours in which to prepare your cars or make last-minute modifications that other teams wouldn't be able to do. For others, all-nighters were to be avoided at all costs, since they resulted in tired mechanics, and tired mechanics made mistakes.

There were a number of reasons why the all-nighter was so prevalent in Grand Prix racing during the 1950s, 60s and 70s. A major factor was the small number of people employed by the big teams, as Tony Robinson points out. "All-nighters were fairly regular; that was accepted. Things were different then. Part of the reason was that, with Stirling and his 250F, and even in the 1960s when we were racing the BRP cars, it was invariably just two mechanics per car." Another reason, as Robinson remembered, was the timing of practice sessions at Grand Prix meetings. "We used to have practice and qualifying somewhere round about five or six o'clock in the evening on a Saturday. I often thought it would have been a good idea to have the last practice at midday on a Saturday, to give a full 24 hours to prepare the car."

Denis Daviss agrees that practice session timing had a lot to do with it; this was a particular issue at Monaco due to the fact that the circuit was on public roads, so sessions were held first thing in the morning and last thing at night. "I used to be quite good at all-nighters; I'd had a lot of practice. Most race team guys worked all night because there was always a late practice. At a place like Monaco, they had an early morning practice, which was fine, then whatever went wrong we spent all day fixing it; evening practice it was the same sort of thing, doing whatever needed doing, meaning working over the next night ready for the next morning. Quite often we didn't even bother to go to the hotel, even though it was just across the road. Fortunately, the garages had a shower ..."

Tony Cleverley notes that another factor contributing to all-nighters in the early years was the poor reliability and build quality of the cars. "The all-nighters came up because cars just weren't made as well as they were later on. The difference between the later cars and an early Cooper or Lotus was huge. The engines wouldn't last as long, Colotti gearboxes would let you down, and you'd be doing an all-nighter to put a clutch and a gearbox in a car. The reliability of the cars was pretty poor, that's where the difference comes in. We used to do a lot of all-nighters, I must admit. You wouldn't think about going to Monte Carlo without knowing you were going to do at least two all-nighters, whatever happened."

Alan Challis recalls that, at BRM, all-nighters were also an integral part of life as a Grand Prix mechanic. "At the time, it was part of the job. You accepted that and, as long as you got the cars finished in the morning, you'd done your job, what you were paid for. The first race I ever did, at Reims, I ended up fast asleep. The first time we'd ever filled this bloody car up was on the Saturday night, and we were about six or seven gallons short to be able to get through the race. Fortunately, we had fabricators with us, and we set to and made loads of little aluminium fuel tanks, which we fitted all around the car, and Bendix fuel pumps to pump it from the little tin tanks into the main tank. Apparently, I was sitting at the front of the car waiting for this bloke to finish off this thing and ended up fast asleep, laid against the radiator. Behind me they were banging a big sheet of aluminium with a hammer but I still didn't wake up until they gave me a kick. I think that weekend we had gone to work Thursday morning and the first time we actually stopped was when we loaded the truck after the race."

Before the Formula 1 teams became sufficiently organised to present themselves as a coherent package, race promoters used the carrot of start money or appearance money to attract entries for their races. This also reflected the fact that there were literally dozens of relatively minor non-Championship races littering the calendar, and sometimes there would be a clash between two far apart events or races on the same weekend.

Many car owners and drivers were able to survive an entire season by moving between races and living off the start money they earned, regardless of whether they managed to finish the races and win some prize money. However, that system meant that it was absolutely essential, at all costs, to make the start of a race. A crash in practice, particularly at some of the more far-flung circuits such as Enna or Syracuse in Sicily – which took the best part of a week to reach – could be financially disastrous, and mechanics would go to any lengths to get a 'start money special' to the grid.

Dick Scammell remembers one such occasion. "You always had to start the car. At Porto [the 1960 Portuguese Grand Prix], with Jim Clark driving, he went off and wrecked the car and we just set to and welded it up. The only trouble was, the only welding wire we could find was in a fence outside. It probably wasn't the best … I can remember Colin saying 'I think we'll just do a couple of laps shall we, gently?' In the end Jimmy finished third. In those days, of course, mechanics got 10 per cent of the prize money shared out between them. It didn't come to much but it all helped."

Ralph Gilbert, who worked as a mechanic for Bob Gerard Racing during the 1950s and 60s, recalls another similar occasion. "Our most memorable all-nighter was in Sicily. One year we went down with two cars for John Rhodes and John Taylor, a Cooper-Climax and a Cooper-Ford with a 1500cc twin-cam engine. Taylor drove the 'twink' and Rhodes was in the Climax-powered car. Rhodes went off and bent it severely. We spent all night repairing it and got it all going. I remember Bob came up to Rhodes on the grid after the warm-up lap and said 'How is it?' John looked at him and replied 'Well, it oversteers a bit.' 'That's normal isn't it?' said Bob, and John said 'Yes, but it oversteers on the straights.' The car looked more like a 45 gallon drum. I think it did 10 laps before it ran out of water. The chassis tubes used to hold the oil and water at that time, and as soon as it got hot, the tubes expanded and opened up the cracks."

Stan Collier also recalls a desperate patching up operation in the same country. "When we were down in Sicily with Formula 2, our cars were going alright but John Campbell-Jones had a shunt and broke his rear upright. Nobody had a spare rear upright with them in those days, we didn't carry them, so he patched it all together, strapped it up with bits of metal and bolts and all that, and put it back on the car, just to get started in the race. He had to do that or else he wouldn't have got any money. To go all the way to Sicily and get nothing, was a long way to go."

Another venue where it was vital to make sure the car started was Watkins Glen, home of the US Grand Prix, and the most lucrative race of the year. Although they didn't actually pay start money, in effect they did because prize money was awarded even to last place. It was therefore essential to at least take the start, as Collier remembers: "Olivier Gendebien was driving one of the BRP cars. We were standing in the pits at Watkins Glen waiting for him, and the first thing we saw was the car coming around the

The tech shed at Watkins Glen afforded fans a great opportunity to see various team mechanics at work on their Formula 1 cars – and was also not a bad place for an all-nighter. This shot, taken in 1976, shows the Brabham-Alfa team, with the car of Carlos Pace in the foreground. Stan Collier is to the left, with his hand on the other team car, while Brabham's designer, Gordon Murray, and owner, Bernie Ecclestone, are deep in conversation with an unknown third party. To the far right, a contemplative Pace reflects on a poor qualifying performance. Starting from a lowly 10th place on the grid, his race didn't get any better, and he retired after a collision with the McLaren of Jochen Mass.
(Stan Collier)

corner, end-over-end. He wasn't hurt, just had a few bruises, but we had a couple of all-nighters getting that car ready for the race. If you didn't start, you didn't get your money. We got it all patched up and he went out.

"I had another one at Watkins Glen with Piers Courage, he had a big shunt in practice and I worked all night there, welding up the back frame and putting everything together." Ex-BRM mechanic Pat Carvath, who was seconded to the Parnell team that was running Courage's BRM at the time, remembers the occasion well. "Parnell said to Stan and myself 'Get that to the starting line and you'll be on a good bonus;' he came eighth in the race. Later, Parnell gave us about US$100. I said 'Are you sure you can afford that, Tim?' He'd promised us about a thousand dollars I think but, anyway …" In the race, Courage stopped first in the pits to change an ignition transistor box and again to replace a missing bolt in the rear suspension, but finally ran out of fuel just before the chequered flag. Being classified eighth was more than enough compensation, however – for Parnell, at least.

That mechanics received a share of the winnings goes a long way toward explaining their determination to place cars on the grid – even if it meant all-nighters – and also why they were so keen to ensure their cars reached the finish through addition of the so-called 'mechanic's gallon' (see Chapter 5).

As Arthur Birchall points out, at Lotus, there was another financial reason as working all-nighters was a way to top up your wages, albeit not by a great deal. "We would do an ordinary working day, which finished at something like 6 o'clock, then, if you worked until 10 o'clock you got something like one and sixpence, which is probably about seven and a half/eight pence, for fish and chips. If you worked from 10 until 2 you got another one and sixpence, and, if you worked every night, most of the night, you could make up probably a quid at the end of your week's work in expenses. It was not a lot, it would just about buy a packet of chips, the one and sixpence. But then, you didn't work there for the money ..."

Sometimes it wasn't just a case of money; pride came into it as well, particularly when a car had made a long journey to get to a race. Bob Sparshott recalls one such occasion when he was running a March 761 for Brett Lunger in the early part of the 1977 season. "We went to the tyre testing in South Africa about two weeks before the race. What the teams used to do was take that opportunity to do some hot weather running, and then stay out there and take part in the race. We were nearly at the end of the testing when Brett went off and did a mighty lot of damage to this car.

"When it came in on the back of the wrecker, I saw that the left-hand side was all stoved in. I said to the lads 'Well, we don't have a spare car, we'll be going home, that's it.' But then, when I went round the other side, it was completely intact. I began thinking 'Hang on, let's have a better look at it.' It didn't look like there was too much trouble with the bulkheads, but all the outer skin had gone, and the left-hand front and left-hand rear suspension, the wing, everything. I said 'If they've got some spares in England and they shipped them out, together with what we've got, I reckon we could make this ready in time for the race.' My mechanics thought I was nuts. I said 'Well, it's up to you guys. If you don't all want to have a go at it, then we are not going to be able to do it.' So they said "Yeah, let's give it a go."

"I did it in the full knowledge that Ken Gillibrand had a workshop about a mile down the road from the circuit. He'd worked in England and he had a European-type shop with proper welding equipment, a flat-bed for chassis, all the kit. I immediately went and saw him and said 'Look, I can only do this with your help.' Of course, he was rubbing his hands together because he was going to earn some money. I worked with Ken on the chassis and left the rest of the team up at the circuit building up bits and pieces, so that when we got the chassis back they'd just be able to bolt it up.

"We just did a 10-day ball-breaker, basically, with no or very little sleep. It got painted on a Sunday night by a local paintshop guy and then taken up to the track and they built it up and we were there for first practice. Even Bernie [Ecclestone] came up to me and said 'That was a bloody fantastic job, I didn't think you could do it,' and I replied 'Nor did anybody else.' And it finished 14th in the race. Not very high but it finished ..."

Mechanics also rose to the challenge when it was a sponsor's home race and a car was damaged, as clearly it was one of the most important races of the year for their backers. Roy Topp remembers one particular instance in Montreal, Canada, when working for Walter Wolf's team. "In 1978, we had Bobby Rahal driving for us and he damaged his car when he went off in a big way. The previous year's WR1 was in Canada somewhere as a show car on display in one of the hotels, and they decided that they would get it out; this was after last practice, with the race the next day.

"It was in show condition, so didn't have a proper engine or gearbox. We got it back to the circuit and worked all night to rebuild this thing into a race car and Rahal drove it. Actually, he was going really well. Unfortunately, it didn't finish. I can remember Jody [Scheckter] saying, 'Don't work on that, work on my car,' because I was chief mechanic. But I had to do what was best for the team."

A downside to working constant all-nighters was that mechanics became tired, crotchety and rebellious. Mike Barney recalls this happening when he was working at Coopers. "When we did the Indy car in 1961, we'd been there for two all-nighters on the trot and were just wiped out. We weren't doing very much by then, we were just too tired. It was silly, really. When you look at it now, it was a total waste of time. Anyway, we'd staggered on and it was a Friday; it had to be a Friday because that was the day *Autosport* came out then, and Noddy [chief mechanic Michael Grohmann] had gone down the road to buy a copy. He came back and we were stood there looking at the pictures when Charlie Cooper came in. He walked up to Noddy, who was already a bit ratty by this time, and snatched the magazine out of his hand. There was then an almighty row, dear oh dear. The language, you've never heard anything like it. The pair of them were effing and blinding at each other, over the chassis of the Indy car. Charlie Cooper went out of the place in a huff and sent the works manager, Major Owens, up. He said 'We can't have the tail wagging the dog, you'll have to go.' But he didn't go because they were just about to go off to Indianapolis."

As former Cooper mechanic Denis Daviss explains, sometimes, if a number of teams were doing an all-nighter at the same time, it was important to gain a psychological advantage over the competition. "With the Lotus 49, when it won its first race out, we were all working in a garage in Zandvoort. Our hotel was across the road, a place called the Myerscough. All the Lotus mechanics were there as well as Chapman and Keith Duckworth, they had been having wheel bearing problems with the 49s. At midnight, I

Taking a break to read the motor sport press in work time was frowned upon at Cooper, but here Mike Barney (l) and Michael 'Noddy' Grohmann manage to sneak a peek at Motor Racing to read all about Graham Hill's 1962 Dutch Grand Prix victory. (Mike Barney)

did a little deal with one of the waitresses across there and she tripped along in all her uniform with a big silvery-coloured tray, a great big coffee pot on it and all the cups round, just for our crew, not for them. Because that's part of the game, isn't it? I had to grease her palm a little bit but that was alright, it was only money."

Just occasionally during all-nighters, inquisitiveness about their working environment would get the better of mechanics, as Roger Barsby explains. "We were at Monza with the old BRM P139 – that was a sod. Surtees was driving for us, and we always used to have the garages in the Parco Hotel Monza just on the entrance to the park. Surtees got in the car and said 'That's well down on power,' so we put the spare engine in. He didn't like that, so we put another one in and he didn't like that either, so we went back to the original. That was four engine changes in three days, and, bearing in mind it took about six hours to change an engine, we got some all-nighters. One night one of the blokes said 'I wonder what's over that wall?' So we stacked up some tyres and looked over the top: it was a wine cellar. We weren't very popular the next morning, but there we go …"

Probably the only thing worse than having to stay up all night and work, is having to stay up all night and sit around not working. Ben Casey remembers when this happened with the BRM team in 1971. "We went to Ontario Motor Speedway in California. It was Formula 1s versus their Formula As, and we had our P153s. At the back, in-between the gearbox and the engine, was a butterfly plate that the suspension used to hang on, and we found that these were all falling apart, cracking. We hadn't had a good weekend; we were working until midnight or more the first two nights, and then this occurred. So we had to strip out all the cars. Aubrey [Woods, BRM engine designer] knew somebody who worked for Boeing or Lockheed, and he went off into Los Angeles with them, got these plates riveted and repaired, and then we had to refit them ready for the race in the morning. That was a long night because, once we'd got everything stripped out, we were sitting about waiting. If you are working, the time goes quicker. We couldn't go anywhere, so just had to sit there and wait for him to come back. It was a bit of a shame really because we were 10 miles from Los Angeles but I never saw the bloody place."

Another cause of greater-than-average team workloads came when two drivers of

Track record
Ben Casey

❝ I lived just down the road at the time, about 50 yards from the works. Being a lad of 16, I used to pop down and see what they were doing and give them a hand. I started an apprenticeship there in 1963 and then when Dennis Perkins decided he wanted to stop racing, I went on the gearbox side, learnt from Dennis, then took over from him. I did ten years as a mechanic with BRM between 1967 and 1977."

Oddly enough, Ben's name isn't really Ben, it is Philip, as he explains. "Ben has been my nickname from the age of 16. I even had Ben Casey on my shirts. In the early 60s, there was a programme on TV, a doctors' series called Ben Casey. I was going up town one night with two mates and they said 'We're going to call you after that fella.' Old relatives and aunts still call me Philip but even my sister calls me Ben."

BRM was the obvious choice for Ben as he lived down the road from the works. (Grand Prix Mechanics Charitable Trust)

very different heights were used and they needed to swap cars. Mike Lowman, who worked as a mechanic for Dan Gurney's Anglo American Racers, vividly remembers one such occasion. "At Monte Carlo in 1967, we had a driver who was 6ft 3in [Gurney] and one about 5ft 8in [Richie Ginther]. After the first qualifying, they decided that the engine in Dan's car was better than the one in Richie's. To do an engine change on it was an all-nighter anyway, so we thought, why don't we change the rest of the car, leaving the engines alone. Put Dan's stuff in what was Richie's and Richie's stuff in Dan's car?

"It turned out that this was no quicker, and we ended up being up all that night and the next doing the same thing in reverse. Because that car was a complete monocoque, to get down into the footwell area was an 'upside-down job,' you used to get into the cockpit upside down and just work above your head inside it, which was not the most comfortable place in the world. There was just so much to change on it but they wanted to feel comfortable in their cars. It was a nightmare changing that. And then Richie didn't qualify …"

Lowman discovered another, altogether different pitfall of working all-nighters later in his career when he was with Don Nichols' Shadow Formula 1 team at the 1973 Belgian Grand Prix. "The first year we went to Zolder, we were working late and [Tecno Formula 1 car designer and constructor] Allan McCall and his team were still at it on the Tecno. We were ready to go and they were struggling, with just tiny little flashlights working on the car. I decided I'd lend them some of our neon lights, so I took them over.

"I went to get out later and the gate to the paddock was padlocked. I went up the control tower, which was about eight floors high, and there was not a soul about. I said to the lads 'OK, get back to the garage and get me my hacksaw.' I cut off the padlock, out we got and just pushed the gate shut. I didn't think any more of it. The next day, we were working on the cars when this police officer came into the garage and said 'I understand you cut the padlock' and I said 'Yeah, we couldn't get out last night, there was no-one there, we were locked in and we needed to go back to get some sleep and some food.'

"He said 'Ah, you cannot do that, I must have your passport.' Fine; I gave him my bloody passport and said to him 'I'll tell you what, if there is any problem, I'll just go back over there and weld it up for you, I don't have the slightest problem in doing that.' So we wheeled the old welder over to the gate and welded the thing for him, which defused the situation a little bit."

It was very rare to find a team that actively avoided all-nighters if it could, though Team Tyrrell was one such outfit, as former chief mechanic Roger Hill explains. "Yes, we had a few all-nighters, everybody does but we tried not to get involved in that. We would work a long day, and you can get a lot done in a day if you really want to. If you think you've got all night as well, that's alright but it's not very good the next day or the day after. We managed amongst ourselves, got stuck in and tried to do the job so it didn't eat into the time when you should be having a rest. We tried to get organised and Ken was the instigator of that. He knew damn well that, if you'd worked all night for a couple of nights or a couple of days, whatever, then you weren't doing such a good job."

The main exception to this rule within the team was with the 1000cc Formula 2 cars, where the highly-strung motors needed a lot of attention, as ex-Tyrrell mechanic Neil Davis explains. "We used BRM and Cosworth engines, and just about every night you had to take the head off the Cosworth engine and do all the valves and springs and God knows what, because they'd been over-revved and the clearances were closed up. It was quite stressful, and it was two or three in the morning before you got between the sheets, and then more or less got out the other side and start work again. But I wouldn't have changed those days because they were an experience, and we were the sort of age that we could cope with it."

A passionate morning in Monza

Tired and hungry mechanics did not make happy people. However, they were still usually able to maintain their sense of humour even under extreme provocation, as ex-Cooper man Denis Daviss illustrates. "In 1966, as soon as we got back from the German Grand Prix, I went rushing off with an engine-less car [a Cooper-Maserati] on a trailer. I arrived in Modena and the engineer, Alfieri, said 'We need to go testing tomorrow.' Just then Surtees arrived 'Yes, we need to go testing tomorrow.' That meant I had to put an engine in. I wasn't alone, I had an assistant this time: Maserati had a roving Alsatian that guarded the place at night. He liked me, for some strange reason, possibly because when I'd been there at other times I'd pinched some stuff out of the restaurant kitchen for him. Anyway, I was laying down on the floor, doing the underneath stuff. To start

Opposite: The arrival of John Surtees following his very public falling out with Ferrari transformed the Cooper team into a force to be reckoned with during the 1966 season. Shown here in the pits at Monza, Denis Daviss is sitting on the rear wheel with Maserati chief engineer Guilio Alfieri next to him in the suit, designer Derrick White kneeling by the left front wheel talking to Surtees, and Jimmy Potton kneeling on the other side of the car. After qualifying fourth, the Englishman retired before half distance with a fuel leak. (Denis Daviss)

Track record   Denis Daviss

❝ *I was working at a place called CVA in Brighton, making tools and dies. I had a friend who was building a Ford Special and I used to make parts for it. Eventually, I had to make my mind up whether I wanted to work on cars or not and decided I did. My first job was for a guy in Kent with an Invicta and an old 4CL Maserati. He said he was in the cantilever business. I found out later he designed brassieres; that was his 'cantilever' … Then I worked for a guy named George Henrott on a Formula Junior Gemini, after which I had a short spell working for the Sirocco Formula 1 team until that folded. I got a job at Cooper's building racing cars with Dougie Johnson, their first employee. After a spell in 1963 working for Willment, I went back to Cooper's a year later and stayed until the end of the 1967 season, when I moved to Honda on their Formula 1 side until their withdrawal the following year. I was a machinist by trade so got jobs because I could get on a lathe and make things. I've never been trained as a mechanic, just knew how to do it, really.*

Denis moved to McLaren, where he became increasingly involved in their efforts to win the Indy 500, a feat he eventually achieved as crew chief in 1974 and 1976. He left the company – and motor racing – at the end of the 1979 season.

Cheeky chappies: Good friends Denis Daviss (r) and Jimmy Potton obviously had some fun in 1966 when they worked together at Cooper. (Denis Daviss)

with the dog would come and lay on me and put his head on me. He got a bit pissed off with doing that, so when I put down a spanner, he'd pick it up and take it away.

"In the morning, when the engineer, Alfieri, and Surtees arrived, I was just about to go and have a shower and something to eat because I hadn't eaten since I'd left Byfleet. They said: 'We need to go testing' and I replied 'I really need to go and get some food.' 'You can have some when we get to Monza" they said, so we loaded up this thing and off we went to Monza, which was about four hours' drive away because it is on the edge of Milan. We got there and they were all fit and ready to go. John got into the car and did a little run to make sure nothing was leaking, because it was getting very close to lunchtime. He did his lap and he's sitting in the car; he said 'You've got some springs and rollbars with you, haven't you?' and I replied 'Yeah, I've got some stuff, not a lot.' He said 'Well, I think we need some harder springs on the front and probably a harder roll-bar at the back.'

"I said to him 'John, bite my ear.' He was wearing an open-faced helmet which he pulled back and asked 'What did you say?' So I said it again: 'John, bite my ear please' and he said 'What the hell are you on about now?' to which I replied 'I like a bit of passion when I'm being f****d about.' With that, he said 'Well, the restaurant is open, why don't you go and get some food and tell them I'm paying for it?'" Never slow on the uptake, clearly, John could see that breaking point had been reached; a meal was the only way that team equilibrium could be restored.

Champagne and oil in Reims

The 1966 French Grand Prix was held at Reims. For the works Cooper team, running Cooper-Maserati T81s, it was an epic weekend. Denis Daviss takes up the story. "Cooper fielded three cars in that race. One for Jochen Rindt, one for Chris Amon, and one for John Surtees. After every day's practice – and there were three – engineer

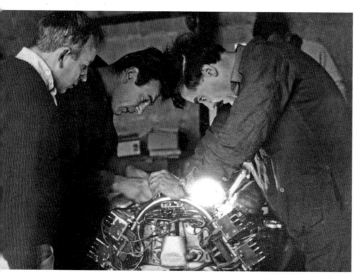

During his racing career, John Surtees was always a very 'hands-on' driver, closely involved in the design, development and running of the cars he drove. Here, he watches intently as Denis Daviss (centre) and Jimmy Potton work on one of the 3-litre Maserati engines used in the Cooper T81 that he drove in 1966. (Denis Daviss)

Alfieri supplied a new specification engine for John Surtees' car; John's engine went into Rindt's car, and Rindt's engine went into Amon's car. Well, as practice was over three days, that made nine engine changes ...

"The Cooper had these booms that stuck out under the gearbox. The engine had to be lowered in so they used to take quite a while to change – eight hours or so. Fortunately, we had two block and tackle sets, plus the one from Cooper. All three cars were having engine changes at the same time, but we still ended up working most of the night, with just two mechanics on each car.

"A big problem was oil, as each car held approximately four gallons in total. At the end of the race meeting, with these nine engine changes, everything that could hold oil was full. Maserati also wanted all the engines back, plus the three race engines – we had their total stock of engines. So the race engines also had to come out, and what did we do with the oil from them? That was a big problem. The oil tank was right at the front and the oil went back down to the engine through an aluminium pipe, about an inch and a quarter in diameter, in a channel in the bottom of the chassis on each side. It was decided to plug these aluminium pipes with rag and hold it on with tape.

"Unfortunately, just as the first car was being pulled up the ramp, the plugs popped out and covered the transporter floor, the ramps, and the road with oil. Before there was time to clean it up, a French cyclist came riding down the road, slowed to look into the back of the truck, and promptly found his bike sliding away from under him. Not a very happy Frenchman. A few racing giveaways made him smile again, however.

"As John was fastest on the first day, he was awarded 100 bottles of champagne – normal for the French as Reims is in champagne country – which I collected and put under the transporter's full-width bench seat. On arriving at Dover, six of us lined up with our duty-free purchases, and the official asked 'Do you have anything to declare?' I told him we had some champagne that John Surtees had won for fastest lap, but nothing purchased. He then asked how much champagne, and I told him there was enough for one bottle each. 'Oh well, that's okay then, off you go,' he replied, thinking I meant enough for the six of us standing there, whereas I had actually meant enough for everyone at the Cooper factory ..."

Lotus: king of the all-nighter

The undisputed king of the all-nighter within the Formula 1 paddock was Team Lotus; just as most teams were knocking off for the night, its mechanics would be making a start on one of Colin Chapman's legendary job lists, as Arthur 'Butty' Birchall recalls. "We used to get people taking the mickey out of us, walking past the door calling 'We're off now, boys!' There was a good rapport with the other teams, but they all knew that Chapman was a pretty hard taskmaster."

Former Lotus Indy and Formula 1 mechanic Hughie Absalom remembers that the constant round of all-nighters took their toll. "At Lotus, we were fairly close to being zombies. Seven days a week was normal, whether we were going racing or back at the factory, you just seemed to be forever working. When Dick Scammell got more of a say as to how to operate the place, it got a lot better, but before that Chapman would just walk all over us."

Scammell vividly remembers the effect all-nighters had on his ability to concentrate

Tired but happy: the Team Lotus mechanics take a well-earned break in Mexico, probably 1964. Left to right: unknown, Nick Garbett, Derek Wild, Dick Scammell, Bill Cowe. (Dick Scammell)

behind the wheel as well. "The first race that I ever went to was at Aintree in 1960. I remember driving up there. It would be terrible today, you wouldn't even be able to talk about it. But everybody worked an all-nighter. I remember setting off with somebody in a van and only being able to drive for about 20 minutes each, we went all the way to Aintree, really falling asleep, which wasn't very clever but that's the way life was."

There were so many Team Lotus all-nighters that it's hard to distinguish them more than forty years on. However, even today, Scammell names the 1967 British Grand Prix weekend as the occasion of probably the team's greatest all-nighter. "When Graham crashed a 49 in the pitlane at Silverstone, we took the wreckage back and had built another car by the following day. That was a huge effort by everybody; a whole mass of people who didn't stop from the time they left Silverstone to the time they got back."

Eamon Fullalove, a fabricator back at the factory, takes up the story. "In practice, Jimmy had pole position and Graham was second. Graham was coming into the pits and hit the pit wall, wrecking the car. That was on the Friday night. We were just going home at about five o'clock when we got a call at the factory to say we had to stay there to rebuild a tub for Graham. The third tub was just done, it had come back from the paint shop. It was painted green, grey inside, but there was nothing in it, only the brake lines. So Graham flew back in his plane and brought a couple of guys with him. Then the truck had to be sent to bring back the wreck. Leo Wybrott and myself started, then Graham got back with a couple of guys, making five of us.

"I asked what we were going to do for food, and Graham said he would go to the shop and get some. He took the two secretaries from Lotus and they all went back to my place, which was not far from the factory, and cooked dinner for us. Then the truck arrived and we had to get the car out and strip it. We worked all night on that. It was a monumental effort, which I don't think could be done nowadays. By Saturday morning we had got the car sitting on the floor. Dick Scammell was running around saying 'Come on guys, you've got to get this in the truck.' We eyeballed it, lined it up, put the strings round it and got the toes right, fired it up – all the functions worked – and loaded it into the truck.

Track record   Dick Scammell

"After my National Service, I knew I wanted to do something with cars so went off to London with a friend and aimed for the Chequered Flag [garage]. My second call was Lotus at Cheshunt. I went into Components and they interviewed me for about three minutes before saying 'You want that lot round the corner.' I duly went round to Team Lotus who were in a huge panic working on a car on the back of the transporter. Jim Endruweit said 'Can't talk now, much too busy, come back in a week'. I went back in a week and they'd obviously all recovered from whatever race meeting it was and I landed a job as a junior member of Team Lotus. It wasn't very big then, the Formula 1 team comprised six of us."

Dick worked his way up to chief mechanic, then racing manager, working with drivers such as Jim Clark, John Surtees, Graham Hill, Jochen Rindt and Emerson Fittipaldi, before finally leaving at the end of the 1971 season. Apart from a two-year interval as manager of the Parnelli Formula 1 team in 1974-76, he was with engine supplier Cosworth until his retirement in 1996, briefly coming out of retirement to oversee the integration of the company into the Ford organisation in 1998.

Under the watchful eye of colleague Dougie Bridge, the Team Lotus chief mechanic rolls the just completed Lotus 49 out of the workshop under its own power for the first time, May 1967. (Ford Motor Company)

Seconds after hitting the wall near the pit entrance, Graham Hill struggles to bring his three-wheeled Lotus 49 under control. The accident would prompt an all-nighter of epic proportions in order to get the Briton on the grid for the next day. (Tim Blackburn)

"Meanwhile, Allan McCall, Jimmy's mechanic, had noticed that the engine mounts on his car were cracking; the rivets were coming loose. It needed to be taken for a spot of welding. There was a garage not far from the track, which they towed it to, using Jim Endruweit's station wagon. Allan, in this little garage with a light bulb, by himself, worked all night and fixed that car. The truck was loaded and headed back to Silverstone and I flew back with Graham, still in our dirty overalls.

"When they got back to the track, someone asked 'What about Allan? He's down in the village with Jimmy's car,' so Jim Endruweit had to go, driving against the flow of people walking in, and the traffic. He finally arrived to find Allan McCall in total panic, thinking they'd forgotten him and were not going to come and get him. They put a rope on and towed Clark's car through the traffic and finally got to the track. Everybody gathered round, working on Graham's car. In the race, Graham had a problem and Jim won. But it earned us the start money and Graham gave the money to all the guys. It was one of those great moments of teamwork."

The 1968 season was a particularly difficult one for Team Lotus. Having had both Jim Clark and Mike Spence die at the wheel of one of Colin Chapman's designs, Graham Hill grabbed the Formula 1 team by the scruff of its neck, restoring spirits by winning both the Spanish and Monaco Grands Prix. However, that year the advent of wings placed a huge strain on drivetrains and suspensions, with the result that new specifications were constantly evolving as the season developed, adding considerably to the mechanics' workload. This situation came to a head during the US Grand Prix meeting at Watkins Glen.

It was common practice in those days for Lotus to field a third car for a local ace in some of the North American races. In this case, it was to be Mario Andretti, though it seems that the news had not filtered through to the mechanics, who were surprised to learn at 10pm on the Friday night that his participation meant that the engines on all three cars had to be changed. With the other teams long since departed, their cars covered and the mechanics tucked up in bed, Lotus mechanics started work, as Graham Hill's mechanic, Bob Sparshott, recounts. "A deal was done with Ford and, of course, he [Andretti] had to have a decent engine, because they demanded he had one. We were short of good engines, and to get Mario a decent one and still give Graham a decent one meant that all three engines had to come out of all three cars, with Jackie's the first car. We did a sort of 'Round Robin' and put a fresh one in Graham's and the best of the bunch – Oliver's engine, which was quite good – into Mario's car. Oliver had to have the worst of the lot, which he didn't like, and whinged and moaned about!

"In the morning, the drivers and the Old Man [Chapman] came back, all fresh and bubbling. We'd gone to have a bacon sandwich and arrived back at the garage as they were all standing around looking at the cars. I'll never forget Jackie [Oliver]; he was looking down at his car, with his hands on his hips, to identify the colours on the springs, because one of the jobs that needed doing on his car was changing the front springs. It was a big job on a Lotus 49, with the inboard front springs. We had prioritised the work and the springs had been left, basically. Jackie didn't say anything to us, not 'Good morning, I see you've been here all night, guys,' nothing at all. He just walked over to the Old Man and said 'Colin, they haven't changed my springs.' Colin went to talk to Bob Dance, I suppose to ask why, took one look at Bob, who was totally wound up, and

Track record
Bob Sparshott

❝I was still at college, aged 18 or 19 when I went to visit my cousin near Chichester. He was very keen on cars and took me to a meeting at Goodwood. I saw these cars racing and thought 'Christ, I've got to get involved.' From that moment on, my whole ethos in life changed. I didn't want to become a scientist or whatever else I was going to try and be, I wanted to be involved in racing. Of course, I didn't have a clue how to do it.

"I rang round the teams and got absolutely nowhere because I didn't have any experience. Eventually I got a reply from Lotus at Cheshunt, who said they couldn't employ me in the racing team because of my lack of experience but they noticed I'd got an accountancy GCE and offered me a job in the office, in Lotus Components. I thought 'S**t, that's the last thing I want' but then I thought 'Hang on a minute, if I get on the team, I'm there.'

"I was travelling from my home near St. Albans by train, bus, then another bus every day and the hours were draconian. I tried for a job on the racing side but ran up against a brick wall because they didn't take people from other departments – it wasn't company policy. I then got myself out of the office into Lotus Service, where I got a good mechanical grounding.

"Eventually I went for an interview with Ray Parsons, who was running the Cortina team. He made it pretty tough for me but I impressed him with what I knew about the theory of various things and he said he would give it the rubber stamp and I was away. That was in 1964. I remember my father died a few months before I got onto the racing team, which was really disappointing because he thought I was wasting my time, he couldn't see the point of it all. I had finally made it and he'd died, it was tragic really."

Bob moved on to the Formula 2 team in 1967, then Formula 1 in 1968 as mechanic to that year's World Champion, Graham Hill, then struck out on his own in 1969. He has worked for himself ever since. In the 1970s and 80s he ran his own team, BS Fabrications, in Formula 1 until 1978 and then in Formula 2 and Formula 3000 under the BS Automotive name, stopping in 1987. Since then he has been involved in manufacturing/fabricating/general engineering work for racing cars and is still active in constructing monocoques, suspension parts and refurbishing components from cars of the 60s, 70s and early 80s through his company, Racecar Work Ltd.

In the mood for mutiny: It's 10pm and the Team Lotus mechanics (left to right) Bob Sparshott, Trevor Seaman and Bob Dance look less than amused as Colin Chapman informs them they have three engine changes to make before morning. Chief designer Maurice Phillippe (right), who stayed to help them that night, looks on. (Bob Dance)

got the vibes straight away. He turned back to Oliver, put his arm round him and said 'I want you to start practice on those, Jackie.'"

Matters then went from bad to worse, as Sparshott explains. "Jackie wanted to get out quickly. I was still finishing my car because I was down on manpower. Graham arrived and asked if he could help. I asked if he'd mind giving it a polish! You always had to polish the car before it went out, but I literally hadn't got time to do it. So Graham was polishing away and everybody else buggered off out of the tech-shed to begin practice. Before we got out, they were back. Oliver had crashed the car, he'd stood on it and a wheel had broken on about the second lap. It turned out that where we screwed up was that a truck came up in the middle of the night from the airport – as they did all through the night bringing parts for everybody – and a load of wheel halves arrived which got shoved in the corner. Nobody said anything about these wheels, so we didn't know anything about them. Afterwards there was an inquest into why we hadn't put on the new wheels, which came to nought because we didn't know about them, or that they had suspected they were going to break."

The team needed an additional complication like a hole in the head, but the decision had been taken to switch to CV-type driveshafts for the US race, necessitating further work for the already hard-pressed mechanics. However, help came from an unlikely source, as Sparshott explains. "We were trying to perfect CV joint driveshafts, which was a new thing and, of course, being Lotus, they were never, ever, man enough for the job, they were always just about there. It was one man's job to maintain all of the joints and Bob [Dance] did it for the race on all three cars. That was a whole night's work. They had to be stripped out, measured, regreased and all the seals put back on. They were all glued on, it was a nightmare of a job. I'll never forget, dear old Maurice Phillippe [Lotus designer] helped us, because Trevor Seaman was ill, which left five people for three cars. Maurice said 'I'll stay and give you a hand.' He worked all through the night with us to make the six."

Among Team Lotus mechanics, the annual visits between 1963 and 1969 to the Indianapolis Motor Speedway during the month of May for the legendary Indy 500 race were another source of sleepless nights.

However, as Bob Sparshott recalls, they also provided plenty of opportunities for mechanics from other sections of the team to get involved and even to go to the races. "During the period that we did the Ford Lotus-Cortinas, I was working with Bob Dance, and we were used to fill gaps when the other teams were in trouble. It gave me the marvellous opportunity of going to some of the races in America with the Indy team. We did a couple of races in 1964 – Milwaukee and Trenton – because they had some crashes and not enough people to do the work. At that time we were somewhere in America, so were shipped up to help.

"In 1965, Bob, Allan McCall and I were in California with the Cortinas doing Riverside and Laguna, two races on the spin. The team encountered all sorts of trouble at Indy with a written-off car, and the Old Man asked Andrew Ferguson who he could get. He said that some of the lads were in California so he told Andrew to bring us over to Indy and just leave one guy to look after the Cortinas. Poor old Allan McCall got left to look after two cars on his own, it being lower priority than Indy, and Bob and I went off.

"That was a memorable day because we arrived at 9 o'clock at night at the airport to be met by Andrew Ferguson. It had been a long day and we were already tired because of working on the Cortinas, so I thought we'd be going straight to the hotel. No fear. We were taken to the garage at Indy, where they were all working away, and Dave Lazenby said 'Put your suitcase over there in the corner, you can check in later when we've finished.' I was thinking 'Geez, when are we going to finish?' We went from the garage at 11-ish to have something to eat, and only got to the hotel after that.

"That was my first day at Indy and every day after that seemed the same. Bob and I ended up there for the entire period, staying for the race and everything. They had me signalling on the wall for the race. With me being the youngest, they told me they had a great job for me. I thought 'Signalling? Oh that's alright, I've done plenty of signalling.' Then I thought 'Hang on, I don't like the look of this wall,' it was a very low wall between you and the track, very isolating. Peter Jackson of Specialised Mouldings did the other board, so I never really worked on the Indy team per se though we worked at odd parts of it."

The 1967 event, when the team went with both Type 38s and 42s (originally designed for a BRM H16 Indy engine), was something of an epic in this regard, as Jim Pickles recalls. "We were building the cars and working reasonable hours, but as you got nearer and nearer the time for shipping the cars, we were working longer and longer hours. However, the really heavy stuff didn't start until we got there.

"We found that we were in a shocking condition and were working all hours then. There were problems with both handling and engines: we blew engine after engine after engine – Ford Quad-Cam 4.2 litre, normally-aspirated V8s. I didn't fully realise why but there was something odd somewhere. We ended up borrowing engines from A J Foyt and all sorts of other people in the end.

"The cars wouldn't handle either. In fact, the Old Man [Colin Chapman] cleared off one of the benches in the garage and actually laid out a drawing board and redrew the rear end. We had to set that up there, we had no special workshop, and had to rebuild the back end and rewind the springs and all sorts. It was grim. But even though I was knackered, I was still enthusiastic about it. I'd learnt very early on that Chapman was so innovative and, in that respect, to be very much admired, from my point of view.

"At some unearthly hour, three o'clock in the morning or something, the cars were on the deck and we were still working on them. I happened to be working on the front suspension and just nodded off draped over the wheel. I did come to, briefly and looked around; everybody else was draped over wheels or the bench, asleep, too."

Dozing 'on the job' was quite commonplace in those circumstances, according to Arthur 'Butty' Birchall, particularly at Indy, and he, too, recalls that year as being especially gruelling. "Falling asleep on the floor or on the toilet was nothing unusual because it was bloody hard work. The worst I ever did was 1967 at Indy when we did three 140-hour weeks."

Birchall also remembers 1969 as another difficult year, not just because of the hours but also the logistics of getting cars and mechanics to the USA, and then moving them around without the use of a transporter. "It wasn't much better in 1969, when we tried to get the Type 64 qualified. We did a couple of weeks of 140 hours then. You'd work on the car at Hethel, get it to the airport to be flown out to somewhere like

---

Track record   Jim Pickles

❝ *When I left school I joined the RAF as an airframe fitter and did a whole apprenticeship and fourteen years there. By the time I was due to de-mob, they asked me if I wanted to stop on but I wanted a change. I'd written to Ferrari, Cooper and Lotus, saying I was interested in motor racing. I knew the cars were monocoque and heading into those realms of aircraft-style structure and construction. I had a reply from Ferrari, nothing from Cooper – I was unaware that they were just about on the way out then. I had a reply from Lotus as well and of course they were in Cheshunt, which is a lot closer than Italy. So I ignored the Italian interview and ended up joining Lotus. I came up to Hethel with them with the Indy team. In those days there were no contracts. After I'd been there for a while, I remember asking Mike Underwood, who was chief mechanic for the Indy section, 'Have I got this job or not?' and he said 'Well, you're still here aren't you?' It was all very informal."*

Jim worked on the Indy section in 1967 and 1968, then ran the Gold Leaf Type 59 Formula 3 cars in 1969 and 1970, returning to the Formula 1 team for 1971 and enjoying the Championship-winning season with Emerson Fittipaldi in 1972, staying with the team until 1974 when he left motor racing for good.

Jim was part of the Championship-winning team which ran Emerson Fittipaldi in 1972. (Jim Pickles)

California or Indy for testing, come back, wash and change and pack a bag and then fly out there yourself. You'd then wait at the airport for it to come in and clear customs and then drive it on a U-Haul trailer to where you were going testing. And that was the way it was done. There were no transporters, you'd hire a car and illegally hitch a U-Haul trailer on the back of it and go."

The fact that Colin Chapman and his chief designer, Maurice Phillippe, were constantly innovating and introducing new designs, made for a much heavier workload for Team Lotus mechanics. Another example of this came in 1970, when the Lotus 72 initially proved recalcitrant and the team had to put in nightmare hours to have the car ready for its debut at the 1970 Spanish Grand Prix, as Eddie Dennis recalls. "We reached Jarama and kept on working and had a period where we just didn't sleep. Herbie [Blash] was the first one to go, we just lifted him into the truck. He hadn't collapsed but just gone to sleep, passed out really. Later in the meeting, I'd gone somewhere to find a bite to eat, sat down and the next thing I knew was back at the garage. Apparently, I'd been helped back there because I'd passed out."

During that season, almost every one of the Team Lotus Formula 1 crew collapsed from exhaustion at some point. After the poor performance of the Lotus 72 at Jarama, and a subsequent non-Championship race, the decision was taken to modify the cars, missing the Monaco Grand Prix and aiming to complete the work in time for the Belgian Grand Prix at Spa. As another mechanic on the team that year Dave Sims explains, it was touch and go whether the car was finished in time. "The rest of the team went on to Spa and left me and Dougie [Garner] behind to finish the latest car with all the mods for Jochen. We had a Thames van and trailer and when we eventually finished at something like four in the morning, set off for Harwich and took the ferry to Zeebrugge. We'd had five days with no sleep and were completely knackered.

"When we reached Spa we had no tickets, no passes, no windscreen sticker, and didn't know where we were going because we approached, somehow or other, from the other side of the circuit to where you would want to go for the paddock. We then got lost inside the circuit; eventually, a marshal led us into the paddock. When we arrived, the Old Man [Chapman] saw us and said 'Get it off the trailer, come on quick, quick, we've got to get it out.' We'd only started it at Hethel, warmed it up, checked that all the systems were working, it hadn't even turned a wheel. The Old Man said 'You've got to change the ratios, it's got the wrong ratios' and the last thing I can remember is trying to take the layshaft off the gearbox and that was it, I passed out. Apparently, the Old Man said 'Put him in the back of the truck, don't let anybody see him.' Eventually I was taken to a hotel."

Evidence of the zombie-like state of Lotus mechanics that year is provided by a story from Dave Sims from that Spa weekend, when they finally made it to their hotel in Stavelot. "There were three of us – me, Joe 90 [Derek Mower] and Eddie [Dennis] in that room. Derek woke me up in the middle of the night and said 'Look what Eddie's doing.' Eddie was crouched at the bottom of the bed. We asked him what he was doing and he said 'I'm changing the roll bar.'"

Later that year, it was Dougie Garner's turn to flake out on the final day of practice for the French Grand Prix at Clermont-Ferrand, although, as it turned out, the end result was a rare period of relaxation. "They took me back to the hotel without me knowing. I woke up in bed the next morning, looked around and everybody else had gone. They had decided to leave me there because I was too knocked out. They all went up for the race and I thought 'Oh God, duty first, must get there.' I got changed into my gear, rushed downstairs and, of course, Clermont-Ferrand was shut. I asked the receptionist to book a taxi to the race track but she said there was no chance. I had got all the passes, I could get in easily but getting there was the problem. In the end, I thought 'What the hell do I do?' and it was getting on because I'd slept quite a long time. I was sat in the bar and looked up at the TV and saw they were on the start line. I thought 'There's absolutely nothing I can do now anyway.' I sat in the bar and watched the race and we won. That was the satisfying part. There I was, drinking a beer and watching the other guys work their socks off. It didn't happen like that very often ..."

Six out of ten ain't bad

Former Cooper and Honda mechanic Denis Daviss recalls one epic period in 1967 when he experienced almost a week of all-nighters. "The first Canadian Grand Prix that year was between the German and Italian Grands Prix but it made lots of extra work packing up stuff for us guys. There being no truck drivers in the good old days, I left Byfleet on a Saturday morning in a brand-new Transit van, with used engines from the last race, to pick up fresh ones from Maserati in Modena for Canada, arriving back at Byfleet around nine o clock on the Monday morning. When you consider there was no Mont Blanc tunnel, so we had to drive all the way down to Provence, then cross over round the back of Chamonix and over the Mont Cenis pass, which leads down into Turin, I guess I probably did 1600-1800 miles. Arriving at Maserati, I unloaded the engines – I didn't even bother to turn off the engine – popped the other ones in and left. That was another all-nighter, on the road. Back in Byfleet, we had to fit the engines into the two race cars that were leaving on Wednesday evening for Mosport Park in Canada.

"I was one of an advance party of two; the other was a Lotus mechanic by the name of Dougie Bridge. All the teams were sending two cars and the instructions were for one car to be in a box and the other car to travel on top of the box. But when it came to it, the transport aircraft was a Boeing 707 with a door in the side, and these boxes with the cars on top wouldn't fit. Dougie and I removed roll-over bars on what cars we could and, if they were in a box, cut the box down a little bit so that they would be lower and we'd be able to put cars on top. That took us just about all night. The plane being a freighter in a strange airport, there were no services, no food, nothing. It didn't even have any seats in it. During the flight, Dougie and I sat on the boxes and occasionally on the co-pilot's seat when he wasn't, and stole sandwiches from the pilot and his mate.

"When we arrived at Toronto, the following morning, we were parked way over the other side of the airport. We then had to get all this stuff out – manhandle it up the plane and out through this door. Fortunately, only one car got dropped and that was a BRM. It didn't hurt the BRM but it made a big dent in the tarmac … Then the organisers dropped another little bombshell: they wanted all the cars on flatbed trucks because they were going to parade them around some shopping malls to pull the crowds in. So that was another all-nighter, taking all the cars out of the boxes and onto these flatbed trucks and then putting the boxes back together so that they could be used again. Everything was then ready for the race teams to reload the cars for the return flights. The cars went on their open flatbeds to the shopping malls and the boxes went to the racetrack. They were all unloaded and just left there.

"The racetrack was a bit of a surprise, too. Our garage was a long tent, about 15-20 feet – long enough to get a car in, including the nose and back, but that was all. There were no services, no electricity to speak of, nothing at all. It was a question of working on the cars and doing what you could. Practice turned into another mini disaster, when one of our cars had its starter ring disintegrate and it came out through these side-pod extensions, which punched a hole on the engine side and another on the outside. So it was out with the engine and the fuel bag and, using a borrowed van and a trailer from a very helpful Canadian team called Comstock, I hi-tailed it off to their workshop with the car on the back of the trailer.

"With the metal tidied up, I riveted patches over these holes, which again took a little time. On returning to our motel, the Flying Dutchman, I had a look around for some of the workers and found they'd all had a meal, along with a little lubrication, and were not in any real fit state to work, so I took the car back to the race track. Finding the tractor used for moving the boxes still had the forks on the back, I re-installed the engine. As there were no lights and the ground wasn't that good in the garages anyway, I found a nice little flat bit of concrete to do that job and, using the headlights of my borrowed van and of some Canadian fans who were camping nearby, I re-installed the engine. It was a bit of a performance because, with headlights, you are always in your own shadow. With the forks, it was a case of gently easing it down on the hydraulics, so that took a little while, too. Without the tractor, it would have been impossible. They were quite heavy lumps, even with people that know what they are doing, it would have taken more than four guys to lower it in and hold it in the right place.

"When the crew arrived in the morning, another two or three hours saw everything left fitted – new ring-gear, gearbox back on and the electrics connected and the car fuelled and ready to run. In the race, Jochen's car retired with a drowned engine and the patched-up car finished tenth. So that was reasonable.

"With everything packed up, the team went off to fly home, leaving Dougie and myself rear guard to help load the aircraft. Flying with the cars, we arrived at Heathrow at 11.30pm on Monday – another all-nighter, by the way. My team manager, Roy Salvadori, had asked me to give him a call as soon as I got in, no matter what time it was, so I called him and he told me to take a taxi home and asked could I be at the workshop at about nine in the morning? I turned up there at nine in the morning and it appeared that all the mechanics were worn out from all this work they'd done, and were all going to have a long weekend. So, with a spare car on a trailer, I was on my way back to Modena. When you think about it, what with the run to Italy and back, then all the messing around at Heathrow and Toronto, fixing the chassis, and my return to Heathrow, I did a minimum of six all-nighters within a ten-day period …

Bernie's good deed

According to Alan Challis, Grand Prix mechanics have Bernie Ecclestone to thank for the easier time they have of it nowadays, and the fact that they rarely work all-nighters. "His deal of getting practice at the same time of day at virtually every Grand Prix was the best thing that has ever happened to the mechanic in Formula 1, because we used to go to Monte Carlo and practice would be Thursday, Friday, Saturday. You'd have practice one first thing in the morning, the next one would be late at night, and the next day it would be 'crack of sparrow's' in the morning, so you could guarantee you were going to have to work all night."

Another Ecclestone-driven development saved his mechanics considerable work at races, as Roy Topp recalls. "Things changed a bit later on. One of the first organised teams was Brabhams, when they came along with a complete back end, just unscrewed it from the back of the tub and slid the new one on, engine, gearbox, the lot. Unfortunately, you can't do that today but there was nothing in those days to stop you changing what you liked."

It is with understandable envy that people like Tony Robinson, who worked in a time when all-nighters were part and parcel of the job, look at today's Grand Prix mechanics. "It is easier for the racing mechanics of today because they lock up the damn cars 24 hours before the race, you can't touch them. In theory, you could go out and get plastered on a Saturday night."

4
One big, happy family

In today's somewhat hostile environment of 'arm's length' relations between the major Grand Prix teams, it is hard to imagine that there was a time when they would happily help out each other. Yet, forty or fifty years ago Formula 1 was one big, happy family, and within the individual teams many mechanics considered their fellow crew members akin to brothers, reflecting the amount of time they spent working and travelling together.

Grand Prix mechanics: This wonderful shot, taken at the 1964 Mexican Grand Prix, captures all of the mechanics working in Formula 1 at the time. From left to right, back row: Ted de la Riviere (Parnell), Sergio Vezzali (Ferrari), Nick Garbett (Lotus), Orio Fossati (Ferrari), unknown (Cooper), Leo Wybrott (Lotus), Jean-Pierre Oberson (Rob Walker), Jimmy Potton (Brabham), John Collins (BRM). Middle row: Carlo Amadessi (Ferrari), J Tonks (Dunlop), W Mincey (Dunlop), Stan Collier (Parnell), Tony Cleverley (Rob Walker), Trevor Orchard (Cooper), Heine Mader (Rob Walker), Anselmo Menabue (Ferrari), Alan Challis (BRM), Willie Southcott (BRM). Front row: Dick Scammell (Lotus), Guilio Borsari (Ferrari), Cyril Atkins (BRM), Dennis Perkins (BRM), Bill Cowe (Lotus), unknown (Ferrari), Gianfranco Tugnoli (Ferrari), Bruno Solmi (Ferrari), Tim Wall (Brabham). A total of 26 mechanics, plus two tyre technicians for the whole grid. Nowadays, there are more than this on each team ... (Dick Scammell)

Tony Robinson sums it up. "In those days, everybody used to help everybody else. It was quite normal for Gurney, if he was short of a gear ratio, to come over and borrow one – which you never got back – or a speedometer or an instrument, if we had it. However, I drew the line at loaning cars to people when they'd shunted theirs. We went to Karlskoga or Roskilde and Jo Bonnier [Swedish Formula 1 driver] was there and had shunted his car. We took three cars for two drivers, one to do Karlskoga and a spare one for Stirling to do Roskilde. Bonnier asked if he could borrow the third one and I said 'No, you can't.' So he phoned Ken Gregory and asked him if he could use it and Ken said 'What did Tony say?' and Bonnier had to admit I'd refused, so Ken said 'Well, that's the end of it.' There was a limit to how far you could go.

"But if it was assistance to get to the starting line you wanted, you'd get it. On that trip to Caen [see Chapter 1, Getting there] with the 250F Maserati, when I arrived, absolutely shagged, it was the BRM boys who unloaded it from the truck, pushed it around and generally gave me a hand. That was the way it used to be, everybody would pitch in. In the 1950s and early 60s, everybody mucked in, it didn't matter who you were."

Former Yeoman Credit and Brabham mechanic Gerry Hones concurs, saying "In that 'family' you could go to any truck, any transporter and borrow anything. If they had it and they weren't using it, they'd lend it to you."

To illustrate the way in which teams used to help each other, Denis Daviss tells of the Belgian Grand Prix at Spa in 1964. "In the race at one stage Jimmy Clark's Lotus was overheating and needed water, so they came down to Cooper's pit and we gave them a big watering-can full. Gurney was leading, then he went; one of the Hills led, then he went out, and Bruce [McLaren] ended up in front. As he rounded the La Source hairpin on the final lap, his engine stopped running. The alternator belt had stopped some time earlier and he had run out of electricity. Had it gone brum-brum twice more, he'd have won the race. Jimmy was running fine, and whizzed past and won – on our borrowed water!"

Derek Wootton, who worked as a mechanic on the Vanwall Grand Prix cars during the 1950s, confirms that, even with arch rival Maserati, there was a spirit of friendly, rather than bitter, rivalry. "I was on quite good terms with Bertocchi of Maserati and would walk down to say hello and ask him 'Have you get anything new?' He would move his head sideways and say 'Have a look, we might have but it's for you to find out.'"

Former Tyrrell mechanic Neil Davis described as marvellous the level of co-operation with other teams in the late 1960s and early 70s. "If we wanted something like tapes or bolts or anything like that, we'd go to Brabham or Lotus, it was no problem. And we'd give it back to them the following race meeting and they'd do the same for us. We socialised together, talked to each other and that was the way it was, just a great time, really."

A good example of this was at the 1968 Mexican Grand Prix, the final and deciding race of that year's Championship, with Lotus, Tyrrell and McLaren drivers all in with a chance of winning the title. Lotus boss Colin Chapman decided to change the high wing on his cars to one that pivoted, so that it could be feathered flat on the straights, reducing drag and gaining slightly on top speed. This was a job which required around 14 hours'

Track record   Derek Wootton

❝I was working for a guy called Ray Martin, when we built the prototype Kieft for Stirling Moss. At that time I was doing some racing with an Austin 7 but it was becoming too expensive so I decided I'd better stop and go and work for somebody who could afford it. When David Yorke was asked by Tony Vandervell whether he would like to put together and run a team, he said 'yes' and invited me to join him. I worked for the Vanwall team between 1955 and 1959, then the Old Man [Tony Vandervell] wanted me to stay on, so I went into the technical sales department.❞

Derek Wootton worked for Vanwall in its heyday and enjoyed the friendly rivalry that existed with Maserati. (Grand Prix Mechhanics Charitable Trust)

work by four mechanics but, more crucially, it also involved the co-operation of all of the other teams in the pitlane, as Bob Sparshott explains. "On away trips in those days we only took a few things because we didn't have a lot of space. We didn't have enough rivets – we needed hundreds – so we went round all the teams and they lent us pop rivets and pliers to put them together. We had to borrow everything but nobody quibbled."

Another nice touch at that meeting is recalled by Team Lotus chief mechanic Bob Dance. "Ken Tyrrell, some of his mechanics and the McLaren mechanics came into our pit late on the Saturday night with a big cake and offered it round, wishing us luck for race day."

This fraternity of mechanics didn't just extend to sharing spare parts; they would also hang around together, as former Brabham and Anglo American Racers mechanic Mike Lowman explains. "The thing about motor racing in my early days was that if you had a spare part and another team needed it and you didn't, you'd give it to them, because you wanted to beat them on the racetrack, not in the bloody paddock. So we used to share ratios and dampers and all sorts of things like that, which obviously would not be contemplated at all today, because there is so much secrecy about everything that everybody does. We had this desire to see a full grid so that we could all go out there and race one another. Then, after it was over, we'd all go and have a beer together."

Stan Collier confirms that it was commonplace for the mechanics to go out together. "We always used to mix in those days. If you met anyone from another team, you'd go out with them and that was the way it was. We always had a good few beers with the other teams, didn't matter who they were. The only team that you'd never mix with too much was Ferrari. We used to talk to them but didn't go out with them because the Ferrari team bosses didn't like them mixing with other teams. But all the other British teams always used to mix."

The only exception to this rule of Ferrari not mixing seemed to come at the US

'Going loco, down in Acapulco:' Every year the Formula 1 mechanics got a chance to let their hair down between the US and Mexican Grands Prix. Here, they pose for a photo after a fishing expedition, probably in 1965. Back row, left to right: Richard Attwood, Tim Parnell, Alan Challis, Roger Bailey, Ted de la Riviere, Tony Cleverley, Stan Collier. Front row, left to right: Jean-Pierre Oberson, Trevor Orchard, Dennis Perkins, Roy Foreman, Cyril Atkins, Jimmy Potton, Heine Mader. (Tony Cleverley)

Grand Prix at Watkins Glen, as BRM mechanic Peter Bracewell explains. "We used to go to this place called Joe's Diner to eat and he would only have BRM and Ferrari mechanics, he wouldn't have anyone else. And the meals they used to prepare, I've never eaten so much food in my life. He was just crazy for racing cars."

Tony Reeson attests to this apparent affinity between BRM and Ferrari teams during the 1960s and 70s. "When we used to go to Grands Prix, the Ferrari mechanics would come to our pit with four or five bottles of Lambrusco or Chianti, every time. Ferrari and

Prize-givings on the Sunday night of a Grand Prix were a regular feature of racing in the 1950s and 60s, and an opportunity for mechanics to relax and enjoy themselves. This is Mexico 1965, with (from left) Bill Cowe, Jim Clark, Mike Spence, Leo Wybrott, Nick Garbett and Colin Chapman, together with their Mexican hosts. (Bill Cowe)

BRM got on very well together because we were the only two teams that made all the components – the engine, gearbox and chassis."

Socialising wasn't restricted to mechanics; it was quite a common occurrence to find drivers out with the rest of the team as well, particularly if there was a prize-giving to be attended on the Sunday night, as Stan Collier recounts. "They [the drivers] weren't like they are now, just flying off, because after the races there used to be prize-givings and the drivers would be there. We used to mix with them quite a bit."

Former BRM mechanic Ben Casey provides a stark contrast between his days and a more recent example that was related to him. "A friend of mine used to be a policeman in Monte Carlo. He had a dog and would go round the paddock, pits and pubs, making sure everything was alright. He told me that McLaren sat in one corner and Williams in the other, there was no way in the world they could converse with each other. Whereas in our days, if we were working at night and we'd arranged to go out with, say, Lotus, and they were doing an engine change and we were finished, we'd go and help with their engine change so we could all get out together."

Of course, having such a tight-knit community did have its downsides, in that it was difficult to keep something secret from other teams. Gerry Hones recalls one example in 1961. "In the workshop at Yeoman Credit, with nine of us, we used to change round. You'd be a chassis bloke for three months and then you'd go on to engines and then gearboxes. I was on engines at the time. With one I'd just fitted, we towed it round and it wouldn't start but I could hear that it was making a funny sucking noise in the carburettors. I got it back into the workshop and thought I'd just change the plugs and have another go and put the slave battery on it. It started like a beauty and was lovely. I made the mistake of not getting in it and trying the gearbox and the clutch. Reg [Parnell, team boss] had said that before we went to Aintree, we would call in to Mallory Park and do a morning's testing. We arrived there, unloaded both cars, towed them round the car park, and neither would start. Jimmy Potton, who was very quick-witted said 'I know what the bloody trouble is – we've got the crown wheels the wrong side of the pinions and we've got five reverses and one forward.'

"We whipped them up onto the ramps on the back of the transporters – we were using the Jack Knight box and it was probably the only box you could do this on – and changed them over. Within an hour-and-a-half it was done and everything was right. Old Reg said to us 'If any of you mention this when we get to Aintree, I'll sack you.' Of course, when we arrived at Aintree, all the mechanics were out at the back of their trucks watching us arrive and, as we came in, they all gave us a clap. Somebody had rung up and told them what had happened."

Looking after the lads

Some of the more enlightened team bosses and drivers realised from a very early stage that hungry mechanics do not make happy mechanics. Similarly, if they feel unappreciated and that their efforts are going unrecognised, they tend to become quickly disillusioned.

On the subject of food, former Equipe Moss mechanic Tony Robinson identifies a surprising trendsetter when it came to feeding the troops. "Stirling's father was always good. When we did Le Mans for a couple of years, Alfred had a caravan and used to

Team catering, 1970s-style: The Elf-Team Tyrrell mechanics take a well-earned meal break. Left to right: unknown, Roger Hill (with back to camera), Roland Law, Terry Coleman, Peter Hennessy (with back to camera), and Roy Topp. (Peter Hennessy)

be the team chef, cooking steaks in shifts, and we would all sit down and have a decent meal, he was always keen on that side."

Chief mechanic with Team Tyrrell, Roger Hill, says that Ken's wife, Nora, was a stalwart when it came to feeding the team. "In the early days, believe it or not, Mrs Tyrrell used to make us sandwiches. On the few occasions when we did work late at the factory, for instance, in the timber yard, at nine or ten o'clock Mrs Tyrrell would walk in with a Thermos flask of tea and some cake on a plate. For some time, even when we were doing the continental races and the flyaway ones, Mrs T used to make sandwiches for us. After that, Ken made sure there were motor homes so that we were all fed and watered. He soon realised that, just as a race car doesn't go without petrol, mechanics don't work well without food, so we were lucky; that was pretty well organised all the way along."

This approach was in marked contrast to the situation with Team Lotus, where the hard-pressed mechanics were often left to fend for themselves, according to Jim Pickles. "The Old Man [Chapman] wasn't particularly sympathetic towards it, not that I recollect. Hazel [Chapman's wife] used to be the one who was always supportive of the lads. She wouldn't overrule him and say 'You've got to let them have a sleep,' but if she came in, she would bring some coffee or doughnuts, that type of thing."

A rare sight indeed: Team Lotus taking a break to eat something during a race weekend.
Left to right: Dick Scammell, unknown mechanic on ground with back to camera,
Ted Woodley, Jim Endruweit, Cedric Selzer. (Tony Cleverley)

Hughie Absalom recalls one occasion at Indy when the Team Lotus mechanics were literally abandoned to fend for themselves with a tornado heading in their direction. "It was my first year there and we had been working forever, seven days a week, before we even got there. The very first day we arrived, we did about five or six laps, and the next thing was they got out all the drawings and began cutting up the suspension, modifying it. Around six or seven o'clock at night, the people next door came in to tell us that there was a big storm afoot, like a tornado. They asked 'Have you guys got some chains here?' and we said 'Err … no.' They said 'You'd better chain down those cars when this tornado comes through.' Hill, Chapman and Phillippe [Team Lotus chief designer] were poring over these drawings and had been ear-wigging when these guys came in. About ten minutes later they wrapped up and just disappeared, leaving us with about one hundred jobs on the list still to do. We were thinking 'Wait a minute now, what about us?' The tornado came through but, luckily, didn't get to the Speedway, passing a mile-and-a-half or two miles north."

Even the arrival of team mobile homes did not prove the lifesaver it might appear, as Arthur 'Butty' Birchall explains. "When I went back [to Team Lotus] in the 1970s, times had changed, they had a mobile home, a Travco that they served the odd meal from. All the food produced there was too rich for us, basically – a working man requires 'meat and two veg.' They would serve rather exotic meals which probably suited the sponsors, but when you are working upside down in the fuel tank after you've had a meal, you don't want to see it again."

Drivers who acknowledged their mechanics' efforts, whether through thanks or financial reward, were appreciated, as Alan Challis explains. "Graham Hill was very good that way. He would always, if we'd had a really shit weekend, buy you a drink or give you some money to share amongst the boys. If he won, he did the same thing.

"Nelson Piquet was like that with us as well. But that was only with his half of the garage. I was always given the cheque or the money and he told me who he wanted to give it to. So it was the case that Nigel's [Mansell, Piquet's arch rival] men didn't get anything."

Gerry Hones remembers that the break between the US Grand Prix at Watkins Glen and the Mexican Grand Prix was always welcome, and that Jack Brabham used to make a point of ensuring that his mechanics were well looked after. "What Jack used to do was to drive in the American race, then take all the mechanics down to Acapulco. He used to send a boat out there, with diving equipment. Betty Brabham was there, more or less looking after the lads to some extent. As they'd worked so hard, the idea was to take them there and make sure that they got a week's rest. That's how Jack was – another good man to work for."

Hones also identifies Jochen Rindt as being very good with his mechanics, too. "If we were building a car for Jochen at Brabham, he'd always be down at night and would take three or four blokes up to town for a quick meal."

5
The mechanic's gallon

Before fuel rigs became all high-tech – well, for most of the time – the process of fuelling a car for a race was a hit and miss affair. In the 1950s, 60s and 70s, a good proportion of the practice sessions were taken up with trying to accurately measure fuel

consumption in order to work out how much fuel would be needed for a car to complete a full race distance.

In those days, there were two schools of thought concerning fuelling cars for a Grand Prix: the first – the 'old school' version – was that it was easier to fill the tanks to the brim, thereby ensuring that the car was more or less guaranteed to make it to the finish. The cars rarely or never ran out of fuel, but they also rarely or never won any races – coincidence? The second school of thought was that, given an accurate calculation of race fuel consumption, it was not necessary to carry excess fuel, which translated to a faster car on the track.

It was an inexact science, however. In a period where tanks regularly leaked or failed to give up their full complement due to surge, faulty valves or pumps, a gallon or so either way often made the difference between success and failure.

The term 'the mechanic's gallon' evolved from the practice of mechanics doubting the calculations of their bosses, and slipping extra fuel into the tank in order to be sure of their car getting to the chequered flag. Team bosses and designers took exception to the practice; they had spent thousands of pounds lightening their cars through the use of expensive materials such as magnesium, titanium and aluminium, and an extra gallon of fuel added 7lb/3.175kg to the weight of the car.

Ken Tyrrell, who won three Formula 1 World Championships with Jackie Stewart in the late 1960s and early 1970s, was most definitely an advocate of only putting in what was needed, as his former chief mechanic, Roger Hill, remembers. "Ken would have only enough fuel in the car to do the race, saying it slowed you down if you had too much; just enough to do the race was all that was required. He issued the amount of fuel that went in, end of story. That was the thing with Ken, you always did what he asked you to do, you didn't think 'Oh, we'd better do that instead.' He needed you to do what you were asked. He did the fuel and it was always dead right, but in Spa [with the Matra at the Belgian Grand Prix, 1968] it was wet so we ran the engine richer than we should have and it used a little bit too much fuel. We did run out there – that was the only time that ever happened.

"Jackie came in and we put some fuel in but it didn't get back to the pump because the old pits at Spa were on a hill. We had to lift the front of the car and managed to put more fuel in it but, of course, it was all over by then." Stewart, who had been leading the race when he pitted with just one lap to go, rejoined to finish a disappointing fourth, missing out on Matra's first Grand Prix win and Dunlop's first victory since returning to top flight racing.

Tony Robinson, who was an assistant to Stirling Moss' mechanic, Alf Francis, and went on to become chief mechanic for the British Racing Partnership team, was another who had a definitive approach to fuel. "Most of the time I was responsible for making sure that the right amount of petrol went into each car that I was involved

Opposite: High-tech stuff: Fuelling Formula 1 cars in the 1960s consisted of pouring churns into a funnel, which ruled out rapid pit stops if cars ran low during a race. Here, Tony Cleverley and Jean-Pierre Oberson fill up Jo Siffert's Rob Walker Lotus 49 in the pits at Watkins Glen at the US Grand Prix 1968. (Tony Cleverley)

with. Even when we were UDT-Laystall and were racing seven cars at one meeting, three Formula Ones, three sports cars, and a GT car, I was permanently in the pits, and I, not anybody else, decided how much fuel was going in. What the mechanics did after that, I didn't know about; very little, I should think, because there would be no reason to. To me, it was cut and dried; we did fuel consumption checks during the practice sessions and that was it."

Mechanics tended to take a more pragmatic view of the situation, as former BRP and Brabham man Stan Collier points out: "The trouble is the engineers or team managers always worked it out that the car was going to do so much to the gallon, and then we put in a different engine for the race. They were never 100 per cent sure, I don't think. We used to work out the fuel consumption ourselves because you didn't have all the people they have now. We used to reckon that we always had to put half a gallon extra just in case we were wrong. Now they can check it because they've got all this telemetry and stuff like that, but we used to cut it pretty fine.

"At Brabham one year [1977] we lost a race with John Watson at Dijon, where the car misfired on the last corner when he was leading and Andretti passed him to win the race. If he'd had an extra half a gallon it wouldn't have happened."

This certainly wasn't the first time a Brabham had run out of fuel on the final lap, either. A famous incident occurred in the 1970 British Grand Prix when, after a race-long battle with the Lotus 72 of Jochen Rindt, Jack Brabham felt his BT33 cough and splutter under him when accelerating out of the penultimate corner on the final lap. He could only coast in, leaving his Austrian rival to take the win. It has been variously suggested that one of the mechanics put the incorrect amount of fuel in the car, or that the car was running too rich. Gerry Hones explains what actually happened. "My two boys were in the workshop at the time and I can remember even now where that car stood and where the fifty gallon drum was, and they carried the gallon cans over to Ron Dennis to put in, and counted them.

"It used to be sent down from the office how much fuel to put in the car, but the mechanics in the garage always shoved another gallon on top for ages and ages. Somehow, Tauranac found out about this. He had this habit of bloody blowing up, he'd go mad, go all red on the back of his neck. After that happened, whatever fuel they ordered from the office, you put that in, because if you didn't and they found out, you'd be down the road. In this case, they discovered that that engine was doing something like four or five to the gallon instead of what it was supposed to be doing, it was running rich.

"Ron Dennis filled it up but my two boys counted the cans. When they blamed Ron Dennis at the works for not putting in enough, I went to them and asked 'How much petrol did you put in that car?' and immediately they knew how many gallons went into that car. So it wasn't the fault of Ron Dennis but Ron Tauranac." It appears that the correct amount – as specified by Ron Tauranac – went into the car but the fact that the engine was running rich meant that it ran out before the finish.

Peter Hennessy also vividly remembers that day and the bitterness of running out. "Just prior to the race, they had to do another lap and I said to Ron Tauranac 'Should we put in a couple more pints of fuel?' and he said 'No, every pound of fuel equals so much time.' As the car coasted to a halt and we realised it had run out of petrol, I said 'I told you we should put in some more fuel' and then thought 'Ooh, I shouldn't have said that.' If only they'd put a bit more in, we'd have been alright ..."

Crucially, there was also a strong financial incentive for mechanics to make sure their cars had enough fuel in that, if their car won, they would get a bonus. Therefore, they wanted to ensure it got to the finish, as former Team Lotus man Arthur 'Butty' Birchall points out. "It was fairly important, apart from the pride of winning, as the financial rewards helped subsidise the wages, which were pretty pathetic in those days."

Alan Challis, a chief mechanic for BRM in the 1960s and 70s, confirms that adding extra fuel was a common occurrence. "It was completely and utterly standard practice. Certainly after I became chief mechanic I did the sums myself. I listened to what I was told I'd got to put in but, if I didn't think that was enough, a drop more went in. Once you've had one run out, you don't want it to happen again."

Former Cooper and McLaren mechanic Mike Barney contends that only at certain races, when consumption was high, did the mechanic's gallon became an issue. "If we had a race that was iffy on fuel we used to cram everything in that we could. Bruce [McLaren] was a bit of a worrier on weight, but we would probably have squeezed another gallon in just to make sure."

Ray Wardell, who worked for the fledgling March team from its inception, and later went on to run Gilles Villeneuve in Formula Atlantic, experienced things from both sides of the fence, as a mechanic and a team manager. "That was a fairly standard issue. The only time I really got to grips with it as far as the management side was concerned was with the Ecurie Canada guys. I used to make sure I got exactly what I wanted, and not what I wanted plus a bit more. That was the first time I became aware that a little less weight really is an advantage; prior to that, we used to just fill the blooming things up all the time – it was very lax."

Someone who was particularly obsessive about the weight of his cars – and had been from the start of his career - was Lotus boss Colin Chapman. Fuelling miscalculations and Team Lotus appeared to go hand-in-hand at one stage, but it seemed that, whatever they did, the mechanics would get into trouble, as Jim Endruweit, racing manager and chief mechanic on the Formula 1 team during the Jim Clark era, explains. "It was the 1965 South African Grand Prix and we were running Jimmy and Mike Spence. The race was on New Year's Day and the cars went beautifully during practice.

"Everything was going well – which doesn't half make you nervous. We took the cars back to the garage and race-prepped them and got it all done by 10 o'clock. We went back to the hotel, had a quick clean up and then down to eat. The Old Man [Chapman] was there, of course, and asked 'What the bloody hell are you doing here?' I told him the cars were finished and we left it at that.

"The following morning I'd done the fuel checks and put in the fuel. According to the calculations we were just on the margin. We were trying to decide whether we needed the top tank [a small tank above the driver's knees], and I had to make the decision because the Old Man didn't turn up. In the end, we had to fuel the cars and he arrived three minutes before they went to the grid.

"Off they went and were running one and two. Mike spun on the last corner before the pits and dropped back to third or fourth, which broke the tension, really. Then the Old Man started on about the fuel:

'Are you sure they've got enough fuel?'
'Yup.'
'Have you got any fuel in the pits?'
'No.'
'You haven't got fuel?'
'No.'
'Well, you'd better bloody get some.'

"So we sent a couple of guys off to get a five gallon churn. You've got no chance of putting it in because it goes into a little filler cap which you screw a funnel on to, and it runs down two little tubes. I mean, if you've got to do a pit stop that's it. And he was all tense: 'You sure he's going to finish?' Jimmy went off at the start of the last lap, into the distance, up the hill, and the Old Man said 'It's a misfire, you bloody ...' I'm getting a roasting and said 'I didn't hear a misfire, he probably lifted.'

"Anyway, he was fine. Jimmy was first and Mike was fourth – he spun again, might even have had two spins. Jimmy came in and joked 'Great, top it up, I'll do it again.' I mean, it was that good, he had no complaints about the car at all, which was quite surprising.

"Then we had to do the fuel check, so we upended the car to drain it out at the back. We did Jimmy's car and probably got out slightly over a gallon. And I got 'You fool, all that fuel, that's an extra 10lb he was carrying.' I'm standing there, getting a rocket for this. And then we did Mike's car and we got about a cupful out of it. So I got another enormous rollocking: 'He could have run out ...' I couldn't win."

Problems with fuel calculations added further to the pressure within the team at the title-deciding 1968 Mexican Grand Prix, already ramped up by having to work an all-nighter to fabricate a new feathering rear wing which could be moved to a low-drag angle of attack on the straights and a high-drag position for improved grip in the corners. The situation reached boiling point on race morning, as Bob Sparshott remembers. "Our nerves were strung out like piano wires at the end of that year. We had a bit of a to-do in Mexico. Bear in mind we'd got a job list a million miles long, and one of the jobs on it was draining fuel – if we could get the fuel out. The Old Man came into the garage and asked what the consumption was, and Bob replied 'I'm afraid it's not come out right.' The Old Man went bloody bananas and began ranting and raving. I spoke out of turn and said 'We can't do a check, Mr Chapman. The only way we'd get a really good check is to stand the car up on end.' He thought that was a real piss-take; 'You bastards, don't blame me if it breaks all the driveshafts on the line' he shouted and stormed out of the garage."

According to Arthur Birchall, many a race was won by Team Lotus with the mechanic's gallon. "He [Chapman] always did his fuel calculations to the third decimal place. We set up the car full and then drained the fuel out to whatever he wanted. And after each practice session, we would fill it up again and take notes about how much it took, from which you could get a fairly accurate consumption figure. We'd probably take 10 or 15 gallons out for the race, depending on what type of race it was, and the mechanics would slip one or two back in."

Hughie Absalom, who worked for Brabham, Lotus and McLaren recalls that, despite the threat of incurring the wrath of Colin Chapman, at Team Lotus, adding extra fuel was common practice. "It was the norm, that's what always happened. Whatever Chapman said everybody always added a gallon. There were several incidents where it had run out during the race, or on the slowing down lap, but you didn't dare tell Chapman what you'd done because he would go ballistic."

However, as former Lotus chief mechanic Dick Scammell points out, the rewards of winning were generally worth the risk of getting a dressing-down. "We did play that game. In general, when you pumped it out at the end, he could have a bit of a go at you if there was more than he thought in there. But we all worked on the basis that it was much better to get a rollicking for putting too much in and perhaps finishing in the first three than it was to run out with a lap to go."

Bill Cowe, who worked on the Lotus Formula 1 team between 1964 and 1969, remembers that, eventually, the situation came to a dramatic head. "At one time, the mechanics used to put an extra gallon in because we knew we were always tight on fuel consumption. Then Chapman found out about this and used to issue the fuel figures with a gallon off. And it got to an almighty showdown one day when we actually put in how much was on the ticket and it obviously ran out way before the end of the race – that was at Silverstone [in 1969]."

The 1969 British Grand Prix at Silverstone had seen a titanic battle between the mercurial Jochen Rindt and champion-to-be Jackie Stewart. Poor Rindt, who had already had to pit to have an errant rear wing end-plate removed, had to come in for more fuel with a whopping seven laps remaining. Rindt's mechanic, Eddie Dennis, takes up the story. "He didn't have the [auxiliary] tank. And because he drove an absolutely balls-out race with Stewart, he ran out." The fact that Rindt's team-mate came in for fuel a lap later, and the other Lotus 49B in the field also had to stop, suggested that fuel was very marginal, even for the Lotuses that weren't running at the front of the race.

This was a point which had clearly not escaped the spectators, as Bob Dance recalls. "In the evening when we were clearing up, I was putting some fuel from a can into the tank of the 10/12cwt Ford van, and a spectator said 'You should have put that in the racing car instead of the van, and then you would have won.' I thought 'thanks very much' but he was right, all the same …"

Another example of hard driving upsetting the fuel calculations was Jimmy Clark's amazing fightback from a pit stop to replace a punctured tyre in the 1967 Italian Grand Prix at Monza. Having made up a deficit of one lap on the leaders, Clark looked set for a sensational victory until his car spluttered on the final lap and he eventually coasted across the finishing line in third, apparently out of fuel.

In the Team Lotus pit, the inquest began into what had gone wrong. Initially, a faulty fuel pump was blamed and it was said to have failed to pick up the final three gallons of fuel. However, Ford Cosworth DFV designer Keith Duckworth, who was present that day, said simply: "He ran out of fuel … Chapman would never have more than the odd ounce of extra fuel in and Clark's absolutely masterful effort – he was obviously going 'Harry Flatters' everywhere – meant that he used more fuel, in catching up this lap and a bit, than he would have done normally. An absolutely brilliant performance."

Chief mechanic that day Dick Scammell agrees: "I do think that a contributory factor was that Jimmy just drove it flat out all the time. To this day, I think there was enough fuel in it, to be driven in the way he had been in practice. The difference between going round the circuit in a reasonable time and really trying is that fuel consumption goes up quite a lot. Jimmy was just continuously driving it right on the edge, which he didn't do all the time, not lap after lap, and that was enough to put it out. Because, quite rightly, we didn't have a big safety margin."

Clark's mechanic, Allan McCall, says that the car would have run out even earlier than it did had not both he and Scammell opted to put in some extra fuel. "Chapman did the fuel calculation and decided that we only needed 31 gallons or something crazy like that! Everybody thought 'f**k off' and Dick Scammell took me to one side and muttered 'Put 33 in it.' I'd done my own calculations and put in 36. I think we were about five or six gallons more than Chapman had calculated. People say we had a fuel pump pick-up failure – that's bulls**t. We simply ran out of fuel because Chapman had screwed up chronically with his calculations.

"After the race, he was shouting 'Who put the fuel in? How much did you put in the car?' I think Scammell spoke up and said 'Actually, Mr Chapman, you said 31 gallons and I told Allan to put 33 in it …' and I added '… and I put in 36.' Then, I got this enormous lecture about not doing what I was f*****g supposed to do. He was saying 'Don't you EVER do that again. If I tell you to put 31 gallons in … blah, blah, blah.' That was the wonder of Chapman: the man was brilliant but, now and again, he had also to realise that some of us had brains. We could calculate – we went to school ourselves, you know."

Even though his obsession with putting in the minimum amount of fuel used to drive his mechanics to despair, looking back, Dick Scammell feels that this was another example of Colin Chapman's advanced thinking. "Each gallon weighs seven pounds. He was ahead of his time. The amount of stuff that's talked about how much fuel they've got in the cars these days, he was on to it then, wasn't he?"

Arrival of more sophisticated means of measuring, monitoring and controlling fuel consumption – such as pit-to-car telemetry and engine management systems – meant that the practice of adding the mechanic's gallon gradually died out. These days, it is a relatively rare occurrence for a Grand Prix car to run out of fuel on the track.

*Denis Daviss tops up the tanks of a Cooper on the night before a race to make sure it has enough fuel to finish.
(Denis Daviss)*

Track record   Allan McCall

❝In August 1964 I travelled to the UK from New Zealand on a ship called the
Northern Star. On board were a couple of London car dealers doing a world
tour. They said that they were race car drivers and over a few drinks impressed me
with great stories of their feats in the sport. At this stage of my life (22) I had zero
experience of motor sport and had only managed to get to Ardmore once with my
mates. These dealers told me to ring up their mate Colin [Chapman] at Lotus when
I got to the UK. They said if I gave their names he would offer me a job as a racing
mechanic which would give me free travel all over the place.

"I rang Colin and he did not know my new mates but suggested I write a letter to
Andrew Ferguson. I did this, then went off and found a job at a Ford garage in Putney
called Adlards. Around December 1964, I received a telegram from Andrew Ferguson
inviting me to come for a test. I understand that I got the job because I was the
only person out of 70-odd applicants who could butt-weld two bits of steel together
without a welding rod. About a month later, I received another telegram asking me
to turn up the following week at the factory to start work with Bob Dance on the
Lotus-Cortina team."

Allan went on to work on the Lotus Indy team in
1966, building the car, with his 17-year-old assistant
Eamon Fullalove, in which Jim Clark finished 2nd.
After Indy he joined the Formula 1 team and stayed to
the end of 1967, working on Jim Clark's Lotus 49. He
moved to McLaren for 1968, then in the early 1970s
became a car constructor in his own right, firstly with
the pretty little Tui single-seaters and also with a
Tecno Formula 1 car in 1973. He completed his final
season in Formula 1 running the Hexagon of Highgate
Brabham for John Watson in 1974.

*McCall working on Jim Clark's Lotus 49/R2 in the
cramped conditions of the Watkins Glen 'tech shed' in
1967. (Ford Motor Company)*

6

The team bosses and designers

Chapman and Team Lotus

Within a decade, Colin Chapman transformed his Lotus marque from a low-volume manufacturer of sports cars racing at club level to a major player on the world stage of motor sport, winning Grands Prix and taking class victories at Le Mans. In 1963, his cars won their first World Championship title with Jim Clark, and the same year they struck out in the USA with the backing of Ford, determined to transform oval racing and conquer the hallowed Indy 500, which they managed to achieve in 1965. The Chapman/Clark/Lotus/Ford partnership was cemented by the development of the Ford Cosworth DFV 3-litre Formula 1 engine. It won its first race in 1967 in the back of a Lotus 49, and went on to record 155 Grand Prix victories – 47 with Lotus – spanning an incredible 17 seasons.

Arthur Birchall, who worked as a mechanic with Chapman on both Formula 1 and Indy, paints a picture of a practical leader who was happy to roll up his sleeves and dirty his hands. "He was an extremely competent motivator who would make you feel wanted. On many occasions, he would work with us through the night, which I can't see any of the modern guys doing. In 1967, we had a very serious problem with handling at Indy on the Lotus 42, which was originally going to be an H16 BRM-engined car. We ended up putting in a Ford engine because the BRM didn't last. We had rear geometry problems, it was bump-steering – not that Indy is a very bumpy circuit.

"The Old Man worked all night with us, tracking up the rear of the car, doing a geometry check on it, and we ended up with him and me fabricating radius arm pick-up points, which needed to go something like an inch below where the designed ones were. We had to move the fuel bag tank out of the way so that we could rivet the components onto the chassis. Things like that stick in my mind. I can't see any of the modern people having the skill as well as the drive to do that. Chapman was intellectual and switched on, but he was also capable. He could pick up a hammer, file or spanner and use it. He was a bloody good leader. We did a lot of fairly risky things that he would condone, like welding up pieces of chassis with full fuel tanks at the circuit in the middle of the night because you couldn't drain them."

Dick Scammell also recalls an occasion when the mercurial Lotus boss got stuck in and demonstrated his tremendous stamina. "When they banned high wings at Monaco in 1969, we decided between us that we ought to have something on the back of the car, so we put a tea-tray-type wing on the 49. Colin had been at Indy and he arrived on the

Lotus boss Colin
Chapman (second
from left), is seen
here with Graham Hill
(left), Dick Scammell
(in the red jacket),
and chief designer
Maurice Phillippe at
the unveiling of the
1968 Lotus 56 turbine
Indy car.
(Arthur Birchall)

A despairing Jim Clark
studies the rear end
of his Lotus 38 in
the Gasoline Alley
garage at the 1967
Indy 500, while a
fed-up-looking Colin
Chapman and Graham
Hill sit at the back,
all of them trying to
work out what they
need to do in order
to qualify the team's
recalcitrant cars.
(Eamon Fullalove)

Track record   Arthur Birchall

❝I started with Littlewoods Pools as an apprentice, working on a fantastic selection
of cars right up from Austin A30s and A40s for the reps, to Rolls Royces and
Bentleys. How I became a racing mechanic was that Nigel Moores from the family
that owned Littlewoods decided he wanted to race a Lotus 7. Lotus wouldn't sell him
one so he built his own, called the Longbacon Mk 1. We built the chassis ourselves in
the Littlewoods Pools garage and it had a coupe-type body in rolled aluminium. We
did some races with it at Aintree and Oulton Park then I went on to work on the cars
of Robin Smith. Robin had a garage called RS Sports Cars and owned an ex-Jackie
Stewart/John Bridges Lotus-Cortina, which I ran for him in 1964.

"I joined Lotus in January 1965 looking after the Type 26R – the Elan – and the
Type 30. I worked with Dave Lazenby and also helped build the Indy cars, the 38s.
Nobody would go home if somebody else was struggling, you just went from one job
to another. I moved from Cheshunt to Norwich with them in 1966. I went out to Japan
to do an Indy race with Jimmy [Clark] and left Cheshunt and came back to Hethel,
because in the two weeks I was away they went through the move."

Birchall worked at Lotus until 1970, mostly on the Indy section but also Formula
1 from time to time. He rejoined Lotus as Formula 1 chief mechanic in 1976, working
with drivers such as Mario Andretti, Gunnar Nilsson and Ronnie Peterson. In 1978,
his final season as a mechanic, he was mainly
looking after gearboxes, after which he set
up his own company doing restorations and
production engineering including the Midas
sports car. His company, Arthur Birchall
Coatings, now manufactures disabled toilet
cubicles for trains.

Arthur Birchall describes Colin Chapman as a hard
taskmaster but an extremely competent motivator.
Here, Birchall is sitting at the wheel of Graham
Hill's Lotus 56, the only one of the three 56s entered for the 1968 Indy 500 with a
strengthened fuel pump shaft, which, unfortunately, crashed in the race. (Arthur Birchall)

Sunday morning of the race. We were in the middle of riveting this thing and he rolled
up his sleeves and gave us a hand.

"To show what the man was like; he went to the race, then flew us home to England
– which was an epic flight – arriving in Hethel at about three in the morning. His parting
words to me were 'I'll see you in the morning, we've got to write the job list.' I was one
minute late, it was a minute past eight o'clock in the morning. I knocked and walked
into his office and he looked at me and said 'Where have you been? Don't be late again.
Now sit down and write this job list.' We wrote out the list and then he got back in his
plane, flew himself to London airport, and caught a flight back to Indy. No wonder he
died young. His energy was incredible."

Job lists were the bane of most Team Lotus mechanics' lives, as Hughie Absalom recalls. "Every car that went out, no matter if it had run two or fifty laps, there always seemed to be about 200 jobs to do. Chapman was very good at writing out job lists." Derek Mower, who worked on the Formula 1 team in 1970, concurs. "I can remember the Old Man coming into the garage and starting a job list. Beginning at the front of the car, he got to the rollover bar and had listed 100 jobs already for that night. He'd come back in the morning – we'd all be knackered from another all-nighter – and say 'I can't see what there is on that list to keep you boys up all night.' He was a bastard but you used to work hard for him. You'd pull your finger out because you knew if you did, you stood a good chance of winning."

Arthur Birchall also tells of how Team Lotus mechanics used the Lotus road car factory as an 'auxiliary stores' for parts. "We used to go and take bits and pieces from Lotus Cars to build the race cars. If we needed a steering rack or something like that, he wouldn't say anything about us stealing them, as long as we weren't caught. It was literally taking from his left hand to give to his right. The race team mechanics were regarded as his blue-eyed boys."

Jim Pickles confirms that they were never reprimanded if they had to go into the factory at night to source parts. "The Old Man got to hear of it but he was very protective of us. On a couple of occasions, the factory had long since knocked off and gone home, and we were still working away. If we needed something that we knew we could find in production, we would break down doors or break locks to get it, and the Old Man would say 'If my guys want something, they can have it' so we had free rein, although we didn't deliberately abuse it, we only did it if there was good reason."

Dick Scammell remembers that, in his early days at Team Lotus, Chapman was quite a formidable boss to work for. "He was quite a frightening character at that time; hugely forceful and always demanding big things from everybody. He used to walk in one end of the workshop and out the other without stopping, along the way delivering a blast to somebody about something that he didn't consider quite right. As a young lad, I found that quite impressive. He didn't suffer fools gladly, that was for sure. He expected everybody to do twice as much as they thought they could do, which was probably quite good for some as it gave us the opportunity to progress. There was always something you could do and if you could do it well enough, that was fine. If you did it and got it wrong more than once, that wasn't fine. Colin was exceedingly bright without a doubt and a very inspiring person to work for, but he demanded a huge amount of effort from everybody.

"If you couldn't take being dressed down reasonably hard on occasion, you couldn't work there. I remember him walking through the workshop one day and giving somebody a horrendous blast, I don't know what it was about but it was aimed at one of the mechanics. It was coming up to lunchtime and this mechanic packed up his toolkit and departed. Colin came through later in the afternoon and said 'Where's Bill?' or whatever his name was, and we said 'You sort of explained the facts of life to him fairly strongly, and he's left.' He said 'I didn't mean that, no, go and find him, bring him back, he's all right' and we did."

Chapman was not just an inspirational leader and gifted designer of cars, but a very proficient pilot, a legacy of time spent in the RAF doing his national service, and an extremely quick racing driver. Dick Scammell tells a story of how Chapman would often embarrass his regular drivers with his own turn of speed when he drove the team's cars. "I can remember times when he would get behind the wheel of the racing cars, with the drivers saying 'For God's sake, don't let him stay out there.' I went to Silverstone with an 18 with Innes [Ireland] and someone else. Anyway, they drove the 18 round and round and round and came in and complained bitterly about it. Colin went to his car, got out his little old crash helmet, put on his driving gloves and Fair Isle pullover, got into the car, did about four laps – and was on their pace. He came in and they asked him what he thought. He replied that it wasn't too bad; 'What about when you brake into so-and-so corner?' they asked, to which he replied 'I'm not a racing driver so I don't brake there, do I?'"

The Lotus boss had an unerring ability to both quickly sum up someone and also persuade people to do things for him without them noticing. Dick Scammell describes one occasion when his wife was on the receiving end of this. "My wife used to say to me 'Why don't you tell him that you're not going to?' and I used to say 'It's difficult,' because I was almost brainwashed. I can remember at Silverstone one day, he turned around and looked at Frances and asked 'Where's my sports jacket?' and I stood and watched in amazement as she rushed off like a demented ferret looking for his jacket. He'd set off for the helicopter, so she ran after him with it and he snatched it out of her hand, shut the door of the helicopter and was gone. When she got back I asked 'Why didn't you tell him to find his own sports jacket?' That's the sort of person he was."

The question of whether or not Lotus cars were too fragile is perhaps one which could be debated for many hours over a drink or two. However, undeniably, several Grand Prix victories were lost due to Chapman's desire to use the lightest possible components on his cars, as Hughie Absalom testifies. "One of the things he was adamant about was driveshafts. Many times we had broken them and he would say they were the right size but weren't heat-treated right, or hadn't been made up of the right material. He had a point there but, in the meantime, he lost many a race by being pedantic like that. At McLaren the cars were always much more bullet-proof, probably because Bruce [McLaren] and Denny [Hulme] were more involved in how they were made, so they were always a lot stronger."

Mike Lowman found Chapman a demanding but rewarding boss. "A lot of people said to me, 'You don't want to go there' but he was fantastic. He made me workshop supervisor, so I was responsible for all of the home-based staff, and making sure that the cars had everything they needed to go out with. I loved working for the guy. I don't think I've ever worked with someone who could motivate people like he could. He was a hard but fair taskmaster.

"My wife became a bit fed up with it at times because, after a race abroad, we'd very often be called at two or three in the morning – he didn't care what time it was in the UK. He'd say 'I want so-and-so done like this, that and the other.' Then I would pick up the phone and call the other guys to say 'Right, I'll see you in the shop in half an hour, we've got to do this and that.' We got the van drivers in to start them off on some of the long trips; that was our biggest problem, being in Norfolk the van driver was about an hour away from anyone at the start of their trip. I stayed there until Chapman died. Peter Warr took over but the soul had gone and it didn't work very well."

Alan Challis was another top mechanic who spent some time in the 'School of

Chapman' and found it demanding. "I went to work at his boat company, for a year. Tony Rudd, who was at Lotus, knew I'd had a falling out at BRM so he offered me a job down there. It was harder than working for a Formula 1 team. I didn't realise how pernickety Colin could be. Obviously a very clever man, a very good engineer, but he liked his pound of flesh. He was certainly charismatic and he knew what made a car work. What he produced compared to the BRM; the BRM was three or four years out of date before it started."

Tyrrell and his timber yard

Headquartered in a modest former timber yard in Ockham, Surrey, the Tyrrell Racing Organisation never lost sight of its humble beginnings and, right to the end, had the feel of a family business rather than a faceless corporation. The team's former chief mechanic, Roger Hill, confirms that Ken Tyrrell was the rock of the family. "Ken was a fatherly-type person. He was the boss but very fair, and you knew where you stood. When I first went there, he said 'If there are any problems, the office door is always open.' He talked to you about anything, whether it was a job or whatever. For all of us who worked at Tyrrell, I would imagine, he was a very good boss. It would be wrong to say that he wasn't mechanically-minded but he attracted guys around him that did the stuff he couldn't do. He was very organised, knew what he wanted to do and was good at leading people, even if he didn't – without being rude – understand what was going on. He encouraged you to get on and do the job. The whole scene was a bit like a family which got on together without any arguments. I know it sounds corny but that's how it was."

Peter Hennessy was another who felt instantly comfortable when he joined Tyrrell in 1971, the reason for which was the welcome from his new boss. "Ken was very nice to work with – until you asked for more money!" he joked. "He always took his tea break in the workshop with the guys, as it was such a small outfit when I started. You'd talk to him like you'd talk to anyone. He took an interest in everything, such as what was happening with your family."

Roy Topp also found Tyrrell an agreeable boss. "He was very easy to get on with. Everybody seemed to respect him. With Ken at the top, although he made the big decisions, he didn't crack the whip or anything, there were no hard words. Nobody told us when to work, only when not to. Roger [Hill] or someone would say 'Right, we'll have this Sunday off.' Ken was a great guy. We had one thing in common: he was a Spurs supporter and I supported Southampton, so we always had a little chat about our football."

Hill tells the story of the building of the first car to carry the team boss' name, the Tyrrell 001, in 1970. The project was kept hush-hush, and the car caused something of a stir when it made its first appearance in practice for the non-Championship Gold Cup meeting at Oulton Park. Ken said 'We are going to make a car. Let's not tell anybody, nobody needs to know.'"

Since Tyrrell had never constructed its own car before, a crew had to be put together to do this. Peter Turland, who already worked for the team, was one of the men chosen. "Tyrrell approached me one day and asked 'Will you build my cars for me?' I replied 'Blimey, Ken. I don't know anything about it, to be honest with you.' He

Track record   Roger Hill

❝My apprenticeship in New Zealand was as a fitter/turner/welder, I'm not a motor
mechanic as such. I came to the UK on a working holiday involving moto-cross
and scrambling. I've always been into something that goes; I don't play rugby or
anything. I did a couple of years of Formula 3 for Charles Lucas
– Piers Courage and Roy Pike were driving for us and knew by
that stage that motor racing was something I wanted to do.

"The Formula 3 thing got me going, then I was introduced
to Ken [Tyrrell] and it started from there really. He was running
Formula 2 and Formula 3 and was going to do Formula 1 in
1968. I went to see him and we shook hands and I had a job.
Later, Ken asked me to become chief mechanic and that went
on for quite some time, almost up to 1998 [when the team was
bought by BAR]. I absolutely loved it. The trouble was, I was
there for a total of about 30 years and, when it stopped ...
Motor racing is almost like a terminal disease; you do it for that
long you can't get out of it and when you do ... I still don't like
watching a race because I'm not there."

*Tyrrell chief mechanic Roger Hill, seen here filling up François
Cevert's Tyrrell 002 in the pit garages at Nivelles prior to the 1972
Grand Prix, says that Ken Tyrrell was very precise about the
amount of fuel that went in his cars. (Roy Topp)*

*The Tyrrell team poses proudly behind Tyrrell
001 after its completion. Left to right: Roy Topp,
Terry Richards, Roger Hill, Derek Gardner, Jackie
Stewart, Ken Tyrrell, Roland Law, Ken Sykes,
John Bullock, Keith Boshier. (Roger Hill)*

said 'I'm asking you, will you build my cars for
me?' I said 'Look, I'll have a go but don't expect
bloody wonders.' 'That's all I want to know,' he
replied; he was like that."

"The first chassis was built at Maurice
Gomm's in Woking. Where the engine fitted at
the back, one of the mounting points was three-
eighths out of line because they built it on a
surface plate, rather than in a jig and hadn't got it straight. When we put that first chassis
in the jig, Alan Stait had to make a special engine mount for it, which was three-eighths
out of line, to level it up."

Unsurprisingly for a brand new car straight out of the box, the 001 had a difficult
debut outing, as Roy Topp relates. "It had never been run before, so we arranged to go
testing at Oulton Park at 6 o'clock on a Sunday morning. You can imagine, a nice quiet

Track record   Peter Hennessy

&6_Working in the motor trade as a trainee apprentice mechanic, I took my final
exams in 1968. I'd come home from the garage every day with the old hypoid oil
stinking in my hair and all this sort of thing, thinking 'there must be something better
than this.' One day I looked in the paper and there was a job for a welder at MRD
just down the road from where I lived._

_"I was into Superstock racing and stock cars and had built a few cars and thought
'I can weld, I'll apply for that and see what happens.' I went down to MRD and found
out that it was for Motor Racing Developments. I hadn't really been into that sort of
racing, I had been so wrapped up in my own formula really. I was told the vacancy
for a welder had been filled, so I mentioned I had just finished an apprenticeship in
the motor trade and asked if they needed any mechanics and they said they'd get the
works manager out to see me. Out comes a very portly chap called John Beasant. We
had a few words before he said he would get the works foreman out to see me, and
out came Gerry [Hones]._

_"I showed Gerry some photos I'd taken of the cars I'd built and he took me
around the workshops, and after about an hour's chat he just said 'Well, if you want,
we'll start you, on £15 a week.' In the motor trade I was earning about £10-£12 a
week so it was quite a jump. I was in the production shop for a few months when
Gerry asked me if I wanted to join the racing team. This was in 1969 and the first race
I went to was the Indy 500. That was quite an initiation, when you've been working
in a garage fitting road wheels on Ford Cortinas and then you've got to put the wheel
on a car that's going to go 212 mph, it concentrates the mind a bit."_

_Peter stayed at Brabham's until the end of 1970. After a short spell in the US
working on the Patrick Petroleum Special
(a Brabham BT32 Indy car), he joined Team
Tyrrell in 1971, as a gearbox mechanic,
where he remained until 1977. A move to
Ron Dennis' Project 4 team followed and he
stayed with the company when it merged
with McLaren, working for it for a total of 28
years, before being made redundant in 2005._

_Hennessy was looking for something more
exciting than working in the motor trade.
(Peter Hennessy)_

day and Jackie's out there thrashing around in a Formula 1 car; it caused uproar among
the locals. Unfortunately, when it came to the race, the engine blew before we had even
qualified it. So he practised in the March 701 and got that well up the grid, but they
opted to start from the back of the grid in the 001. It got fairly well up but it was a two-
part race in those days and, as he crossed the line at the end of the first leg, the engine
blew again. So that was the 001's first outing.

"It never won a race and very rarely finished. We sorted out the problem with the engine blowing; it was surge in the oil tank. In those days, the Cosworth used about six pints of oil in a Grand Prix. There was one stage where we had a collector on the back and a little pump sending it back into the oil tank. That was why some people used to put soap powder down the trumpets of a DFV, to try and gum up the rings and stop it using oil. Then he went to Monza and the hub broke, and in Canada at St Jovite the front beam across the top, where the dampers fitted on, came away from the chassis. At Watkins

Six wheels on my wagon: The radical Project/34 Tyrrell Formula 1 car, was introduced to a stunned press audience in September 1975. It is shown here in the pit lane at Silverstone during early testing, with Patrick Depailler at the wheel, Ken Tyrrell (left) and the car's designer Derek Gardner. (Roy Topp)

Glen the engine blew. He led the race, he'd lapped everyone. An oil pipe rubbed through on the exhaust. From there it went to Mexico and I think a dog jumped out in front of him. That was the life of 001. Entertaining but with no results."

Secrecy was also paramount five years later, when the radical Project/34 six-wheeler was unveiled in late 1975, as Roger Hill explains. "We managed to keep that a secret, and even when it was under wraps at the launch, we had a lump of wood between the two front wheels, which made it look like a front wheel; when the cover came off, nobody could believe it."

Peter Turland remembers that there was a good financial incentive, in the form of

Track record
Roy Topp

❝I'm a motorcyclist at heart and used to do trials and scrambling. One day I was riding at Beaulieu and doing very well but there was this other little guy on a Bultaco Metisse who kept beating me. At that time I was a charge hand at a welding place and a bloke came in wanting a job. I said I would give him a welding test, we got talking and it turned out he was the guy who kept beating me. This was John Bullock, who later went to work for Tyrrell's because he knew Roger Hill and all the people who were there.

"When Tyrrell's built their first car, the 001, they needed a welder/fabricator and John said that if I wanted to get into Formula 1 or motor racing, I should write a letter to Ken – he must have had a word with him. I did and Ken gave me the job. I was heavily involved with building the Tyrrell 001 and obviously in those days there were very few of us. Although Maurice Gomm did the chassis, we did most of the other work. After 001, I worked on Jackie Stewart's car with Roger Hill until I became number one on Jackie's car and somebody came and worked with me."

Roy also worked with François Cevert, Jody Scheckter and Patrick Depailler at Tyrrell. In 1977, he moved to the nascent Wolf team with Jody Scheckter staying there through Jody's two seasons and into 1979, when James Hunt quit the team mid-season. At the end of the year, he moved to ATS, where he stayed for two seasons, working with Marc Surer and Jan Lammers. A year with the Fittipaldi team in its death throes followed, after which he returned for a final season with ATS in 1983.

Roy Topp works on Tyrrell 005 during the 1973 season. Thirty-six years on, he is restoring this car to tip-top condition. (Roy Topp)

a bonus, to keep the six-wheeler project secret. "Ken gathered us all together and said 'We're going to build a six-wheeled Formula 1 car. I don't want anyone else to know about it so, if it gets out, I'll know it's one of you.' We began building it in the February and finished it in August or September, managing to keep it quiet. We got a good bonus for that."

Tyrrell's gearbox man, Peter Hennessy, nearly inadvertently rumbled the project in its very early stages. "During development of the six-wheeler, old Keith Boshier made the mock-up in the fibreglass shed. If you had to pass through there for any reason, you had to knock on the blacked-out door; they would cover up the project and you could go in. I had to go through to fetch something. They had this funny thing covered up and, as I walked past, I casually asked 'What's that – a pair of front axles?' I didn't think any more about it but I'd hit the nail on the head; I could see their jaws drop when I said it but it was only a throwaway line."

Roy Topp recalls that the idea behind the six-wheeled format was that it would reduce drag while increasing grip at the front of the car. In practice, however, it did not seem to offer many advantages. "There weren't a lot of gains. One of the reasons for doing it was to increase the contact patch, but also the theory was that a lot of the drag came from the front wheels because they were the biggest things to hit the air going forward. The idea was to put the smaller wheels as low as the top of the nose so that you'd generate less drag but more contact. But it wasn't quicker on the straights. It was no harder to work on but it was more difficult to balance the braking with the two sets of wheels on the front. If the front pair locked, the back ones didn't touch the ground, or vice versa. We had a double balance bar on it, one for the balance between the front brakes and another for the balance back to front. Jackie [Stewart] drove it at Paul Ricard. He said it felt no different to the four-wheeler but that you couldn't see the front wheels."

Although it was an interesting experiment, the car was a relative failure, scoring only one win in two seasons of competition. Topp attributes the sensational result at the Swedish Grand Prix at Anderstorp, where the cars scored an impressive 1-2, to nothing more than tyres. "Goodyear did some special tyres for us, something a little bit better that seemed to work very well there, so that win was down to the tyres more than anything."

Although Ken Tyrrell usually played the paternal role within the team, he wasn't

Jody Scheckter (3) and Patrick Depailler (4) stunned the Formula 1 world with a dominant 1-2 victory in the 1976 Swedish Grand Prix, but it was a false dawn and mainly attributable to special tyres produced by Goodyear. They are shown here two races earlier, during the Belgian Grand Prix at Zolder. (Roy Topp)

averse to giving his drivers a rocket if he felt they weren't putting in sufficient effort, as Roger Hill relates. "Ken certainly used to have a go at the drivers occasionally, with his famous 'froth jobs.' He would become revved up sometimes and he'd be squawking so much that occasionally a speck of saliva would fly out of his mouth. I've seen him do that to a few drivers, especially if they hadn't done something he thought they should have. Ken was good at making his point and if he thought that somebody didn't understand, he made sure that they did."

Neil Davis, who worked for Tyrrell between 1968 and 1973, is glowing in his praise of his former boss. "He was the most straightforward person you could ever wish to meet, or work for. He was approachable, there was no side to him, and he and his wife, Nora, would make sure all the mechanics were well looked after. He would often take us out to dinner. I didn't work for anyone else because I didn't want to; he was a fantastic boss as far as I'm concerned.

"He was a great man, a great organiser, everything was in place. You always knew what you were going to do, where you were going to go and when, he was so precise, and this is what made him. There was nothing left to chance. He was absolutely brilliant. The day they made Ken Tyrrell they broke the mould, he was that good."

Bruce McLaren: engineer extraordinaire

Bruce McLaren first struck out on his own as a Formula 1 constructor in 1966, after seven and a bit seasons racing for the Cooper Car Company, which had included three Grand Prix victories, the first at the tender age of 22. In 1968, he became only the second driver ever to win a Grand Prix driving a car bearing his own name. Sadly, he was killed in an accident while testing a Can-Am McLaren M8D at Goodwood in June 1970.

Ray Rowe worked for him at both Cooper and McLaren, and found him very easy to get along with, although the close-knit nature of the team perhaps meant they got too close to their drivers. "Bruce was good. You could relate to him and he to you. With

his being an engineer, you knew what he was talking about and we could understand each other. Normally, the driver is the driver and I'm the mechanic. With Bruce and Denny they were different, we were more of a family then. But later on, when we got taken over, we weren't quite so friendly with the drivers and it was a different set-up."

Hughie Absalom identifies McLaren's willingness to share his line of thinking with his mechanics as a key way in which he differed from other team bosses. "Bruce was the guy I learnt the most from. He was more receptive to telling you what he was thinking out loud – he would explain his train of thought. With Chapman, you did as you were told. There was never enough time to question why we'd done this or that. With Bruce, it was an ongoing thing. I probably learnt more from him than Brabham or Chapman."

McLaren: Engineer, constructor, champion and friend.
(Mike Barney)

Mike Barney was another who worked with Bruce at both Cooper and McLaren. He had a particularly personal reason to feel grateful to the boss, but also found it a great place to

Track record   Ray Rowe

❝I started as a race mechanic when I went to Cooper. I had a 750 special which
I had built but didn't get to race. I went to work for Cooper instead because I
couldn't afford to, racing was expensive then, as it is today.

"Cooper happened to be close to me – they were in Surbiton and I lived in Sutton.
I went along and met Roy Golding, who was the foreman there, about a job. There
wasn't one advertised but I guess he took me on because I already had a grounding
in mechanical bits and pieces.

I started at Cooper in early
1961 then moved to McLaren
in 1965 and I'm still there.
I do two days a week now,
helping with the gearboxes.

*Ray Rowe, shown here fitting
a nose to a McLaren M15 Indy
car; he worked with Bruce at
Cooper, and McLaren found
him easy to relate to.
(Ray Rowe)*

work. "He was the best. When
my wife and I married in 1964,
he took us to Watkins Glen for
our honeymoon, as part of the race. Having got there, he said 'You might as well come
to Mexico' because they'd got airline tickets that the race organisers had supplied. We
got to Mexico City and that entitled us to a free trip to Acapulco, so we had 10 days
there as well.

"On his memorial stone at Goodwood, it says 'Engineer, Constructor, Champion
and Friend' and that sums him up. He had his foibles, as we all do, but it was a good
team and he was a good bloke to work for. It was full of switched-on guys, even in those
early days."

Talking of foibles, Barney remembers a good example of McLaren stubbornness
from the 1967 season. "There was a classic scene with him in Canada with the V12
BRM-engined McLaren. We were a bit marginal on fuel and Bruce suggested we took
the alternator off to save a bit of weight and fuel and produce more power. We said that
there was no way you could do that, because the battery would go flat. He said 'No it
won't, if we charge the battery fully it'll be alright.' We argued and argued.

"We had the engine off to do something or other and that was the only time we
could fit the alternator back on. We were trying to move him out of the way so that we
could put the bloody thing back on and put the belt on it so that it would actually charge
in the race, but he didn't go, so Wally Willmott and I couldn't. Two-thirds of the way
through the race, the battery went flat. Jack Brabham told him, we all told him it would
but he would not listen. He drove into the pits and we stood there looking at him. There

Track record Mike Barney

"I'd done an apprenticeship in the late 1940s/early 50s at a Ford garage, Dees of Croydon. In fact, a lad that used to work with me, in 1958, was Peter Gethin. We got fed up with that and he wanted to be a racing driver and I wanted to do something else so I went to Cooper in Surbiton. I walked into the workshop, having come from a 'proper' firm, Dees and asked to see the works manager. A couple of blokes looked at each other and said 'Who's the works manager this week?' Then they said 'Well, Burgess is here' so I got talking to Ian Burgess and told him 'I just want to work here, see what it is like'.

"I had been there about three or four months when there was some sort of ruckus on the race-team, I never did meet the guy that they chucked off but found out it was because they couldn't keep him out of the driving seat, he kept on wanting to drive them up and down and they didn't look too kindly upon that. So I got that job because I was too big to fit in the cars. My first race was Aintree 59, which we won and I never looked back. My time at Cooper was the best ever."

Mike subsequently moved to McLaren and later in his career enjoyed spells at Williams and Brabham. He finished his work in the sport in 1991 when the latter team folded.

Mike Barney: His time at Cooper was 'the best ever.'
(Mike Barney)

was nothing we could do. We changed the battery but that was a lap and a half gone: him out of the car, battery out, new battery in, him back in the car, it was ridiculous."

When McLaren died, it devastated the team, which only survived due to the efforts of people such as Denny Hulme, Teddy Mayer and Phil Kerr, along with the commercial agreements the team had in place with sponsors, as Mike Barney explains. "The death of Bruce was a hammer blow. We'd spent so much time blasting those cars around Goodwood, we became a bit blasé about the dangers. The place stopped dead but it was down to people like Teddy Mayer and the fact there was money from the likes of Reynolds, Gulf and Goodyear that the team kept going."

Rob Walker, Gentleman

Rob Walker was heir to the Johnnie Walker whisky fortune and spent his money wisely – running a racing team out of his Pippbrook Garage in Dorking, Surrey. Although he began entering cars in his name in the early 1950s, Walker first came to international prominence when Stirling Moss drove his tiny 1.9-litre Cooper to victory in the season-opening Argentinian Grand Prix of 1958. Moss and Walker struck up a great partnership

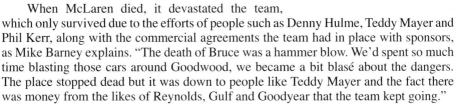

which resulted in six Grand Prix wins, including the first-ever for a Lotus, before Moss suffered his career-ending accident at Goodwood in 1962.

A host of other famous names drove for Walker, including Maurice Trintignant and Jo Bonnier, before he linked up in 1965 with Swiss driver Jo Siffert, who stayed with the team until the end of 1969. In an era where it was harder and harder for privateer teams to remain competitive, Walker's swansong season was 1970 with Graham Hill. Tony Cleverley, who worked for Walker between 1955 and 1970, has tremendously fond memories of his former boss. "Rob Walker was a great guvnor. We got peanuts in those days, but we would have worked for nothing for him, he was that sort of guy, I had great respect for him. We weren't on the greatest of expenses, and we might have had to eat tripe now and again, but he always made sure we were looked after and had a

Gentleman Rob: Rob Walker briefs his mechanics in the narrow pits at Monaco while driver Jo Bonnier sits on the pit counter. (Tony Cleverley)

proper hotel and things like that. The money he threw into motor racing, he should have been knighted."

Stan Collier, his colleague in 1969 and 1970, agrees with that assessment, and also sheds some light on why Walker closed down the team at the end of the 1970 season. "Robbie was lovely, he was a real gentleman. We had Siffert, then Graham, but that all folded because Rob Walker was very friendly with Graham, that was the trouble. He wanted him to pack up racing but Graham said no, he wanted to carry on. So Robbie virtually said 'Right, I'll pack up the team and that was it."

Fearless Frank Williams

Starting Frank Williams Racing Cars in the mid-1960s after a brief career as a somewhat brave but accident-prone driver that earned him his 'Fearless' moniker, Frank Williams spent more than a decade ducking and diving in an attempt to establish himself as an entrant in the top flight – Formula 1. He first came to prominence in the winter of 1968/69, when he ran Piers Courage in the Tasman series in Australia and New Zealand, where his Brabham BT24 was the closest opposition to the dominant Lotus entries of Jochen Rindt and Graham Hill.

Bob Sparshott, who left Team Lotus at the end of 1968, explains how he began working for Williams around this time. "In 1969, I got involved with Frank, doing a Brabham-DFV conversion. He rang and said he had an interesting project if I wanted to have a look at it. He had this Brabham BT26. The first conversion – on the BT24 – had been done for Frank by Johnny Muller with a 2.5-litre Cosworth DFW. After the Tasman series, Frank needed the money so he sold it, confident that Johnny Muller was going to come back to England and build him an F1 version. But Johnny said he was retiring and not coming back; even Frank couldn't convince him to return.

"So there was Frank, he'd got nothing to go on – there weren't any real drawings or anything – and he was committed to converting this car. I took it on and obviously it was a hell of a lot of work. I was travelling up and down to Frank's place in Slough every day from Wheathampstead in Hertfordshire – which was a nightmare journey – and doing long days as well. It went on and on and on. He used to come in every evening to see how it was going, and one night said 'I've got an idea; why don't you move into my flat?' which was above the workshop. 'I'll go and stay in London with my girlfriend and it'll save you travelling time and you can go home at the weekends.' So that's what I did.

"I'd been in there about a week, at which point he hadn't paid me any money, and I'd done about three or four weeks' work. The deal was that I was supposed to be paid at the end of every week, or at the worst, every two. I decided to tackle him. He came in one evening and was typical Frank Williams, dressed up to the nines, in an immaculate suit, saying 'I love the way you've done that water rail' and all this soft-soap crap. Anyway, I said 'Frank, about the money, I haven't had any.' 'Ah,' he said 'Yes, I thought you might be asking me for some. It's a little bit tight at the moment. I'll tell you what, have you had a look in my wardrobe in my bedroom?'

"I said 'No, of course not, I would never dream of doing that.' 'You ought to have a look' he said 'because there are some Saville Row suits and you can have a couple of those.' I said 'Frank, I don't want suits, I want money. Firstly, they won't fit me because I'm much bigger than you and, secondly, I need to buy things with money.' 'Oh' he said 'I thought you'd see it that way, I'll see you tomorrow.' The next day he paid me, up to date. But if I hadn't said anything, he'd have gone on for months. Anyway, we got it all done and it was alright and it went quite well."

Williams is not short of admirers, both for what he has achieved in his life and the way he did business, even if it was, at times, not exactly 'by the book.' Mike Young is one such fan. "Frank Williams is absolutely fabulous. One of the things I've always liked about him is the fact that, although Frank took liberties, he never did actually let a company go. I can think of one instance, after two years of not paying somebody, Frank finally got cornered. He had the money but said 'Look, I'll pay you in cash but is there any chance of a discount?' so he was a salesman to the very end. I used to go down to the Sheriff's Officer for Berkshire probably at least once a fortnight with a briefcase full of money, and we'd sit down with his bottle of Scotch and go through who was giving him the most hassle. We'd have these High Court and County Court writs laid out on the floor and be putting money on each of them. It'd be a case of 'That one's not going to last any longer, so he can have a big amount.' So many people asked Frank why he didn't wind up the business and just start again, but he wouldn't do it; hats off to him for that. But it did make life very difficult at times."

Later on, Young returned for a second spell with Williams, and tells of how somewhat unconventional means were utilised to install Frank's new company in its premises. "When we started up Williams Grand Prix Engineering in 1977, he got a deal with Patrick Neve [to run a March 761 in Formula 1] and we virtually opened up with nothing – an empty factory and no equipment – but we had a car on the grid fairly soon afterwards. With all the faffing around trying to sign the lease for the factory at Didcot,

---

Track record   Mike Young

❝I was brought up in the city, working in the Stock Exchange in London. In the 1960s most stockbroking companies were partnerships. Every partner had about three sons of limited ability but because they were sons they were just being brought in one after the other, so there was no future for me there. One day, I saw an advertisement for a storeman/gopher at Team Lotus and thought I would apply. Very kindly, Jim Endruweit decided I fitted the bill, which was the start of 30-odd years of motor racing."

Mike worked for Lotus from 1964 until the end of 1968. He then moved to Frank Williams, where he worked with drivers such as Piers Courage and Brian Redman. A short-lived spell with Graham Hill's Embassy Racing came to an untimely end following Hill's death in a plane crash and in 1975 Mike returned to work with Frank Williams, who had linked up with Walter Wolf. When Williams struck out on his own in 1977 to form Williams Grand Prix Engineering, Young went with him and helped set up the fledgling company. He finished his mechanic's career with a spell at the underachieving ATS team between 1982 and 1984, working with drivers such as Manfred Winkelhock and Eliseo Salazar.

Working for Frank Williams meant there was never a dull moment. (Grand Prix Mechanics Charitable Trust)

---

there was only one way to get going and that was to kick in the door and hope the owners didn't turn up and find we'd already moved in. That was quite an achievement, especially on such a small budget. After that season, they started building the first Williams car with Patrick [Head], and it went from strength to strength. I left at the end of that year, because with the great foresight I had, I couldn't see Frank going anywhere, apart from back to his old ways …"

Reg Parnell, forward thinker

Reg Parnell was a British racing driver of some repute who competed before and after World War II, making sporadic appearances in Formula 1 (although he never won a Grand Prix), and establishing a strong relationship with Aston Martin, for whom he drove sports cars. When he retired in the late 1950s, Parnell became team manager for Aston Martin, guiding its sports car team to the 1959 World Championship title and a famous victory over Ferrari in that year's Le Mans 24 Hours. Sadly, he died in 1964, aged 52, when a routine appendix operation went wrong and he contracted peritonitis.

Gerry Hones worked with Parnell, in both the Aston sports car and the Yeoman Credit Formula 1 teams, and remembers his attention to detail as being outstanding. "I often wonder what Reg would think if he came back now, because he died very young. He was one of the best managers I've ever worked with and was dedicated to motor racing. He had his farm up in Derby, with something like 1600 pigs, and used to come down from Derby on the Monday morning. He was a real forward thinker on everything.

"A typical example was with Aston Martin when we did the Tourist Trophy at Goodwood [the deciding round of the 1959 World Sports Car Championship]. It was all manual quick-lift jacks in those days, shoving them under the car. He came in one day with some hydraulic jacks. They were off a 1937 Wolseley 12, which had fitted what was known as a 'Jack-All' system. There were four hydraulic jacks on the car and between your legs on the floorboard was a little trap door. When you lifted that, there was a dial marked F, R, and A – for front, rear and all. A lever was strapped to the side of the upholstery where your leg went down. If you had a puncture on the front, you turned the dial to F, sat in the car and used a lever to operate a pump, whereupon the front of the car would lift while you were still sitting in the dry. Then you'd jump out and change the wheel.

"Reg came in with four of these and said 'Make up all the bracketry and fit these on one of the cars.' He got an expert in to talk about these hydraulics. He asked the bloke 'Can we blow these up with air?' and was told that it would be better if we inflated them with nitrogen because, with the oil in them, there's no risk of it igniting or exploding. At Feltham [where the team was based], we worked in a big hangar with a large apron outside, where we could work if the sun was shining and could also do test runs for pit stops. When we flipped the lever, these jacks were so quick, you couldn't time them. Pitstops at the time with the manual quick-lifts were around 54 seconds. With these air jacks, we got it down to something like 22. In a 1000km race, there's a minimum of four pit stops and the possibility of five, so that is a big time-saving. Your first pit stop was usually 55 minutes into the race, by which time your tyres were stuffed.

"Avon built us some special tyres with a white 'breaker strip' moulded into it for when the tyre had two laps' worth of tread left. We had two blokes laid in the grass with binoculars at the right-hander before the chicane at Goodwood [Woodcote], watching the cars go by, around about the time we thought the tyres would be showing this strip. When it appeared, they immediately got on the walkie-talkie to us in the pits, so we could give a pit signal to the driver to come in on the next lap – because he'd got just two laps of tyre left – and in he'd come.

"When you worked it out, we very nearly gave our drivers a lap's advantage over

Not even fire could upset the carefully laid plans of Reg Parnell to help secure the World Sports Car Championship for Aston Martin at the 1959 Goodwood Nine Hours.
(LAT)

our rivals and that was it, we were well away. The tyre changes were going well and it was definitely our race to win; and then we had a fire in the pits. Anyway, it didn't matter because we still won the race [with one of the other team cars]. But that was typical of old Reg's innovative thinking."

Around the same time, Aston was working on its Formula 1 car, a front-engined machine introduced much later than intended, by which time it was apparent that rear-engined cars were the way to go. However, it is a little-known fact that Aston Martin actually constructed a rear-engined Formula 1 chassis in 1959, as Gerry Hones explains. "We had a rear-engined car on the jigs. But then we won Le Mans and the World Championship [with front-engined sports cars], and so the rear-engined Aston Formula 1 was cut up, which is a terrible thing." Definitely a case of 'what might have been …'

Hones recalls another project that was a good example of Reg Parnell's forward thinking, although today he remembers it more for its name than anything else. "When we were at Yeoman Credit he got the idea of taking a Formula 3 frame and building it up into a Formula 1 car, with a one-and-a-half litre engine. We were on an aircraft one day. Jimmy Potton and I were sitting in two seats and Reg and William Samengo-Turner [one of the brothers who owned Yeoman Credit, the Parnell team sponsor at the time] were sitting behind us. They were talking about this car and the subject cropped up of what we were going to call it. Jimmy leant over and said 'We'll call it the VR.' I said 'What's that?' and he said 'VR for Virgo Reluctarum. That translates from Latin as the reluctant virgin because it's bloody hard to get into.' It was always referred to in the press as the

Track record   Gerry Hones

❝ *When I left the army, I spotted a job advertised in Stockholm with the main Citroën agents. The managing director was into rally work and I worked on the rally cars for some time, then went to another firm that used to do ice racing, as well as rallying. After four years, I came back to England and there was a job advertised for a racing mechanic with Frazer Nash. Tony Brooks was the driver and I did Silverstone with him and the 1954 Le Mans 24 Hours with Maurice Gatsonides (inventor of the Gatso speed camera) and Marcel Becquart as the drivers.*

"Then the job came up with Aston. John Wyer had just been promoted to managing director, Automobile Division, and Reg Parnell had taken over the racing side. We used to do something like 11 championship races every year and some non-championship. In 1959, we won the World Championship with the sports cars, not thinking at the time that we were just working ourselves out of a job. In common with a lot of manufacturers, once Aston was on a high spot, that's when it moved out of it. That was it; we were all made redundant.

"Reg urged us not to take another job as he had something in mind, but Jimmy Potton and I were offered positions with Ogier, the Essex millionaire who was going to race two GT Astons. He promised us £1000 a year and a cottage on the estate, so we went back to Reg and told him. He countered with £900 a year, so, after we'd laughed at him and he'd upped his offer to the same, we agreed and found out it was the Yeoman Credit team, in Formula 1."

In 1964, Gerry moved to Brabham where, after a few years of travelling, he elected to be home-based, becoming workshop foreman, staying with the company until 1970. He moved to Frank Williams for a year before emigrating to New Zealand, where he stayed until 1997. He returned to work for McLaren for eight years as maintenance fabricator, finally retiring in 2005, aged 78.

Hones has enjoyed a lifetime of racing. (Grand Prix Mechanics Charitable Trust)

VR and I don't think any of the journalists knew what it stood for ... Jimmy was a very witty sort of bloke."

Black Jack Brabham

Jack Brabham enjoyed a remarkable career as a driver, winning the Formula 1 World Championship in 1959 1960 and again in 1966, the third time in a car of his own name and construction. With fellow Australian Ron Tauranac, he established a very successful racing car production business, selling customer versions of cars that he and the other works Brabham drivers raced. Gerry Hones rates Brabham extremely highly, observing that the success of the relationship between Brabham and Tauranac was built on clear demarcation of their roles. "Jack was one of the best to work for, very steady. The workshop was divided into two; a smaller section for the Formula 1 team and a bigger section for production. Jack never interfered with production, Tauranac wouldn't have allowed that, it was very fiercely protected. Ron could be a little troublesome or excitable at times but he was alright."

Master and apprentice: Team boss Jack Brabham points out something to his pensive- and youthful-looking mechanics Ron Dennis (r) and Peter Hennessy in the Nürburgring pits at the 1969 German Grand Prix. (LAT)

Recalling his days as foreman at Brabham, Hones talks of the extraordinary output of the production side of the company during the late 1960s. "I went back to work for Brabham and Dennis Reid had taken over as manager. One day he said to me 'You old bastard, you never told me you made 115 cars when you were foreman here.' We used to do Formula 3s, 2s and 1s, a couple of Indy cars, and in the winter when there wasn't much to do, we'd do hillclimb cars. I remember we did one for Sir Nicholas Williamson – another cracking bloke – but he used to have a terrible stutter. He came in one day and said 'C-c-c-c-c-can I t-t-t-t-take the wheels?' and I said 'If you want, what do you want them for?' and he said 'I'll get the 'effin b-b-b-b-b-butler to polish them.' When these wheels came back, they were magnificent. You could imagine this old butler, polishing the wheels in the kitchen at night ..."

Perhaps one of the reasons for the prodigious demand for production at Brabham – as well as the fact that the cars were extremely good – was the way in which Hones used to deliberately 'leak' details of upcoming test sessions for new models. "All the drivers would come in and ask 'When are you testing?' and I'd say 'I can't tell you that.' They'd say 'Go on, tell me, when are you testing at Goodwood?' And I'd say 'Friday.'

"Friday would come and I'd take the transporter down and Jack would arrive a bit later. All of a sudden, these young drivers would turn up. Jack would go out and do a few laps and his times were always bloody good. When he came in he said 'How do these blokes know when we're going to be here?' and I'd say 'I don't know, they must have heard it from someone.' Then he'd say to them 'Of course, if you had your helmet and your gear, you could have a go and try it' and they'd all say 'Actually, we've got them with us.' They'd go out and try to beat Jack's time but couldn't. Then it was a race back

Brabham production staff pose with foreman Gerry Hones and some of the cars they made in 1969. Left to right: Norman Brewer, Preston Anderson, Hugh Owen, Gerry Hones, Dave Luff, Dave Kaylor, Alan Burrows, Lloyd Owen, 'Bill the van driver.'
(Gerry Hones)

to the works, to put in their orders, because the person who put the first order in received the first car."

Murray, Barnard and Head: the new breed

In the 1970s, a new generation of racing car designer emerged, one that placed more emphasis on aerodynamics and the overall packaging of the car. In the vanguard of this group were designers such as Gordon Murray, Patrick Head, and John Barnard. Murray first came to prominence as the designer of the 1972 Duckhams Special Le Mans car, and again later as chief designer at Brabham. Head spent his early years at Lola but blossomed when he joined Frank Williams at Williams Grand Prix Engineering in 1977. Barnard established himself in the US working on Indy cars before going to McLaren and introducing one of the earliest carbon fibre composite tubs, and, later still, the semi-automatic gearbox for Ferrari.

Stan Collier, who worked with Murray at Brabham, remembers him as the mechanic's friend. "Gordon was a nice, down-to-earth bloke. When he was going to alter something on the car, he would come round and ask if it would make life easier for us, which most designers didn't even think about. They didn't worry about that sort of thing but Gordon always did, he was very good."

Hughie Absalom also identified Murray as a designer who gave a lot of thought to how easy it would be for mechanics to work on his designs, but rated Barnard and Head, too. "Probably the two guys I can think of that were good in that respect were Gordon Murray and John Barnard. They realised that the easier you make it to work on, the more reliable the car becomes. When Patrick Head came out with the FW07, you'd look at it and think 'Wow, there is a whole bunch of stuff missing on this thing, compared to everybody else's – it was so simple the way he had packaged everything. Barnard was of the same ilk."

Ray Rowe worked with Barnard at McLaren, and has great respect and admiration for how he put together his design team. "John was 'the man.' He looked after the engineering and cars and Ron [Dennis] looked after the PR and bringing in the money, so they were a good combination. They were actually very good years. John was the chief designer on the shop floor, designing the cars, in amongst it. He obviously had the right people he could go to. You can't play cards unless you've got a decent hand and he picked the people he wanted."

7
Letting off steam

Working in such a high pressure environment – the long hours, constant travelling and danger of their drivers being killed or seriously injured – meant that mechanics and drivers in the 1950s, 60s and 70s led a life akin to World War II fighter pilots: they worked hard and played harder.

Tony Robinson, who travelled extensively as assistant to renowned mechanic Alf Francis as part of Equipe Moss when it was running a Maserati 250F, and later on his own as Bruce Halford's mechanic on a similar car, sums up their attitude. "In those days, before and after the race most people in Formula One and Formula Three who were running around at the time – those living like gypsies out of trucks and cars in Europe – were basically hellraisers. They were a different breed; there to have a damn good time. And how did they enjoy themselves? Nightclubs, bars, doing everything other than behaving themselves."

Former BRM chief mechanic Alan Challis points out that much of the hellraising among mechanics was attributable to a combination of the fact that prize-givings were held on the Sunday after the race, and, in some instances, it was cheaper for mechanics to stay in places like North America between races than fly them home. "In those days nobody went home on Sunday night, so at least you could go out then. Sometimes, though, it was not a relief on Monday morning, when you had to try and get up with your head still attached to the floor. In the 1980s and 90s, when we started flying everywhere on longer trips, we'd always get a week off and often go to Florida. In the BRM days we used to have a week in Acapulco because it was cheaper to keep us there. Nowadays, it's cheaper to fly people home."

More often than not, mechanics would let off steam on the Sunday evening by drinking too much. As Challis alludes to, most of the time this was high-spirited and resulted in nothing more than a crashing hangover the next morning. However, on one occasion, Challis thought matters had really gone too far. "I was woken in Monte Carlo, on the Monday morning after the race, by a huge banging on my bedroom door. I staggered out of bed, opened the door, and there was a Gendarme standing there. With his lack of English and my very basic French, it seemed he was telling me somebody was dead and that I'd got to come with him. So I got into his car and we went across town to the hospital, with the siren going, with him trying to explain what was going on.

"Anyway, we got there and a doctor took me in and there was one of the BRM mechanics lying on a slab. As I opened the door, the stench of booze was horrifying. He'd actually been walking on the sea wall, early in the morning, supposedly trying to get back to the hotel, and fallen off the wall, over the sea side onto one of those big rocks, and broken his leg. Luckily, somebody had seen him fall, some local. How they got hold of me, I don't know. I remember ringing [BRM boss] Mr Stanley to tell him. The mechanic survived on the team, actually. But that was down to me, as Stanley didn't get 100 per cent of the truth, rather, my edited version ..."

Occasionally, the drinking began on the way to events, particularly with the trips to races that were further afield. Tony Reeson recalls one journey where Mike Hailwood came up with an ingenious solution to a shortage of alcohol onboard a flight. "In 1972, we went to the Canadian Grand Prix. We used to go on charter flights sometimes and this was with British Caledonian, from Scotland, the first one they flew on that route, so everything was free on it, drinks and everything. We got about three-quarters of the way across and they ran out of drink. Mike Hailwood was on the plane and said 'You've got plenty of duty-free' and they said 'You can't drink that on the plane.' So Hailwood said 'If we pay for it, we can.' He went and bought the lot. The Grand Prix was sponsored by Labatts, so when we landed in Canada they'd laid on this big 'do' in the hotel with food and drink, but nobody wanted any and they couldn't figure out why – everybody had had their fill on the plane."

One team even had its own personal supply of alcohol, as Gerry Hones recounts. "UDT were terrible p***heads. Tony Robinson [the team's technical director and manager] used to have to lock them in their rooms at night. Watney's was one of their sponsors, and they used to have a barrel of Red Barrel bitter in the back of their transporter. When they came back from a race, the brewery would come down, take the empty and put in a new one, ready for the next meeting. Those that were in the know could get in the back of the transporter after practice and sup a few pints in there." Robinson confirms the team had unlimited supplies of beer as part of its arrangement with Watney's ...

Mechanics liked nothing more than a challenge or a bet as part of their night out, too, as Ray Rowe relates: "We went to Monza and outside the hotel where they had the prize-giving on the Sunday, there were two big fish tanks with trout in them. The chefs would go and fish them out so that you could have fresh trout.

"We were on the way out and we'd had a couple of drinks by then. I looked at these things and thought 'I wonder if it's possible to get one out?' Not only did I manage to catch one but landed two. They flopped onto the floor and poor old Mike [Barney] was fumbling around trying to pick them up and put them back in."

Travelling through many foreign countries, the language barrier was a constant problem, and occasionally led to misunderstandings, as Tony Robinson relates. "Alf [Francis] and I stopped off once during the daytime in Bologna at what I thought was a bar, but which turned out to be a clip joint. We sat down with a couple of girls to a table and when the bill came it was for 26,000 lire. The girls had drunk 26 double whiskies between them, so they said. We refused to pay and Alf and I got locked up for a small time. We were in this cell, and they wanted us to pay and I said to the fellow in the prison 'We are not going to pay that, but I will spin you – double or nothing.' Of course, I lost and they put us back in the bloody cell again." Today, a very dim view would be taken

Track record   Tony Reeson

❝I did an apprenticeship in a garage, as a motor mechanic, then went to work in
the garage at Raymond Mays. When I wanted to go into BRM – I wasn't bothered
which part – they wouldn't let me transfer from the garage, so I left and had a year
at Fiat Allis, who were in earthmoving equipment, as a staff inspector. Then a vacancy
came up at BRM in engine development, so I put in for it and got the job and was
there for four years on and off.

"Glen Forman was in charge of the engine shop and I was second in command.
There were six of us building the works engines. There were two engine shops – one
which built customer engines and another that built the works ones. When we had
engine problems, Glen used to go to one race and I went to the next, so we always
used to go racing but were engine rather than car mechanics."

Tony started at BRM in late 1962 and stayed there until the end of 1968, working
with drivers such as Graham Hill and Jackie Stewart. In 1969, he was asked to run
Colin Crabbe's Antique Automobiles team, which was fielding Vic Elford in an ex-works
McLaren M7A and he stayed with the team in 1970, when it ran a satellite March for
the young Swede, Ronnie Peterson, in his debut Formula 1 season. He returned to
BRM at the start of 1972, as chief mechanic of
the BRM B team, running three of the team's
five cars that year and stayed until it went into
liquidation at the end of 1974, working with
drivers such as Jean-Pierre Beltoise, Peter Gethin
and Niki Lauda.

*Tony Reeson, seen here with Ronnie Peterson
(left, in car) and Peter Bracewell (right) at the
1970 Belgian Grand Prix. (Peter Bracewell)*

of mechanics and team bosses spending time behind bars, but fifty years ago things were
a little more relaxed. "In those days it was permissible to enjoy yourself, to have a drink
and work – that was what motor racing was all about" says Robinson.

Certain circuits seemed to encourage the letting down of hair more than others,
often because of the generous hospitality of the hosts. A good example of this was
Reims, where perhaps the copious supply of champagne may have been a contributory
factor. One episode has established itself in motor racing folklore, although determining
the 'who, where, what and when' of the incident has proved more difficult. It seems
that it occurred in 1963, at a sports car race, the date of which I have been unable to
pinpoint.

Denis Daviss was working at the time for the Willment team and attended the event
with its newly-built Cobra Coupé for Frank Gardner to drive, although it retired in the
race. He takes up the story. "The prize-giving was in a big chateau just out of town, with
a great big room upstairs. It had a staircase, with potted plants all the way up each side

– very swish. They were giving away champagne; every time you took a sip, somebody filled your glass again. Pretty soon it was time to leave. As we were traipsing out, one of the drivers – I think it was Trevor Taylor – picked up a pot plant and off he went down the stairs singing *Onward Christian Soldiers*. Now all the mechanics had to have pot plants.

"We ended up at Brigitte's Bar and continued our little impromptu party there, during which David Piper's mechanic, Fairfax Dunne, got up on a table and decided to do a striptease, which upset the lady of the house but he wasn't about to stop, he was being egged on anyway. Brigitte called the police and, when they arrived, it was all kicking off and Fairfax was keeping out of the way, as it was their intent to arrest him. They finally got him, took him outside, popped him into their vehicle and off he went. But when they got to the first corner, all the wheels fell off because some mischievous little bastard had undone the wheel nuts while they were inside ...

"Now there was a real problem. The police began arresting anybody who looked or spoke English. There were guys hiding in bushes and behind walls. By then, the fountain in Reims had received a good helping of washing powder and since it was a recirculating type of thing, it was overflowing soap bubbles everywhere. They weren't very happy about that, either. Bit by bit they were picking up guys and throwing them in the calaboose. One guy was hiding in the awning above the hotel entrance. Well, they spied him because they could see the big bump he was making, so they poked him out and slung him in jail. A lady who used to go to all these types of races was also thrown into jail; Graham Hill got to hear about this and – her would-be knight in shining armour – went off to the police station to explain things and maybe get her out. As he seemed to know a lot about it, they threw him in jail as well!" As to the identity of who removed the wheelnuts, Stan Collier suggests it may have been Michael 'Noddy' Grohmann, former chief mechanic of Cooper.

Monaco was another place where mechanics tended to let off steam, either at Rosie's Bar, which used to be on the left, halfway up the climb from St. Devote, or in the Tip-Top Bar, on the left on the run down from Casino Square towards Mirabeau. Mike Lowman remembers one particular spot of relatively harmless fun. "One Monte Carlo, it must have been 1967, we were in the Tip-Top Bar after the race. It was a fairly narrow bar that went a long way back, with a white-and-green decor. We were in there drinking away when this white-and-green 2CV pulled up outside. Two guys got out and came into the bar. I looked over at Bob Dance, the same thought in our heads:'That's too good an opportunity to miss.' We got four chairs – I suppose there must have been eight or ten of us – went outside, picked up the car, put the chairs under the wheels, gently dropped it down, left it standing there on four white-and-green chairs and went back to our drinking. The two guys came out, went absolutely ballistic and called the gendarmes. Of course, no-one would own up to doing anything. In the end we helped them put it back down on the ground; it was a good laugh."

This would not have been the first time that Team Lotus mechanic Bob Dance was involved in a little frivolity. In fact, he was widely regarded as the ringleader of practical jokes in the Formula 1 paddock, while within the team he was also involved in several pranks which the Anti-Terrorist Squad would probably take a very dim view of today, as Alan Challis recalls. "Bob Dance? If he was going Grand Prix racing today, he'd get

Track record   Bob Dance

66When I left school, I became a trainee mechanic though I never had an apprenticeship. I was
not entirely self-taught but with assistance from some mechanic friends I started to learn the
ropes. Then National Service got in the way, although I was fortunate enough to be sent to a
vehicle battalion in Germany, where I was taught to drive and maintain the army trucks. After I
came out, I ended up going back to the same garage I had worked at before. I wanted to get
into racing but it seemed difficult to achieve.

"I went for a job with Lotus at Hornsey in 1958 but they didn't pay very good money and
couldn't match what I was earning at the time. Then they moved to Cheshunt and I tried again.
Roy Badcock offered me a job with Lotus Components building the five-speed queerboxes. I
thought if I got to Lotus I could move into the racing department from there but found it more
difficult transferring from one department to another than I thought it would be. They were
going to put me on to building Formula Juniors but I saw it as a retrograde step, I wanted to
go racing, so they transferred me to Lotus Developments, working on Hewland, Colotti and ZF
gearboxes, development of the Lotus twin-cam engine and Lotus Elans. I used to see quite a lot
of Colin Chapman at that point and was in a position to talk to him. I asked him about getting
into racing and he replied 'What do you want to do that for? It's a dead-end job'. I told him that
the reason I came to Lotus was to get into racing, so he said 'If you must, I'll see what I can
do,' and I ended up going to Team Lotus racing in 1963 with the Lotus-Cortinas."

Bob worked on the Cortinas until the end of 1966 but often found himself seconded to the
Formula One or Indy sections and was present at Indy in 1965 when Jim Clark won. He stepped
up to running the Lotus 48 Formula 2 cars in 1967, then became Formula 1 chief mechanic in
1968, a traumatic year when the team lost both Jim Clark and Mike Spence before Graham Hill
went on to win the World Championship. In 1969, he worked on the four-wheel-drive Type 63
and 64 cars, then moved across to the nascent March concern the following year, where he was
seconded to Mario Andretti's car and involved in building McNamara Indy cars. After returning to
the works March Formula 1 team for 1971, he moved to Brabham in 1972, which had just been
bought by Bernie Ecclestone.

Working with greats such as Hill, Carlos Reutemann, Carlos Pace and designer Gordon
Murray ("one of the best designers of all time for my money") eventually the lure of his first
love, Lotus, proved too much and he returned for a second spell as chief mechanic, staying with
the team until its unhappy demise at the end of 1994, working with drivers such as Andretti,
Peterson, Mansell, Senna, Piquet and Häkkinen. He then moved to Toms GB, which was bought
by Audi in 1998 and renamed RTN, to develop a Le Mans coupe,
which became the basis for the design which won Le Mans in 2003.
When RTN closed in 2004, Bob – at the age of 69 – completed
the circle by going back to work for Colin Chapman's son Clive, at
Classic Team Lotus, fettling many of the cars he worked on thirty or
forty years ago for historic racing or museum collections and he is
still there today. Not bad for a 'dead-end' job.

*Bob Dance (r) with Jim Clark after the 1968 South African
Grand Prix: Dance worked hard and played hard.
(Ford Motor Company)*

arrested and charged with being a terrorist. Team Lotus were bloody mad, how they didn't kill somebody is beyond me."

Dance expresses surprise at having such a reputation, saying, no doubt with a twinkle in his eye: "I can't quite come to terms with why they should say that." However, he did concede that Monaco was a favourite place for a spot of 'high jinks.' "We used to try and do things like put the small cars up on chairs outside the Tip-Top. The Armco outside there used to be only two strips deep, so it was at a very convenient height for all of the drinkers to sit on and see what mischief one could get up to. Virtually across the road was the little police station, slightly to one side of the Tip-Top. They never used to really do anything much, just stayed out of the way. But if what we did began to block the road, then of course they would come out after people; if you were pretty shrewd, you could keep out of trouble and watch innocent bystanders being caught up in it all."

He remembers several instances of mischief, invariably arising from a night at the Tip-Top or somewhere in the surrounding area. "There was another little bar next to the Tip-Top, not quite of the same quality, shall we say. The Tip-Top was the place where people went, with perhaps a bit of an overspill to next door. Well, fairly late one evening we were there. The bar had a swinging sign outside which was square mesh, you could see straight through it. It was like an open Venetian blind, with another laid across it at right angles, so it made squares with sharp edges. We bought a jar of Scotch eggs and enquired of the crowd if anybody had a catapult. And do you know what, some bloke said he'd got this metal-framed one. We borrowed it and were firing these eggs into the sign; of course, they were shredding and disintegrating all over the people outside.

"Then there was ducting the water from the fire hydrant, which was up the hill a bit more. We managed to turn that on and, by pulling a plastic advertising sheet off the railings of the park opposite, were able to put that in the gutter and duct the water, which was flowing down the gutter, over the pavement and into the nightclub next door, which was below pavement level, so they had water cascading in the front entrance.

"Also, somebody put black driveshaft grease on the nightclub door handles, so people going in ended up with driveshaft grease all over them ..."

Occasionally, even the best laid plans would go awry, with disastrous results, as Dance explains. "Outside the Tip-Top, there used to be two huge round pots with conifer-type trees in them. They were about two foot across and stood about two foot six high, so heavy you could hardly lift them. One Sunday night after the race, we decided to try and get them over the Armco to block the road. We had the idea of using a length of loose Armco, putting it across the other Armco so that it was like a see-saw from the pavement to the road and, if we could tip the pot up slightly, once we got it onto the Armco, we could slide it up, over centre and then down the other side.

"Some blokes from the American Navy were there and were well out of control as well. We let them in on what we were going to do and they were quite helpful. We got the pot on the go and over, which was the reason for a lot of cheering, which drew the police outside to see what was going on. We decided this was a good time for us to not be involved, and left the pot in Navy hands. They lost control of the pot and it fell on its side, in the road. Being round, the pot rolled all the way down the hill to the right-hander at the bottom [Mirabeau], where it hit the barriers with a resounding crash and broke. The bosun of this American Naval craft was arrested and the police completely lost control, hitting people with their batons, one of whom was James Hunt's girlfriend of the day. The Monday newspaper reported that she was in an 'arrest drama' outside the Tip-Top Bar. Well, that was something we'd engineered."

Although Dance and his Lotus mechanics were often the instigators of many pranks, Tony Cleverley of the Rob Walker team says his was the first team in the paddock to harness the power of explosives for a spot of mischief. "We were the first ones to do it right in the very early days, at the Watkins Glen track. We always made a fairly big bang there and had all the police running around, looking for who had done it. We filled a 50-gallon/227-litre barrel with oxy-acetylene and detonated that; they heard it down in the village of Watkins Glen itself. The bloody drum went sky-high – everybody was on the run after that one ..."

Home-made cannons were a popular diversion for mechanics in the 1960s, ammunition ranging from swedes to rolled-up newspapers, and even custom-made shells. The Team Lotus device was developed at its Cheshunt base in the early 1960s, as Bob Dance explains. "It was a very long piece of thick-wall tube, which we used for making the bearing housings in our suspension uprights. We made projectiles in aluminium, or used swedes or rolled-up newspapers, and fired these off from the mezzanine floor at Cheshunt. Unfortunately, there was a housing estate at the back of the factory and missiles often used to head in that direction. When we moved to Norfolk, we took it with us; it gradually became shortened when a piece of material was needed to machine up for a bearing housing."

Jim Pickles joined the Indy section of Team Lotus in late 1966 around the time that it moved to Hethel in Norfolk. He remembers that, for someone with an interest in guns and explosives, the team represented a surprisingly good opportunity to further pursue his hobby. "I was always interested in guns and used to make them in my spare time. At lunchtimes I'd be hacking away at bits of steel; I used to make pistols and things like that, so liked explosives. They already had the cannon from the days in Cheshunt, a massive, long piece of good quality steel pipe with a wall about half-an-inch thick and a bore of about three inches. They had welded a base plug onto it, put a sparking plug in the base, strapped it to one of the trolleys we put the cars onto in the workshop, and presented it at an angle of about 30-45 degrees.

"What we used to do was get a very large tip of a welding torch, something like a 10 or something. We'd get it going with a nice, even blue flame so that it had the right combination of oxygen and acetylene, then we snuffed out the flame onto a steel bench. The gas was still coming out and we poked the gas torch down the muzzle of this device, leaving it there for half an hour or more, so that it filled up with an explosive mixture of oxygen and acetylene.

"Ted Fleet, dear old Ted, he's dead now but he used to make up some aluminium canisters that were a nice rolling fit down the bore and then fill them with gravel, so you had something like a missile. They were about five inches long and three inches in diameter. We used to ram them down, with a bit of wadding around and, of course, that compressed the gas that was in there. By the time it got to anywhere near the bottom it was a potent affair. Then you just flashed the sparkplug across the back and off it would go. God knows where they ended up ..."

According to Bob Dance such wild behaviour was tolerated – if not approved – by

Lotus boss Colin Chapman, who actually came across the cannon one day in Hethel. "I'll never forget, in the middle of the workshop at lunchtime, Willy Cowe was busily charging it up and the lads were standing around it. It was probably one of its early firings in Norfolk. Chapman came into the workshop and people sort of drifted away from it quickly, leaving just Willy in the middle of the shop, still with his welding torch, preparing it. The Old Man stopped and looked at it and said 'What's all this, then? And Willy said 'I don't know, I've never seen it before.' And the Old Man just went past and never said any more. He knew what we used to do because when there was a big bang or something went wrong, he knew it was his blokes."

Team Lotus' incendiary activities were not restricted to Norfolk either, as Jim Pickles explains. "I remember making a device in Madrid, at Jarama in 1972. It was after the Spanish Grand Prix but before Monaco. We were preparing the cars in Spain, ready for the race, before we loaded them on the transporter. After the race, everything was very casual. We'd have a nice break for lunch, that sort of thing. At the time we used methyl-bromide fire extinguishers in the cars, which came to us in very thick, stout cardboard boxes. I looked at one of these boxes and thought 'Cor, that'll make a good bomb.' What we did was the same as we used to do with the pipe, using the oxy-acetylene torch, that was our propellant.

"We punched a small hole in the box and fed in a loop of ordinary car electrical wire, which was stripped down bare, took the insulation off the top of the loop and cut all the strands away, so there was only one very thin strand left. We poked that into the box, charged the box with gas and bound it up very strongly with black tank tape. Then we went and put it under a whole heap of rubbish right at the end of the garages, where the sweepers had been round after the race, sweeping up all the sweetie packets and coke cans and whatever. It was a huge mountain of rubbish. We stuffed the box at the bottom of the pile, took the leads back to the garage, which was about five or six garages away, and just flashed it across the battery. Of course, that burned off the little loop of wire and set the thing going. It went off with an almighty bang and the whole sky was filled with debris, littering the entire circuit, just about. All we had to do was just pull the wires back in and act all innocent."

Occasionally, things didn't go quite to plan, as Pickles explains. "We did this at the factory once; under the canopy, which ran all the way along the back of the building, over all the entrances to the workshops. We set off this bomb underneath there at about six o'clock in the evening. There was an almighty bang when it went off. Unfortunately, the air pressure from the explosion managed to get through into the roof space of the factory, especially our workshop. All the roof panels came down, the striplights were dangling by one lead, and it was filled with dust. Freddie Bushell, who happened to still be in the factory, came storming in saying 'What was that?' Everybody was at their benches filing away and pretending to be busy, and we just said 'What? What's the matter?'"

Bob Dance also recalls another incident which incurred the wrath of Bernie Ecclestone. "We had one of our aerial acetylene bombs go wrong at Monza: it landed on Bernie's canopy and burnt a hole in it. This was on the Saturday night. They knew it was us who'd done it; we were next to them in the paddock. On the Sunday morning, I was coming up the stairs before warm-up and the Old Man said 'You put me right on the line last night, didn't you?' I wasn't ready for it and asked 'Why, what's wrong?' He said 'Why is it your lads always manage to do things better than everyone else?' adding 'I've had Bernie after me – you burnt a hole in his canopy last night.' 'Oh that' I replied and he said 'I'm not paying, you're going to have to pay for that yourselves.' But he was quite impressed, really, he always liked a bit of a laugh and a joke anyway, so we did lead a bit of a charmed life. I think in the end it was lost somewhere in the expenses ..."

It seems that there was a natural affinity between mechanics and missiles, for Team Lotus wasn't the only one up to something. Mike Barney recalls similar shenanigans at Cooper. "There was always somebody making a gun or a rocket projectile somewhere. We [the Formula 1 team] were at Langley Road, which was about a quarter of a mile up the hill from Hollyfield Road, where the main Cooper headquarters were. Noddy Grohmann had a three-inch diameter tube which we converted into a mortar.

"We used to try and hit the design office, which was on the top floor of the Cooper building, by aiming swedes at it. We would phone Eddie Stait who was in the office, to say 'We're aiming one now' and he would give us feedback such as 'Well, it fell short and it's too far to the left.'

"We also used to make aerial bombs at night. We would fill a child's toy balloon with coal gas, so that it would float, then fix two small balloons dangling underneath, charged with oxy-acetylene, and a Jetex fuse taped to it. We'd light it and just send it up in the air and it used to make tremendous explosions, I mean, if we did it today ...

"One time, we misjudged things. We were floating one off towards Cooper's when the wind changed and it blew up over Surbiton Hospital. They were straight onto the police because they didn't know what the hell was going on, there was just this huge bang. When the police came round and asked if we knew anything about it, we said 'Oh no, we thought we heard a bang, it was quite late at night and we wondered what that was.'"

Over at near-neighbour Brabham, acetylene bombs were also the weapon of choice when mischief was in the air, as former mechanic and foreman Gerry Hones reveals. "In the Formula 1 shop, they had a print room in the corner, a wooden building which was about eight feet square, and they used to take drawings in there and print off copies. Peter Parrot, who was a Formula 1 team mechanic, made a balloon bomb. When the drawing office bloke Mike Hillman went in to print off something, he tossed this balloon in there with the string alight and leant against the door so he couldn't get out.

"Hillman came out a shaking mess. He came to me as foreman, ranting and raving – it was definitely a sacking offence and he wasn't going to let it go. I had to go and see Pete and I said 'The best thing you can do is go into that drawing office and see Mike Hillman and kiss arse. Unless you can talk him out of it, he's going to have your guts.'"

Antipathy between the white and blue collar workers at Brabham was the motivation for much mischief, with the unfortunate Hillman on the receiving end of many of the pranks. "This Mike Hillman, he used to come up from Godalming or somewhere on the train carrying a briefcase and umbrella, and wearing an office worker's hat. When he came into the drawing office, he would hang up this umbrella in a small porch by the door. I said to Nick Goozee one day 'Go over to the sweet shop and get some confetti, two or three bags. Get the nice stuff with the hearts in it.' Then I told Nick to take the umbrella, open it up, put all the confetti in and roll it up again. The story goes that he was standing on the station at Godalming – and all of his movements would be very elaborate – and a few spots of rain came down. So he undid his umbrella, shook it, then swung it up and opened it and all this confetti went all over his head."

Acetylene bombs were a useful way of shaking the members of the Brabham drawing office out of their post-lunch stupor as well, according to Hones. "When Tauranac was away, at lunchtime they'd all go up to the pub and have a couple of pints. Around half two to three o'clock, they'd all be dozy and we'd shove an acetylene bomb under the drawing office. It was a wooden building that stood about four inches off the ground and so was like an echo chamber: the entire drawing office leapt in the air."

World Champion-to-be Denny Hulme was another to attract the attention of the local constabulary when he set off a particularly large explosion, recalls Hones. "In front of the Brabham works there was a lot of old scrub. Denny put this inner tube bomb out there and we all ran back into the workshop. When it went off it made an enormous explosion and cleared about 20 yards of scrub. About 20 minutes later, the police arrived – somebody had reported a big explosion from the works. We told them it was kids mucking about with fireworks."

It wasn't always the mechanics who instigated practical jokes; just occasionally they were on the receiving end and it was the drivers who had the last laugh. Tony Robinson remembers one episode during his time as BRP chief engineer/designer when the joke was on him. "It was in 1964, on a trip to Watkins Glen and Mexico City – more or less the last Formula One races of BRP. Innes Ireland, Trevor Taylor and I arrived in New York on the Wednesday before the race. We stayed the night in a hotel in Manhattan and had a good evening. The following day we collected the usual brand new Ford courtesy car that they supplied to all the visiting Formula 1 people and drove up to Watkins Glen. We were staying at the Hotel Jefferson, with an old friend of everybody in Formula 1, Bob Kelly, who used to be the barman there.

"On the Thursday afternoon we had to go through the ritual with organiser Cameron Argetsinger, collecting all the necessary passes and paperwork, checking-in for scrutineering and unloading the cars ready for practice on the Friday morning. That evening we had dinner in the restaurant and, just before we went to bed, Innes and Trevor asked what time practice was the next day. It wasn't scheduled to start until midday but I told them 8.30 in the morning and arranged to meet them at 7.30am for breakfast.

"The following morning, bright and early, they arrived in the dining room in their racing overalls with their crash hats, all spruced up and ready to go. I was just about finishing my coffee. They sat down and Trevor asked where everybody was as there were just the three of us in the restaurant. I told them most people had finished their breakfast and gone to the circuit. Innes said 'Maybe we had better go now because we don't want to be late,' so we went out and got into the courtesy car, with Innes driving this Ford as if he was already practising for the Grand Prix. There wasn't much on the roads so we got to the circuit nice and early. It was only then that they twigged that the laugh was on them.

"We did the practice and, in the evening, Innes and Trevor had to do some promotional work. Later on in the evening, the three of us had a bit of a drink and then I went up to bed. Needless to say, when I got into my room I couldn't believe what I saw – practically everything had been rearranged. There was straw everywhere, the mattress was hanging out of the bed and it was really in a mess. It was payback time. But that was fine, now we were square, or so I thought.

"Next stop was Mexico City. Innes and Trevor went off to stay in Victoria, Texas, for a few weeks with a fellow called Tom O'Connor. We loaded the transporters and headed off to Mexico. We ended up staying in a hotel called the Del Prada, all bored to tears for weeks [there was a three-week gap between the two races]. Practice was on the Friday and the race was on the Sunday. I received a telegram from Ken Gregory on the Friday asking me to collect him from the airport, as he was arriving at 9.50 in the evening. If you've ever driven around Mexico City, you'll know it is bedlam. Arriving at the airport to collect Ken after a crazy drive in the hire car, there was no sign of him on the flight, so I hung around for a couple of hours and then came back.

"I got back and sat down again with the few around the table, I think Jimmy Clark was there as well. I said 'I can't understand it, Ken wasn't there' and then one of them, I think it was Innes, turned to me and said 'Oh, by the way, there is a telephone message for you at the desk, it arrived after you left.' I went over to the desk and picked up the telephone message that had arrived at eight o'clock that evening. It said 'BOC public relations office, October 23, 1964. Mr Gregory arriving Mexico, Western 791 0519 October 24.' [5.19am the following morning]. I went back to the table where we discussed it; it appeared that Flight 791 was from Los Angeles. I thought to myself 'What the bloody hell is Ken doing in Los Angeles?'

"Anyway, I went to bed shagged and the following morning was up incredibly early to drive to the airport again, where I waited for a while but Ken wasn't on that flight either. I drove back to the hotel just in time to join Innes and Trevor for breakfast. I began to explain the latest twist to the story but noticed a twinkle in their eyes. Finally, the penny dropped: Innes had organised the scam, the bugger. The girl that he married, Edna Humphries was our secretary, so he had been on the phone to her, getting her to send telegrams and false phone messages. They got their own back and the last laugh was on me."

8
The Champions

Mechanics are in a unique position to observe the characteristics of the world's best racing drivers, when things go their way and when they don't. Forty or fifty years ago, they were extremely close to the drivers they worked with, very often the only person, or one of a handful, that worked on each car, and so struck up strong relationships, many of which endure to this day. In addition, because they would attend tests as well as practice and race sessions, they encountered new talent before the outside world read, heard about, or saw it.

A question always asked is whether a common thread links the great champions; whether it is immediately obvious that there is something special about them, that they have 'it' – whatever 'it' is. Alan Challis, who worked for both BRM and Williams during their heydays, thinks there is. "The first time Jackie Stewart ever sat in a BRM, at a wet test-day at Silverstone, it was very obvious that he had 'it.' At the time Graham was the acknowledged 'rain-master' but Stewart was quicker by the end of the day. I feel very fortunate that I was there the first time he drove a BRM.

"There is something different about the really good ones, you can sense it. With Fangio there certainly was an aura about the man. He was obviously quite old when I first met him and I was only a young man. But every time I met him after that, he still knew my name – amazing." Former BRM mechanic Dick Salmon, who worked with Fangio, also has fond memories of the man. "We couldn't talk to him because he didn't speak English, but we conveyed messages to one another, so that you could understand what he did and didn't want.

"He was so easy-going. If he asked for something and you couldn't do it, he'd shrug his shoulders and that was it, he'd get on with it. An amazing man, really. I believe he said the V16 BRM was the most incredible car he'd ever driven. He was the best driver that raced it. It was so bad on roadholding and handling but he seemed to manage it. He was a big, strong man and wouldn't have fitted in today's cars. The best moment was at the Albi Grand Prix in 1953, when Fangio led Ascari in the works Ferrari. He drove it the year before but we had problems with the cylinder head studs breaking, and then in 1953 we had the tyre treads throwing off, which was a shame because he would have won the race."

Briton Mike Hawthorn was known as the Farnham Flyer and took his only World Championship title for Ferrari in 1958, by virtue of consistency rather than out-and-out speed – he won just one race that year, while Stirling Moss won four.

Track record   Dick Salmon

"I went to BRM to work on the maintenance of transport, which included three Austin Loadstars and the Commer workshop wagon. There was a Dodge lorry with a canopy, which we used to transport personnel, various vans and a motorbike and sidecar. I hung about the racing section a bit and visually familiarised myself with the cars.

"Then, Peter Berthon overturned his Vanguard van and it was upside down all night. We rolled it upright but the engine wouldn't turn. They were scratching their heads and I said I thought it was a hydraulic problem – oil that had drained into the cylinder heads. I don't think they expected me to come up with this, especially when that was exactly what it did turn out to be.

"Whether that had any effect, I don't know but they asked me if I'd go to Monza, for the testing sessions with Moss and Wharton in March 1952. I didn't have to be asked twice ..."

At BRM, Dick was privileged to work with names such as Juan-Manuel Fangio, Froilan Gonzalez, Ken Wharton, Ron Flockhart, Peter Collins, Harry Schell, Graham Hill, Richie Ginther and Jackie Stewart, until he left the team in 1968.

Dick Salmon, shown second left with his hands on the tail of Harry Schell's BRM, worked with greats such as Fangio, Gonzalez, Collins, Hill, and Stewart. Also in shot are (left) Phil Ayliff, Gordon Newman in hat, Maurice Dove and Pat Carvath (behind Dove with hands on hips). (Pat Carvath)

Fangio used his strength to tame the BRM V16; here he is at Albi in 1952. (Pat Carvath)

Phil Hill endured a disastrous season with Cooper in 1964 due to a problem which was not identified until the following year. He is shown here in the paddock at Silverstone prior to that year's International Trophy, where he finished 4th. This shot clearly illustrates the conditions mechanics had to work on in those days, kneeling on a dusty, cinder-covered paddock with tools strewn on the ground. (Gary Critcher)

Derek Wootton remembers that, like many top drivers, he could be fun *and* difficult, depending on his mood, and recalls one particular incident when he drove for Vanwall at Spa-Francorchamps in 1955. "We had a hell of a time at Spa because we ended up doing just about everything on the car. We were in a garage next to a hotel with one light bulb hanging on a bit of flex. We had our own lights and things but nothing much. Hawthorn was wearing white overalls. We had an oil gaiter go at the back and oil came up and some went on him. God, he was very upset. He was alright and could be quite jovial and everything else but he could be very temperamental, too."

Three years after Hawthorn took the title for Ferrari, the American driver Phil Hill regained the Championship for the Maranello concern, driving the rear-engined Ferrari 156 'Sharknose.' However, an ill-judged switch to the ATS team saw his fortunes dip and so, when he went to Cooper for the 1964 season, Hill was looking to revive his career. As Cooper mechanic Mike Barney explains, it did anything but. "He was a lovely bloke. To this day I feel we really screwed him, we really let him down. With the V8 1.5-litre cars at that time there were only two of us on the team – me and Hughie

Frankland. Hughie was prepping Phil's car and was taping the front throttle cable anchor to the chassis tube. It was an old-fashioned, two-piece Bowden cable with an inner and outer like you'd get on a motorcycle. In those days the water ran through the chassis tubes. When the tubes heated up, it melted the adhesive on the tape, released the cable and gradually the car lost power until there was nothing. Phil would come in and say the engine had gone, so we would take it out and send it back to Coventry Climax, which would say there was nothing wrong with it."

Incredibly, the reason for this perplexing state of affairs did not become apparent until 1965, as Barney explains. "How we found out what had happened was with Jochen [Rindt] next year. We took the same cars to Monaco and Bernie Ecclestone was managing Jochen. He didn't qualify and was absolutely devastated; he couldn't make out what was wrong. In the evening, Bernie and Jochen came round to the garage and it was just me there, tidying up. They asked if they could have a look at the car, so we took the bodywork off and, of course, found the melted tape." The 1964 season was Hill's last full year in Formula 1 and it was therefore on a sad note that the former champion bowed out.

Every now and then, a driver comes along who isn't, perhaps, a raw natural talent in the mould of Clark, Stewart or Senna, but who, by sheer bloody-mindedness and determination, makes the grade. Phil's namesake, Graham Hill, was one of these. Mike Costin, who worked with him at Lotus in Hornsey in the mid-1950s (where Hill was employed in the gearbox shop), remembers that, in those days, it wasn't evident that Hill was a potential World Champion. "It wasn't clear at all. Graham was a pretty hairy driver in his early days, a lot hairier than he was later. But even at Hornsey, he quite seriously told me that his aim was to become World Champion, and he'd done absolutely nothing. He used to cadge rides off Dan Margulies and John Coombs, and anybody else that would give him a drive.

"I remember saying to him that, financially, anybody who had become World Champion had started out with a lot of money and therefore wished him the best of luck. But he actually achieved it; he never gave up, nobody was more concentrated than Graham. When he began to climb the ladder, even before he was on the second rung he was totally committed to every aspect, whether or not he knew what he was doing. He would make notes of everything in a notebook: the names of everybody he spoke to, their telephone number, everything about them, for future reference.

"He would also jot down the first lines of jokes because, as soon as he became known, people began asking him to speak at dinners. The man of the moment for after-dinner speaking then was Stuart Turner. Well, Graham 'out-Stuarted' Stuart. As an ambassador for motor racing, he was incredible. He must have had some raw talent for speaking, but he developed the gift in just the same way as he developed his racing, by sheer hard graft. No stone was left unturned."

Costin also remembers Hill as being fiercely competitive, and recalls a little technique used by Lotus boss Colin Chapman to keep his driver on his toes. "When we were testing something, Graham always used to muscle in and come with Colin and myself. We'd be changing the odd thing and Graham would want to change 20 things. David [Phipps, a photographer closely allied to Lotus at the time] told me that if Graham was not going quickly and Colin couldn't make out why, he would say to me 'Hey Mike, get in and have a few laps and see what you think of it.' If I went faster than Graham had been, the old moustache would twitch a bit and he'd get in; there was no way that he'd have me being quicker than him. I didn't realise Colin was doing this, it was David Phipps who pointed it out to me, because he'd observed it."

The consensus of opinion among mechanics who worked with Hill is that he was something of a complex character – sometimes difficult in the car but a barrel of laughs outside of it. Pat Carvath, who worked with Hill at BRM in the first half of the 1960s, has tremendous respect for him, even though his constant tinkering with settings could be maddening. "Graham Hill was a hell of a man. He would come back to the garage and tell you exactly what he wanted and you had more respect for him. He struggled to set up the car initially, at Silverstone and Goodwood. Once he had it set up, though, especially the V8, it was good.

"Initially, when he first joined BRM, I think he thought 'Christ, what the hell have I let myself in for here?' because it was a bit of a pig. He realised that the cars were a little bit better built than the Lotus, strength-wise anyway. One of the things with Graham was that, when he pulled into the pits, he'd ask us to alter the tyre pressure, or whatever but, of course, we didn't dare do a thing without asking Tony Rudd or Peter Berthon. Eventually, he did get that altered, he had a big meeting with them at Zandvoort and they decided it was time the mechanics were allowed some responsibility; they wouldn't even let us start the engines initially, it was a bit of a bind.

"But he was a devil for making last-minute changes. I can't remember which race it was but I said to Graham 'You'd better give me a fiver. He said 'What for?' and

Victory at last! Graham Hill claims his first Grand Prix triumph at the 1962 Dutch Grand Prix, beginning a run of results that would secure him the world title that year. Left to right: Cyril Atkins, Pamela Rudd, Bette Hill, Pat Carvath, Roy Foreman. (Pat Carvath)

Track record   Alan Challis

"*I was a local lad and joined BRM in 1958, straight from school. I did an engineering apprenticeship with them, so went through the factory, the whole college and learning bit. I moved on to the Formula 1 team the year after Graham won the Championship, in 1963."*

Alan worked for BRM until its eventual demise, later joining Lotus but to work on their boat-building business rather than racing cars. A move back to racing saw him join the Shadow team until the end of the 1979 season, the following year he moved to Williams, where he became chief mechanic. In the early 1990s, he transferred to a factory-based role and finally retired from Williams in 2006.

Challis' (standing by car nose) near 50-year career included stints at BRM, Shadow and Williams.

I said 'I'm going out to buy a wheelbarrow.' He said 'What the hell do you want a wheelbarrow for?' and I said 'I'm going to put a bunch of roll bars and springs in it, wheel them all to the starting line and see which ones you want to put on.' I didn't get the wheelbarrow ..."

Alan Challis, who also worked with Hill at BRM, reckons that much of the need for constant adjustment was psychological. Indeed, many times he would ask for something to be changed before a race that simply couldn't be done in the time

Gritty Graham: Hill drifts his BRM P57 on his way to third place in the 1963 South African Grand Prix. (LAT)

– and he knew it. "Graham was always fiddling. His was the first car I was number one mechanic on and I was with him until he left for Lotus. There were things he would want done on the startline that couldn't be changed in an hour, let alone the quarter of an hour you were on the grid. But he wanted them done there. I thought 'Hey, no problem, if it makes you feel better.'

"There were times when he wanted something changed right down in the cockpit, and you'd pour yourself in through the top, down to the front, rattle your spanners about, come back out and tell him that you'd done it. I'm certain he knew that you hadn't because he knew it couldn't be done. But if it was something to boost his confidence, that was good enough for me."

Occasionally, Hill would catch himself out. Tony Reeson recalls one such incident while Hill was driving for BRM. "We went to a race, which he won quite easily. Afterwards, he came in and he said 'When my car goes to the next meeting, I don't want it any different to what it is now, I want it setting up exactly the same.' One of the mechanics said 'You don't want your front roll bar re-attached then?' It had broken off on the first lap, the ball-joint had come undone. Graham just grinned and walked away."

While some BRM mechanics humoured him, others were driven to distraction by his behaviour. Roger Barsby explains. "Graham was a nice enough bloke but he was a twiddler. He wanted an eighth of an inch stiffer on his front roll bar or quarter of inch on the rear roll-bar, and it never made a blind bit of difference, it was all in his head. We'd rattle about at the back of the car and say 'Right-ho, Graham, try that' and he'd come round and say 'Oooh, that's better' and we'd done sod-all, so we knew what his game was. Once, when we reached the startline and he wanted his roll bar moving back a quarter of an inch, one of the mechanics quipped: 'Hill, if I brought all the f*****g spanners you wanted, I'd be a walking toolbox, just get in and drive it.'"

Dick Scammell found Hill, for all his faults, one of the most enjoyable drivers to work with. "Graham was such a character. He used to drive people to distraction because he would adjust the car endlessly, almost adjust himself off the pace, too, and he had a little book which he wrote it all down in so he knew it all off by heart. But he drove pretty well.

"The Sunday night after the race was always looked upon as the night you all recovered a bit and went and had a drink. All the teams turned up, and you were either drowning your sorrows or celebrating. Graham would turn up to those and he was a laugh, a real entertainer."

Tony Reeson, who worked with him at BRM, also remembers post-race drinks with Hill. "Graham in particular and Jackie [Stewart], were very friendly people. I remember going to Monaco with Graham and he'd come out at the end of the race, buy us all a drink in the Tip-Top Bar, and we'd sit in the middle of the road until three o'clock in the morning with the traffic trying to pass by. And many of the things he was given as prizes, he passed on to the mechanics."

Bill Cowe, Hill's mechanic at Team Lotus in 1969, also found working with him a pleasure. "I did a fair bit with Graham and quite liked him. He was different, let's say, to the culture we'd been used to with Jimmy. He and Colin sometimes had a bit of a 'set-to' as to how he wanted the car set up. Graham wanted things his way and Colin would say

Graham Hill: Bill Cowe (shown here on left with Herbie Blash in the background) worked with him at Lotus and says that he was 'different to the culture we'd been used to with Jimmy' (Clark) because he wanted the car set up his way, which caused a number of 'set-tos' with Lotus boss Colin Chapman. (Ford Motor Company)

'Look, I designed the car, I know how it should hang out and what bits should be on it. But although Graham was a hard taskmaster, he was alright to work for.'"

Stan Collier, who worked with Hill towards the end of his career, when he was driving for Rob Walker, found him tough going. "Graham was hard to work for and was the worst one. He wasn't a natural driver, he was self-taught. In practice he would go round and round and round. He used to work out the best way round each corner, as he went. Then he would put them all together and go quickly. He used to come in and ask for a quarter of an inch on a roll bar, the pedal was too high, it just went on and on and used to drive me mad. He was sort of two people, Graham; a great bloke outside the car. but when testing or practising, he was a different man, as though his personality had changed."

Jim Clark was the dominant driver of his generation and, but for being let down by his machinery on too many occasions, probably should have won successive World Championship titles between 1962 and 1967. Instead, he had to settle for victories in 1963 and 1965, as well as winning the Indy 500 on his third attempt, an achievement which cemented his position as a household name around the globe.

Mike Costin, who raced against and worked with Clark in the early years of the Scot's career, remembers him as someone who didn't realise what a special talent he had, wasn't a great 'fiddler' with the settings of his car, and rarely drove at the limit. "Jimmy didn't have to concentrate because he didn't know what all the fuss was about. He just got on with it and enjoyed it, he was a fantastic character. There's no doubt about it, he was something else, just totally naturally gifted.

"If you sent Graham [Hill] out for five laps in a car, he'd want at least 10 things changing, whereas you could send Jim out and he'd come back and couldn't think of anything. He had to be prompted with 'What's the braking like? Is there a bit too much on the front or the back, shall we shift it a bit?' or 'What's the understeer or oversteer like?' He very rarely had a specific hard and fast thing he wanted doing.

"There was only once I saw Jimmy a little bit upset. Mike Beckwith and Tony Hegbourne used to run the Normand Racing team with Lotus 23s and, somehow or other, they nailed another car together for the three hour race at Snetterton and asked Jim to drive it. This car was a dog. All day they were after me, saying 'Can you come and have a look at this?' I forget what I was doing but I was involved with something else and too busy to help them.

"Right at the very end of practice, Jim put it on pole position. I shall never forget, as Jim came into the paddock, Mike

Clark: Mechanics who worked with him describe him as 'a special person,' 'a gentleman' and a 'wonderful man.' Here, comfy in his trademark cashmere cardigan, he snoozes as mechanics work on his Lotus 40 during testing at Snetterton in 1965.
(Arthur Birchall)

The expression on Jim Clark's face says it all: he didn't have to 'hang it out' in a racing car very often but, on this occasion – one of only two when he drove a single-seater other than a Lotus – he has just had to push his Vollstedt Indy car to the limits of its capabilities in order to qualify on the front row, alongside Dan Gurney, for the 1967 Rex Mays 300 event at Riverside Raceway. (Eamon Fullalove)

Beckwith said 'Great, Jim, we sorted it then.' And I've never seen Jim like that. He had a sort of ashen face and said 'Look here, I had to hang it out to do that.' That was all he said. The thing was, he didn't hang it out normally."

A good demonstration of Clark's superiority behind the wheel of any vehicle came on the weekend of the 1964 Belgian Grand Prix at Spa-Francorchamps, as Denis Daviss relates. "After practice, we had the day off. There was no running this particular day. Round the old circuit, near Stavelot, there was a little tunnel under the railway, which went to a place called Coo. A bunch of us guys, along with Jimmy Clark, went there and, amongst other things, there was a go-kart track.

"We had a little play on these go-karts and an impromptu race amongst ourselves, which Jimmy won, cheeky bastard. We thought somebody had given him the better kart, so he got into the one that had come last and we had another little race, which he also won. On the third race, he was getting a bit carried away; coming up to pass me we locked wheels, which had him off in the dirt, tipped it right up. He had gravel rash down his side and up his arm, and the people at the track covered him in all this red dye stuff. Come race day, Jimmy was there bright and early, sitting in the car, long before anybody else because he wanted to be in before Chapman arrived, as he was not supposed to do go-karts. Chapman never, ever knew about it."

Cooper mechanic Ray Rowe was also there and confirmed Clark's superiority, whatever kart he was in. "After so many laps, everyone was asking which one Clark had and trying to get that kart, but he'd still come past you on another machine."

Dick Scammell, who worked with Clark throughout the time he was at Team Lotus, describes him as an inspirational character. "Jimmy was such a gentleman and did his job so well. When you have a person like that driving for you and the team, it inspires everybody. You knew very well that, if you did your bit the best you knew how, he would

The Champions

A gravelly, dusty paddock was the usual working environment for mechanics during the 1950s and 60s. Here, Dick Scammell tends to Jim Clark's Lotus 33, while the Scot looks on. (Dick Scammell)

wring out the last drop he could from it, and therefore encourage everybody in a way to do a good job.

"I used to say I didn't think I could ever work for one of the teams there just to fill the grid because I would have found that very difficult. You knew he would do his utmost and if he started the last lap in third position, you had no doubt who would come round first over the line, he was that sort of person.

"He was fun and drove all sorts of things, which was nice. Occasionally, he'd take us for a ride. Up to the time I first had a ride with him I thought that I was probably the next World Champion. If I could have driven that quickly, I'd have thought I was wonderful but he was still laughing and joking.

"He was a gentleman with it, in that he was nice and cared about people. When we won the World Championship in 1963, Jimmy gave all the mechanics a watch to say thanks for their efforts. I had a pretty major motor accident and was in hospital for quite a long time, and he actually came to the hospital, fought his way in because visiting time was over, to give me my watch. I thought he was a really special person to do that."

Alan Challis did three Tasman series with BRM, and perhaps saw a more relaxed side to Clark than did most of those on the European circuits. "Jim Clark was a wonderful man. When we used to go to the Tasman series, the social side of it – our drivers and their drivers – were as one. Plus, the teams – because there were only three of four people per team – sort of worked together. When Jimmy was socialising, he was as big a playboy as anyone I've ever come across. But obviously, when he was racing, he was deadly serious."

To win a World Championship in any form of motor sport is certainly an achievement to be proud of, but to win titles on two and four wheels is something that only one man – John Surtees – has achieved, when he took his Championship with Ferrari in 1964.

Although he was very quickly competitive when he made the switch, sometimes his way of doing things didn't sit well with his mechanics, as Dick Scammell, who worked with him at Lotus in 1960, recounts. "I was John Surtees' mechanic when he came in. He'd come from being World Champion on motorbikes. But in motor racing, that meant nothing to us.

"He used to turn up with his mother and father. Other people will tell you that in those days, with Weber carburettors, to get the engine to run properly you had to change some of the jets in it. He'd say 'You have noted which hole the jet came out of and which carburettors, haven't you?'

"It was utter nonsense but was a sort of ritual with him. That was the way they had run the bikes and that was the way they were going to run the cars, so you had all these little jets that you had to keep numbered as to where they came out of the carburettors, because they had to go back in the same holes. It was quite tricky, especially with John's father looking over your shoulder all the time. Colin [Chapman] didn't get too involved in that bit, so we were left to our own devices. The easy way was to do what John wanted because it would only upset him if you didn't and that wasn't a good thing to do either."

Although it was Team Lotus that gave Surtees his first Grand Prix outings in 1960, Reg Parnell and Aston Martin were very much involved in encouraging his transition from two to four wheels. In fact, as Gerry Hones explains, they tested Surtees and another established motorcycle racer, John Hartle, at the same time. "We [the Aston Martin sports car team] were the first team to try John Surtees, in 1959. We had two of them down there – Surtees and John Hartle – both motorcyclists. We had a problem with the transaxle on the Astons – it would try and select fifth and fourth gear at the same time and used to blow the gearboxes to pieces. This John Hartle came down the straight at Goodwood, changed down and selected two gears, and it spun like a top. They had no harnesses in those days and I can remember him going up in the air, the car spinning and him being six or eight feet above the car in the air going sideways. But he was alright. We knew that Surtees was quicker than Hartle and, from then on, John [Surtees] was, for quite some time, Reg's man."

Pat Carvath was another mechanic who was lukewarm about the former motorcycle champion. "John Surtees didn't rate very highly in my book. He was a good driver but he seemed to get the mechanics' backs up a bit." Roger Barsby felt that Surtees' uncompromising approach sometimes got in the way of things. "He was always right, he just wouldn't listen to anybody. He knew it all, and if you tried to suggest something to him, he would just say 'No, that won't work.'"

However, Denis Daviss, who worked with Surtees at both Cooper and Honda, saw another side to the man, one that was very generous. He tells a story of the 1966 Mexican Grand Prix, when Surtees met the President of Mexico twice in one day. "John qualified on pole and that night we changed the engine which meant another all-nighter. Race day came and in the warm-up the engine was not running well, it was slow on the pick-up and blowing out clouds of smoke, and all sorts of nasty things. It was decided that it was running too rich and that, maybe among the panic at Maserati [Cooper's engine supplier], they may not have fitted a high altitude fuel cam. We tried to fit the cam from the practice engine but it was a little different on the bore size, and we couldn't do it.

"John obtained permission from race officials to use the straight at the back of the circuit to see if he could sort out the mixture problem. The people involved were John, the Champion sparkplug engineer – who, I believe, was Bobby Strollman – and myself. The plan was for John to drive the wrong way down the circuit to the start of the straight, then drive back towards us the right way, and do a plug cut, with the Champion man looking at the plugs and me altering the shims to make it weaker. After a few plug runs the engine was beginning to perform better and I made the last available adjustment to the shims we had.

"On his way to turn round and make his final run, Surtees met the Mexican Grand Prix entourage – including the President – in a limousine on a track inspection. We were out of time and had to go round and park ourselves on the starting grid. At the start of the race, John was passed by Brabham and Rindt as the thing was running like a dog, as – we later realised – the mixture was now too weak. Maybe I had gone a bit too far but there was no fixing that now. Three or four laps later, when the engine had reached the same sort of temperature as it was when we were round the back, the car suddenly came to life and John passed Rindt and Brabham, stayed in front and won the race.

"That's how he came to meet the President for the second time that day – for the prize-giving. John was really happy with his first Grand Prix win since leaving Ferrari, and took all of us mechanics to a fancy place in Mexico City to eat and drink a little. Suitably lubricated, he wandered over and asked me what this win was worth to us. I told him and he said 'Well, I'll double that when we get home.' Two weeks later a cheque arrived in the post at Cooper's, to the value of double the prize-money, proving that not all drivers have short arms and long pockets."

Jack Brabham championed a number of new young drivers in his cars, such as Dan Gurney, Denny Hulme and Jochen Rindt. Like all great drivers, he had a very good feel for the cars he was driving and any subtle changes that might occur. Peter Hennessy, who worked at Brabham in the late 1960s and early 1970s, recalls one such instance. "With Jack, we were running a car at Indy. He came in and said 'There is something tightening up in the transmission.' What we found was that the input shaft bearing had turned blue. How could Jack feel that? That always sticks in my mind."

1967 World Champion Denny Hulme was a very relaxed, down-to-earth character who, after moving to McLaren to drive with his good friend Bruce, did a lot to hold the team together in the wake of the death of its founder. Mike Lowman remembers him as being completely without pretension and not afraid to get his hands dirty. "Denny was so laid-back it was unbelievable. When I was at Brabham he and Jack were running the Formula 2 cars with the Honda engine in the back, and they were just about unbeatable. I was looking for him one lunchtime, going around the factory calling out 'Denny, where are you?' and eventually heard 'I'm over here.' Outside was a transporter we'd borrowed from BRM for the Formula 2 cars, and he was underneath. Apparently, it had a two-speed rear axle that didn't work very well and he was under there trying to fix it because, when he was a lad, his father had a transport business and Denny used to work on all the trucks. He was that sort of a guy, he would do what he had to do."

Gerry Hones also remembers Hulme with great affection. "Denny was another cracking bloke, a good one to work with. He was so laid-back. In the summer months he used to walk about without any shoes or socks on. We would say after practice 'What

Brabham had fantastic 'feel.' (Indianapolis Motor Speedway)

Denny 'the Bear' Hulme (l), shown here at Indy in 1971 with team-mate Peter Revson, was a 'cracking bloke,' a loyal team player and very laid-back, but could also pull some mischievous pranks. (Eamon Fullalove)

do you want me to do with the car tonight?' and he'd say 'Aw, s**t, just give it a polish and stick it away' and that was it. A magnificent driver."

On many occasions, Hulme played the dutiful number two to his team leader Brabham, as they swept home 1-2. However, one time, as Gerry Hones recounts, temptation got the better of him. "One day Denny was working with me on the car and he said 'I can beat that old prick.' I said 'Yeah, of course you can.' And he said 'Yeah, I just sit behind him.' Anyway, he must have got a squib up his backside because pow – he went by Jack and won it. and Jack wasn't expecting it." As they pulled out of this right-hander, Denny gave it some stick and went past him and led him over the line. It was a silly thing to do because, obviously, Jack was the Guvnor, owned the works and owned Brabham. If you're number two, you stop at number two. Whether you can beat Jack or not, doesn't make any difference.

The next day he came into the workshop with a big smile on his face and said 'How about that then?' I said 'Yeah, great: Jack wants you in the office.' When he came out, I said 'What did he say?' and he said 'Well, I had the stony silence for a long time and the black look and then he looked up at me and said 'What are you trying to do, make a c**t out of me?''"

Like many Kiwis, Hulme wasn't averse to a prank or too, either, as Hones recounts. "Denny was always up to something. You know how, with a can of Evostik, after a period of time you get all this glue that has gone a bit dry around the cap? Denny made a habit of sticking one of these dry bits on the end of his nose and talking to people.

"He was unbelievable on acetylene bombs. Between the Formula 1 shop and the production shop there was a brick missing out of the wall. One day I saw this brown paper bag with a string attached to it coming through this hole where the brick was missing. As it dropped through I could see the string had been soaked with petrol and was alight. Then, ker-boom. That was Denny."

Over the years, it hasn't just been the approach of top drivers like Stewart, Senna and Schumacher in the cockpit that has marked them out as different. Each one had an amazingly perceptive grasp of the power of marketing and the importance of presenting themselves in a professional manner. Mike Lowman, who began his career as a race mechanic at the legendary Scottish team Ecurie Ecosse, remembers well the young Jackie Stewart. "During the course of my fairly short tenure at Ecurie Ecosse – I was only there for about a year – Jackie joined us. He used to have to drive under a pseudonym because his mother was not terribly happy as his brother, Jimmy, had been hurt quite badly in motor racing. He was very good and, even then, had ideas for marketing himself. I helped him to fit the first tartan band – it was just a ribbon – to his helmet. We cut and fitted it around the helmet and then taped it on. I was the new lad in the team and he was the new driver and we struck up a good friendship, which endures to this day."

Dick Salmon remembers that, for the young Stewart, making his Formula 1 Grand Prix debut was quite a big step up, physically. "I was mechanic for Jackie on his very first World Championship Grand Prix for BRM which was in South Africa, in 1965. He finished sixth and after the race said that he hadn't realised that these Formula 1 cars were so bloody heavy. But it was obvious from the start that he was something special. He was always hovering about the car looking and asking questions, and you sensed that he was going to be very good."

Track record   Mike Lowman

❝❝I had a season ticket to Brands Hatch in the 1960s and had gone to a sports car
race there with a friend. We were standing where the little circuit joined the big
one when Jack Fairman in an Ecurie Ecosse Tojeiro whistled round the corner, lost it in
a big way and hit the marshal's post, which substantially destroyed the car. The next
week in Autosport there was a job advertised under a box number and I thought 'That
sounds interesting'. At the time I was a workshop foreman in a crash repair shop in
Guildford. I was invited to a job interview which turned out to be with Ecurie Ecosse
in Edinburgh, was offered the job and my first challenge was to repair the car that I'd
seen crash at Brands."

For 1965, Mike came back down south and joined Brabham, at first in the
production shop, then later on the race team, working with Tim Wall on Dan Gurney's
car. When Dan left to set up Anglo American Racers in Rye, Mike went with him and
later, after the demise of the team's Formula 1 programme, went to the States to work
on its Can-Am operation. Staying with Can-Am, he joined Peter Bryant's Autocoast
outfit, then moved to Don Nichols' Shadow team, returning to the
UK to help set up and run the new Formula 1 effort in 1973. A
brief return to AAR was followed by a break from racing, restoring
imported sports cars, before the lure of Formula 1 saw him come
back to the political turmoil that was the Shadow team around the
time of the Arrows breakaway. In 1980 he moved to Team Lotus,
where he stayed until the end of 1984. Mike has continued to work
in motor sport and is still involved today, building A1GP cars.

Mike Lowman's first job in racing was with Ecurie Ecosse – and he's
still involved today. (Grand Prix Mechanics Charitable Trust)

Stewart acted as a great motivating force for his mechanics, in
much the same way as other drivers who were considered 'unbeatable' on their day,
such as Stirling Moss and Jim Clark, as Neil Davis explains. "Jackie Stewart was the
main man. You knew that if you gave him the right car, he would win the race for you,
or certainly finish in the first three."

Roy Topp, who got to know the Scot very well after joining Tyrrell in 1970, has
nothing but praise for him. "Jackie Stewart was a very good driver when I went to
Tyrrell. He had such a lot of natural talent, and a feel for everything: he was smooth;
really good on the cars and the tyres. He was so precise with his driving and could get
in the car and detect tiny little things that other drivers wouldn't have worried about. He
stood out from everyone else; it was such a natural thing for him and he made it seem
so easy."

It was Ken Tyrrell who gave Stewart his first break in single-seaters and, after his
spell in Formula 1 with BRM, they renewed their relationship to devastating effect,
winning three World Championships in 1969, 1971 and 1973. They were, as Roger Hill
observed, the perfect partnership and the Scot also gelled with his mechanics. "Jackie
and Ken understood one another. Jackie was a very reasonable guy – I still know him

well – and he never grizzled at us. He was alright. We got on and did our job and he got on and did his job and Ken made sure it was all tied together."

Jochen Rindt was another extremely talented driver. Born in Germany but raised in Austria by relatives after the death of his parents, he burst onto the scene in 1964 with a stunning Formula 2 victory at Crystal Palace, eclipsing all the established stars of the time. His bravery and car control was unquestionably exceptional, but some people, including noted *MotorSport* magazine journalist Denis Jenkinson, doubted he had what it took to win a Grand Prix (Jenkinson promised to shave off his beard if this ever happened). By 1969, aboard a very competitive Lotus, Rindt looked as if he would silence his critics on several occasions but was denied victory until the penultimate Grand Prix of the season, the US round at Watkins Glen, when he finally broke his duck. Jenkinson was forced to eat humble pie and, true to his word, shaved off his beard.

That first victory opened the floodgates and, armed with the Lotus 72, which finally came right after a sticky start, Rindt dominated the 1970 season, winning four races on his way to the Championship before his untimely death in a practice accident at the Italian Grand Prix. Jim Pickles did not work with him in Formula 1 but witnessed a superb example of his bravery at Indianapolis at the wheel of a Brabham. "I saw him at Indy in 1967. This was in the evening when we'd finished work and were sitting in the stands. There was Dick Scammell, Butty [Arthur Birchall], Hughie [Absalom] and myself. We watched him qualify in the wet, on slicks as there were no wet-weather tyres. God, that was an exhibition. And he qualified too. That guy had skill, no question."

Laid-back Kiwi Denny Hulme was team-mate at McLaren to laid-back Brazilian Emerson Fittipaldi in 1974. While Denny 'The Bear' was in his final season and slipping gently into retirement, Emerson took the World Championship title to add to that he had won with Team Lotus in 1972. Jim Pickles worked with Fittipaldi during that Championship year with Lotus and remembers him as being good to deal with. "Emerson was the easiest driver to work with, no question. Most of it was through the chief mechanic but, even so, I had a direct relationship with him as well. He was a fine interpreter of what a car was doing.

"I can remember Emerson coming in to Lotus. He'd been doing Formula 3 so we knew him to say hello and chat to because he was with Jim Russell in the 59s. He came into the factory and did a little test drive round Hethel in the 49. When he came back into the workshop afterwards, I managed to talk to him and asked how he had found it. He replied 'Ooooh, so much power.'"

Nonetheless, few people could fail to be impressed by how quickly he came to terms with the 'grunt' of a Ford Cosworth DFV, winning only the fourth Grand Prix he started and going on to take nine Grand Prix victories at the wheel of a Lotus 72, and a further three in a McLaren M23. Steve May, one of the mechanics at John Player Team Lotus in the title-winning year of 1972, likens Emerson's feel for the car to that of a skilled horseman. "I have horses and watch people ride them and say 'That person's good, they have soft hands.' 'Soft hands' in the equestrian world means you can make a horse do what you want, you don't have to kick it to make it go, you don't have to keep pulling on the bit to make it stop, it's just natural, they flow, they gel. That's how I saw Emerson. A very fluent sort of driver, kind to his car. He'd feather the throttle rather than accelerate-brake-accelerate-brake. Ronnie [Peterson] was fluent as well, which made them both

Emerson Fittipaldi: A very fluent driver with 'soft hands.'
(Ford Motor Company)

stand out. Emerson had the slight edge but Ronnie had bigger balls."

Fittipaldi's successor to the Championship title in 1975 was the young Austrian driver Niki Lauda who, only three years before, had struggled along at the back of the field in an uncompetitive March. His springboard to greater things was a BRM drive for the 1973 season, which led to a berth at Ferrari the following year, but it was in Formula 2 with March that Lauda really made his mark. Mechanic Ray Wardell worked with him in those days and saw early evidence, not just of talent on the track, but also his ability to manipulate things the way he wanted them. "Niki had a tremendous talent for thinking things out and for being a politician within the team. He worked hard to get what he wanted. With the Formula 2 programme, we were running Ronnie Peterson and Niki side-by-side, but even though Ronnie was very much the number one, Niki was not going to accept second-best, that was for sure. You knew he was going to manoeuvre to make sure he had *the* best.

"A very bright guy, so intelligent about what he was doing, he thought everything through and had ability. I was manager for the Formula 2 team at the time when Max [Mosley] asked me to pick up this guy at the airport. I'd never heard of him, and trundled down there not knowing who I was fetching or why. It turned out to be Niki Lauda turning up with a briefcase full of money to buy the Formula Two drive. He was very personable as well, he made an effort to get on with the team. Apart from occasionally stirring things on the political side to get what he wanted, he was a charming guy and good fun to be around."

Former BRM mechanic Tony Reeson agrees with the 'friendly but determined' epithet. "We were at Nivelles for the Belgian Grand Prix and Niki came out with us. There was one of those machines that tested your reactions, where it dropped a coin and you had to catch it before it reached the bottom. We had a bet on, and I beat Lauda every time. He said to me 'I think you'd better drive tomorrow, your reactions are quicker than mine.' He was like Peterson but more demanding. Everything had to be right. You could see he was going to get there because he was really dedicated to the sport. He wanted the best of everything. If we hadn't got enough tyres, he was there asking 'Where are my tyres?' The others would just sit back and wait for you to give them whatever we had but not Lauda. He'd be asking 'Is his engine better than mine?' He wanted the best one. At BRM you had to look after yourself, especially when you had four drivers and then Louis Stanley to deal with."

Peter Bracewell who, during his time as a mechanic for BRM, worked with Lauda, also remembers him as being decisive about setting up the car. "We had Niki before he went to Ferrari. He would tell you what he wanted you to do to the car. There wouldn't be any scratching heads about it unless we were in real trouble. He'd come in and say 'Do this or do that.' He'd go out and if it was instantly quicker, we knew we were going the right way. If there was no difference, we'd put it back to where it was."

After dominating the 1977 season with the revolutionary 'ground-effects' Lotus 78, only for poor reliability to rob him of the title, Mario Andretti made no mistakes in 1978 with the Type 79, a refinement of the concept, streaking to the title with six wins, ably backed up by team-mate Ronnie Peterson. Bob Dance found working with the American, which renewed a relationship first begun at the 1968 US Grand Prix, particularly satisfying. "I always enjoyed working with Mario, with his technical knowledge. He was very determined, good for morale, could motivate people and [Colin] Chapman liked him. Then, of course, Ronnie came along and Mario became number one, so everything revolved around Mario winning the Championship." The fact that Peterson was more than capable of taking the title – but as number two in the team was contractually unable to – caused some intra-team factions to emerge, as Dance recalls. "There were the Ronnie mechanics and the Mario mechanics. Rex Hart and Nobby Clark were Ronnie people and Glenn Waters and Phil Denney looked after Mario with Gilbert Sills on the spare car, which Mario used a lot. As chief mechanic, I had to divide my allegiance but I was always a Mario man, I suppose."

A driver whose meteoric progress through the ranks inevitably led him to Formula 1 was the South African Jody Scheckter, who finally won the title with Ferrari in 1979 after earlier spells with McLaren, Tyrrell and Wolf. Roy Topp, who worked with him at Tyrrell and Wolf, says it was clear straight away that he was something special. "With Jody, it was immediately obvious he was World Champion material. You could tell that when he was driving the McLaren [he had several outings for McLaren before signing for Tyrrell]. Although he caused a big shunt at Silverstone, he obviously had the talent. They always called him 'Sideways Scheckter,' which was one of his downfalls. There was one occasion when we went to Goodwood with a brand new car. I don't remember whether it was after one or two laps, but he put it in the bank. It was probably the new Tyrrell 007.

"We had two different types of driver because he came in at the same time as Patrick [Depailler]. Patrick was very smooth, he braked quite gently into the corner and accelerated quickly, whereas Jody would hare into the corner, brake like hell, hit the throttle and go sideways. It was two contrasting styles of driving. They were very equal on times, although Jody was the more fortunate to win the races and he finished third in the Championship in his first year at Tyrrell."

Nelson Piquet was another to make an instant impact on Formula 1 on his debut in 1978, firstly with a one-off drive in an Ensign, and then with a three-race deal to run a McLaren M23 with Bob Sparshott's BS Fabrications team. "We did a deal with Nelson when he had stitched up the Formula 3 Championship by about three-quarters of the way through the season. We went to Brands Hatch and asked 'Would you like to drive a Formula 1 car?' thinking he was bound to say 'I've had 85 offers already,' but he said he would love to. We did a deal to do the Austrian, the Dutch and the Italian Grands Prix. He was incredible. When he first drove the car it was so heavy compared to his Formula 3 he could do just ten laps before he was absolutely knackered. He used to get out and lie in the back of the garage. I said to him 'You'd better get a bit fitter to do a Grand Prix season.' He was a real laugh, fast and a very quick learner, too.

"For the start in Austria it rained and they went off the line up the hill, and more or less straight on at the top. Alan Jones, who went on to become world champion in 1980, said to me 'Your bloke came past me so quick, I thought I'd stopped.' He was just a complete racer, Piquet. He'd hit all the kerbs and bent all the rockers on the front suspension so they were like a cartoon rocker, all curled up. We didn't see that at first. He came back to the pits with the thing dragging it's arse on the ground and said 'It's alright, I only went over the kerbs' and I said 'It's not alright, it's wrecked – you can't race in this.'

"One of the things that really made an impression on me about the man was during that terrible accident at Monza [which led to Ronnie Peterson's death]. In all that carnage, Nelson had started from a few rows back and driven blind through mist. He ran over a bit of debris but squeezed through. Then they red-flagged the race because of the accident and, I'll never forget, he came into the pits and stayed in the car. I asked him 'What are you sitting in there for?' and he said 'When is the race going to restart?' I said 'If there is a race, which is doubtful, it won't be for an hour or two – haven't you noticed what's happened?' He clearly had shut it out of his mind. That impressed me because, to be a race driver, you have to be able to do that."

Sideways Scheckter: Jody demonstrates why he was given the moniker as he struggles to eighth place in his home Grand Prix in 1973. (Roy Topp)

9
The contenders

Mechanics' opinions about those drivers who impressed them but never quite managed to secure the title, or died before they had a chance to do so, are particularly fascinating and often poignant.

Former BRM mechanic Dick Salmon remembers with fondness the Argentinian 'Pampas Bull' Froilan Gonzalez, though found that his Latin temperament didn't always sit harmoniously with the working methods of BRM management. "He was possibly a bit harder on the car than Fangio. Peter Berthon [BRM engineering director] was inclined to upset him. On one occasion at Boreham, Gonzalez said after practice 'It's OK, leave it as it is,' but PB had to do something, change the carburettor needles, I think it was. Gonzalez eventually found out, went a bit haywire and crashed it – whether deliberately we don't know. He was a good driver but not quite as good as Fangio."

Derek Wootton, who worked as a mechanic for Vanwall, found Gonzalez quite obstinate, which didn't work in his favour on his one outing for the team in the 1956 British Grand Prix at Silverstone. "He came all the way from Argentina to drive for Vanwall and he did 100 yards. We had 650 rear tyres on it and he wanted 700s. We didn't like 700s because of the loads put on the transmission. He said 'No, no, I'll be alright, I'll take it easy.' Of course, the Bull let the clutch out, snapped the transmission, and that was the end of that."

In 1953 and 1954, Tony Robinson worked alongside legendary mechanic the late Alf Francis, tending to the cars of Stirling Moss – including two different Cooper-Altas and a Maserati 250F. He found it extremely rewarding working with such an obviously talented young driver. "I enjoyed working with Stirling because he was so popular and so good. Stirling had a way of making a bad car look good, and his success took everybody along with him. With Stirling you knew that only he could put the car on pole position, only he would coax it out to a win. Anybody else, you'd be wasting your time."

The great season enjoyed by Moss in 1954 led to him being signed by Alfred Neubauer to drive for the factory Mercedes team in 1955. After the Stuttgart firm withdrew from motor sport in the wake of that year's Le Mans tragedy, Moss returned to Maserati and then had two seasons driving for Tony Vandervell's British Vanwall team. Derek Wootton had the privilege of working with him at Vanwall, and makes an interesting point about the impact of the Briton's spell at the 'money no object' Mercedes team. "Having known Stirling from the early days with Kiefts and things, when he went to Mercedes, everything was expendable. He came back a harder driver [on his car] than perhaps he was before. I'm not saying that against him but, where he might have taken it a bit easier if he'd been with his own team, when he went to Mercedes it didn't matter, they simply pulled another part out of the stores."

Tony Cleverley, who worked with him in the Rob Walker team, is another Moss fan. "Stirling was the driver I enjoyed working with most. Whatever you did for him he used to put it into practice, and if he couldn't make it work, you knew it never would. He used to say 'I don't think this is going to work' and that was it. No question about it, he was always great with a car, making it last and look good. He drove so nicely, it made life so much easier, as a fitter."

Wootton was particularly impressed by Tony Brooks, who drove for Vanwall in 1957 and 1958, and – sharing with Moss – scored the marque's first Grand Prix victory in the British event at Aintree in 1957. He then went on to win three Grands Prix in 1958 and was unlucky to miss out on the Championship title. "Brooks was very quiet, he got on with the job. He didn't want engines swapped around and things. Moss, being the number one driver, if there was half a second or a second in a car, between him and, say, Brooks or Lewis-Evans, he would think they had a better engine and he'd want the engine out of the car. In the end it reached the stage where the others kept quiet."

Stuart Lewis-Evans was a quiet, unassuming driver who initially made his name in the 500cc Formula 3 category. He was offered a drive with the Connaught team in late 1956 and, around this time, met up with Bernie Ecclestone, who became his manager. Impressive drives in the Connaught saw him promoted to the Vanwall team in 1957, with the highlight a pole position at Monza for the Italian Grand Prix, as part of a Vanwall 1-2-3 on the grid in Ferrari's backyard. In 1958, he continued with Vanwall and also drove in Formula 2 for the British Racing Partnership (BRP), as well as sports cars for Aston Martin but, sadly, perished from burns incurred in a fiery accident in the Moroccan Grand Prix at Casablanca. Tony Robinson got to know Lewis-Evans well in his role as chief mechanic at BRP. "Stuart was such a nice man, a gentleman. When Ken started up the British Racing Partnership we had a Formula 2 Cooper, which he [Lewis-Evans] drove quite well. But he never complained, up to the point that I said to him 'Stuart, when you come in, if you can't find anything wrong at least say you haven't any power.' But he just drove the car and thoroughly enjoyed himself. It was sad when he was killed."

Although he was a very slightly built man, there were many in the paddock who felt he had the raw talent to go on and challenge for the World Championship title, Derek Wootton among them. "If Lewis-Evans had been a bit fitter, he certainly could have [gone on to be a really top-line driver]. Tony Vandervell sent him up to Harley Street or somewhere to have him okayed. Lewis-Evans was a very smooth driver, he was one of these guys that had come up quickly and was probably the least well-off of the lot. It was because of this that he had his nylon overalls on when the car caught alight. The nylon burnt into his skin and that was what caused him to die of secondary shock. Nobody really knows [what caused the accident], we never got to the bottom of it. It hit Tony Vandervell hard, he couldn't believe it. He hired a plane and flew him back from Casablanca straight to McIndoe, the guy at East Grinstead who treated all the airmen in the war who got burnt. Apparently, Stuart was talking to one of the mechanics saying 'I should be out of here in a week or so, can you ready the car', but then suddenly died."

Many drivers in the 1950s and 60s shone fleetingly before their lives were snuffed out by a tragic accident. One example was the American, Herbert Mackay-Fraser, as BRM mechanic Dick Salmon recalls. "A driver who looked like being very good was Mackay-Fraser. He drove for us at Rouen and was mixing it with the big boys and then the following weekend he was killed. He would have been a good driver, he was very promising." His appearance in the 1957 French Grand Prix marked his Formula 1 debut, but it would be his one and only Grand Prix, an accident in the Coupe de Vitesse sports car race at Reims in a Lotus XI ending a promising career.

Likeable Swede Jo Bonnier is probably best remembered as the man who finally scored the BRM team's first Grand Prix win. Pat Carvath, who worked as a mechanic for BRM in the 1950s and 60s, tells an amusing story about that weekend. "I was in charge of Bonnier's car at Zandvoort in 1959 when it won, and Dick Salmon was in charge of Harry Schell's. Harry had brought a brand new road car there and said to Dick 'If I win on Sunday, you can have the car.' I said to Jo 'Did you hear that?' Jo had a Porsche there and he thought for a moment before saying 'I don't think so.' I said 'Tell you what, Jo, I've worn out that many pairs of bloody shoes pushing you, you can buy me a new pair if you win' and he said 'I'll do that.' Then he went and won the race. In fairness, I did eventually receive the shoes."

So many top drivers died in racing accidents during the 1950s and 60s that Derek Wootton is hard-pressed to decide which had the biggest impact on him. "Jean Behra's death at AVUS was one of the ones that hit me really hard, also Marquis de Portago and Harry Schell. I remember being with Behra, looking at something on his car, and in the next race he had an accident and was killed. That shook me up quite a bit because I'd just been talking to the guy. We were staying in a hotel at Silverstone, and de Portago was there and I happened to talk to him for about half an hour. The next thing I knew, he'd had this big accident in the Mille Miglia." I got on very well with Harry Schell. He was a real jester. Harry was probably the most likeable of all the drivers. He was very flamboyant, really good fun.

Tony Robinson can never forget the day that Schell died in 1960, the start of a difficult year for the Yeoman Credit Racing Team which would lose another of its drivers, Chris Bristow, only a month later. "Harry was killed at Silverstone on Friday May 13th – that is still my unlucky day, I never do anything then, no matter where I am. I'm superstitious on that one. It was raining on that particular day and I was the last one to speak to him. He had already put up the quickest time in the wet and wanted to go out again. You say to yourself 'Maybe I should have told him not to bother ...'"

Bristow was one of two young British drivers – Alan Stacey being the other – who died during the tragic 1960 Belgian Grand Prix at the high-speed Spa-Francorchamps road circuit. Robinson feels that Bristow was destined to go a long way. "He was a great young man and I was very sad about him because he would have been out at the top, had he lived. He was a brilliant little driver, full of life. We had some good times together. I was very close to Chris and was actually responsible for him driving for BRP. George Wicken was driving for us in the early days and wasn't really doing the job. We were testing down at Brands Hatch one day and I saw this Chris Bristow running around. He was driving very well and I suggested to Ken [Gregory, boss of BRP] that he had a word with him and he signed him up. We travelled around together: he had a Mark II 3.4

Harry Schell, seen here in the centre of a posse of BRM mechanics with a bouquet, was tremendously popular with all of the mechanics who worked with him, and his death in practice for the International Trophy at Silverstone in 1960 was a big blow. Left to right: Maurice Dove, Gordon Newman (behind him in hat), Phil Ayliff, Willy Southgate peering round his shoulder, Arthur Hill in peaked hat, Dick Salmon, unknown Lockheed brakes engineer, Pat Carvath, 'Sergeant Bilko' in hat, Roy Foreman behind him, Dennis 'The Sheriff' Perkins in hat and sunglasses. (Pat Carvath)

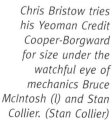

Chris Bristow tries his Yeoman Credit Cooper-Borgward for size under the watchful eye of mechanics Bruce McIntosh (l) and Stan Collier. (Stan Collier)

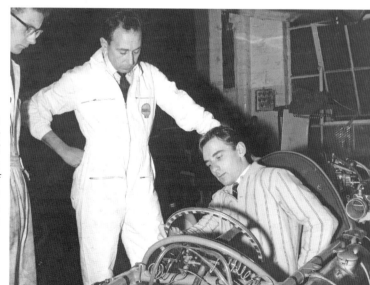

Jaguar that he had bought himself now he was moving into professional racing, and at that time I was running a three-litre Rover. If we were going to Aintree, we would go up in convoy. He was very young [aged 22 when he died], full of life and always laughing, but a damn good driver. I was very close to him and it was incredibly upsetting when he was killed."

Stan Collier, who worked for Robinson at BRP, was also quite affected by Bristow's death. "I felt sorry for Bristow, that really did upset me. He was one of the boys, used to mix with us, and he was young. He became tied up in the race with Willy Mairesse, who was renowned for cutting up people. That was the worst one, really."

Although he took part in nearly 50 Grands Prix, Roy Salvadori never managed to win one, despite coming close in Germany in 1958 when he was a member of the works Cooper team. Richard Watson worked with 'Salvo' during 1957, when he was also driving for Cooper. "Roy was alright. We had great fun with him. He was very fussy about his tyre pressures. He would tell me what pressures he wanted and I used to kneel down with the tyre gauge and pretend to put it on. I knew what they were and that they were good enough. He used to come in again and I'd ask him how it was and he'd say 'That's better.'

"The other bloke who worked with me, a chap called Ray Gibbs, used to say 'I think old Roy is going a bit faster [revving the engine more] than he makes out.' Roy came in and the rev counter was below the mark and I thought 'No, you're definitely going faster than that' and I said to Ray 'I'll soon put paid to that.' Now, on the back of the rev counter there was a trip button, so I took the button out. After that, he was going round like the Harry Dingbats and we could see him coming down the straight. I said 'Look, look, watch him' and he was fiddling about trying to re-set this rev counter. We could see what he was doing, and he was going over the mark."

Gerry Hones, who worked with him at Aston Martin on both Formula 1 and sports cars, feels that, while he was very competent, Roy simply excelled more in other classes of racing. "Salvadori was never really a top Formula 1 driver but as a saloon car driver he was unbeatable, magnificent."

Some drivers were quite superstitious, particularly about numbers. Ivor Bueb, who had established himself as a top-class sports car driver, had occasional outings in a variety of Formula 1 machines (including a drive in a Connaught in the 1958 British Grand Prix, entered by Bernie Ecclestone), and for 1959 secured a place in the BRP Formula 2 team, driving a Cooper-Borgward. Stan Collier wonders whether his superstitions may have unsettled him the day he died, in the Auvergne Trophy Formula 2 race at the Clermont-Ferrand road circuit in France. "Ivor hated number 7 for some unknown reason, and when we went to Clermont-Ferrand he was given that number. Stirling said 'I'll change with you' so he took number 7 and they gave Bueb 34, which added up to 7 so that upset him, too."

Innes Ireland and Trevor Taylor both made their Grand Prix debuts with Team Lotus but each justifiably felt that they received something of a raw deal from Colin Chapman's outfit. Ireland scored the team's first ever Grand Prix victory before being callously cast aside in favour of Jim Clark, while Taylor was always going to play second fiddle to Clark. In a neat twist, both drivers moved to the British Racing Partnership after their spells with Lotus came to an end and, in 1964, were team-mates, a combination which Tony Robinson found most agreeable. "Now they were a couple of nice people, full of life. With Innes it was a thrill a minute on and off the track, and Trevor was the same. Innes was my favourite. At the end of the day, he was my man. He was a terrific character, who could be serious and funny. He liked to enjoy himself, have a bit of a laugh and a drink, but he wasn't a mercenary person.

"Trevor went into the Lotus team and ended up as team-mate to Jimmy Clark. His problem was that, in his last year or so with Lotus, he had had quite a lot of accidents and it affected him, his confidence went. Our job at BRP was to slowly overcome that and try to bring him back to how he had been. If he had got a couple of races under his belt without having a major off, things could have been different. We nearly reached that point when he started having the odd accident again and that's basically how it ended up, it was unfortunate." The 1964 season would be Taylor's last full year in Formula 1, although he continued to drive in sports cars and, later, Formula 5000. Ireland continued into 1965 with Reg Parnell Racing but failed to score any Championship points: his topline career fizzled out with a pair of retirements at the end of 1966, driving Bernard White's privately-entered BRM.

Mike Costin was a key figure in the early development of Team Lotus who would later find fame as a partner to Keith Duckworth at legendary engine-builder Cosworth. He was another fan of Ireland and felt particularly bad about the way in which the Scot's services were dispensed with, which led to a rift between Innes and Chapman that would never heal. "Innes Ireland was between the two [Jim Clark and Graham Hill] in terms of ability. He was very gifted but didn't pretend to have any technical knowledge. I used

Innes Ireland developed something of a reputation among his mechanics for crashing. Fortunately, in this instance (practice for the 1961 German Grand Prix at the Nurburgring), he appears to have spun into the shrubbery without doing too much damage. Innes is visible second right in shot (partially obscured by the marshal in sunglasses) while mechanic Ted Woodley (left front wheel) supervises retrieval. (Dick Scammell)

to have to spend some time getting him out of various scrapes – what a character. Innes never concentrated on anything but used his gift. I spent quite a bit of time with Innes at the races, one way or another. I was terribly sad when Colin did the dirty on him. In terms of signing Jim to drive instead of Innes, Colin did do the right thing, but it was the way in which it was done. Innes left the country and went to South Africa or somewhere for the entire winter and was never told that he didn't have a drive. When he came back, he didn't have enough time to organise another, which was why he never spoke to Colin again."

Former Team Lotus chief mechanic Dick Scammell remembers Ireland as being somewhat accident-prone, which didn't always endear him to his mechanics, as it made a lot more work for them. "At Solitude Innes had run the car off the road yet again and I thought I'd tackle him about it. I told him I thought he was an idiot and that, if he couldn't drive any better than that, he should give up. Innes, being Innes, caught me by the throat and was going to fill me in and we had this stand-up row in the middle of the paddock. I was probably tired at the time and Innes said he wouldn't have me working on his car any more. Colin said that was not up to him and he resolved the problem by sending Innes and I off together on the Tasman series. But he was a great character, another one who enjoyed life."

Although Graham Hill probably had the biggest reputation for being a settings fiddler, other drivers were capable of challenging him on that count, one of whom was Dan Gurney, as Hughie Absalom, who worked with him at Brabham, explains. "Dan was probably much more difficult to work with than Jack [Brabham] because he was learning his business as he was going along. He would be forever wanting to change springs and roll-bars and things like that. There was always a bigger workload on his car than on Jack's. Jack knew what he wanted a lot more than Dan did."

Gurney's propensity to tinker is confirmed by Mike Lowman, who worked with the American when he ran the Eagle in Formula 1. "He used to fiddle a lot. If we reached the stage where we were ready to start an engine in a car when we were preparing to go to a race and he was there, after you'd started the engine, you'd be holding the throttle steady while it warmed up and he'd come out, take it from you, and start playing with it, bruumph, bruumph, bruumph. One particular time he sent over some really trick oil hoses for us, they were early Typeflex lines, which were fairly low pressure. They would be fine once the engine oil temperature reached its proper level but, when the oil was cold, you used to have to hold the engine at really low rpm and let the temperature build slowly. This was in the days before things like oil warmers.

"We had these things on and were holding the engine at about 800rpm when he came rushing out, grabbed hold of the throttle, hit it hard and the pipe burst. He was covered in oil from head to foot. We had a laugh and then he went away but we had to do a bloody engine change because you could see the pipe but you couldn't insert your hand down between the side of the monocoque and the engine. The engine was not a stressed member, it had the monocoque running along to the back. That meant we had to work all damn night to do that job."

Gurney evidently didn't want the rest of the paddock to know the extent of his obsession, as one story from Lowman illustrates. "We were testing at Goodwood one time and he was in for a spring change. We must have had probably two dozen sets of springs for each end of the car and he wanted to see them all, so we had what we called the 'spring mine' in the back of the truck. Jo [Ramirez] and I were taking out all these springs and putting them on to the back end of the truck so he could come and look at them, when the Brabham truck arrived for Jack to do some Goodyear tyre testing. Dan came running across and saw we had all these springs out and was so embarrassed, saying 'Put them away, I don't want Brabham to see all those.'

"Brabham would probably have only had four springs for the car and that would have been it. With Dan, anti-roll bars used to go up in something like 60 thou increments. We had masses and masses of those sorts of things. Then he would fiddle about with exhausts, saying 'let's shorten the tail-pipes' and stuff like that. We were down there at one test and had only one set of titanium exhausts for the car. They were actually on the car, rather than the test set and he wanted to start hacking around the tailpipes. We refused to let him touch them because, in the UK, we didn't have a purge tank or the ability to do titanium welding, it was done in the States. At times that used to be a bit frustrating with Dan, waiting for him to finish fiddling. But when he had a good result, it used to make you think 'To hell with it, look what he's done.'

"I'm still a huge Dan fan. He's my absolute hero, closely followed by Jackie [Stewart]. There's something about the pair of them. At Zandvoort, the year the Lotus 49 came out, we shared a garage with Team Lotus, and thought that there was no way that car was going to finish. They were going through wheel bearings like they were going out of style. The night before the race, they had used so many that they didn't have enough to build Graham's car – they were rummaging through all the old ones to pick out the best ones. We thought 'All we have to do is keep going and they will fall apart.' Nothing happened – but we broke a damn metering unit, not very far into the race; about seven or eight laps.

"Dan decided he wanted to do some testing the next day, so we went back to the garage and, while everybody else was packing up and putting their stuff away, we were doing an engine change. We went to the circuit the next day and that guy drove his heart out, I felt ten foot tall. He would have put that car on pole, the time he was doing round there. It was awesome to watch; he was going round and round and round. He obviously had to work it out of his system as well as us."

Lowman tells a tale of a last minute adjustment Gurney made to his Eagle before going out to win the 1967 Belgian Grand Prix at Spa-Francorchamps. "We were in a Mobil garage in Stavelot at the other end of the circuit. What was nice in those days was that you would drive the cars from the pit to the garage where you were working on them at night, and then in the morning you'd take them back to the pits, so you were able to drive the circuit in the race car, which was really good. We went back to the garage and prepped the car for the race, going through the bump steer and everything, and it was fine, we were ready to go motor racing. We reached the paddock – the old paddock at Spa was on the hill down to Eau Rouge – and were sitting in the back of the truck when Dan came in. He was standing there looking at the car, which was facing us, and I said 'What's up, Dan?' and he said 'I want some more toe-in on the left front.' I said 'Pardon? It's the set-up from last night.' 'I don't care,' he said 'I want some more toe-in.' I went over and did it, thinking 'If you want it, you want it.' He actually went out and won the bloody race …"

Lowman counts the years with Anglo/American team Eagle amongst the most special of his career, "It was such an achievement in those days, for him to build his own car with his name on it. Every time we used to push out those cars, as you went onto the grid they'd play the car's national anthem and you used to feel ten foot tall when the old 'Stars'n'Bars' came on."

Richie Ginther was perhaps slightly in the shadow of some of the higher profile American drivers, such as Gurney and Phil Hill, who came to Europe to compete in Formula 1. Nonetheless, he drove for top teams Ferrari, BRM and Honda (scoring the latter's only victory in the 1.5-litre Formula 1 era in Mexico in 1965). BRM mechanic Roger Barsby remembers him with great affection. "A lovely guy. He was never any bother, he used to jump in the car and drive it."

Ginther's Grand Prix career stalled in 1966, then petered out in 1967, despite his seeming to have a top class berth driving an Eagle alongside Gurney. Mike Lowman thinks he lost the hunger to take risks. "He couldn't cope. It was funny, it first came to light when we should have been 1-2 in the Race of Champions at Brands. He gave up with a vibration in the car which turned out to be a wheel weight missing on one of the fronts. I thought 'Come on, you have to grin and bear it.' Then we went to Monte Carlo and he failed to qualify and that was it." Ginther formally retired from racing during practice for the '67 Indy 500, and briefly went into team management, most notably in the Can-Am series, looking after the Porsche of Jo Siffert.

Ginther, Phil Hill and Gurney were examples of Americans who successfully made the transition to Formula 1, but there were plenty of formidable drivers who never made the switch. Bob Sparshott had particular admiration for two such gentlemen. "Back in the Lotus days, we had the chance of working with a lot of drivers. On the American front, we had A J Foyt and Parnelli Jones drive for us. Parnelli was a cool character. At Milwaukee, he was doing some testing when he came off turn four and spun. It went round about three times but he never hit anything. When we reached him, the right wheel was hanging over and the steering arm had broken. He was still in the car. Chapman was all over him like a rash, saying 'What's happened, Parnelli?' Parnelli simply pointed to the steering arm, turned to him and said 'Colin, I think you're trying to kill me.' And the Old Man went 'Oh no, we have some stronger ones, we're going to put them on,' and all that bullshit that used to come out. Parnelli was cool. A J Foyt and he tried to cut off my hair at Indy with wallpaper scissors because I had a Beatle haircut, chasing me all up and down the garages. Old Foyt was built like a bloody wrestler but they were only mucking about, fortunately."

Someone who began their career with Team Lotus but seemed to blossom after he left for pastures new was Mike Spence, who spent two seasons largely in the shadow of Jim Clark and then, after a spell in the wilderness with Reg Parnell Racing, came good at the wheel of the difficult H16 BRM in 1967. He was brought back into the Lotus fold for Indy in 1968 after the death of Jim Clark but, tragically, died in a testing accident before the start of official practice, by all accounts going into Turn 1 too fast while trying out a sister – and therefore unfamiliar – car to his own. Bill Cowe, who worked with Spence at Lotus in Formula 1, was an admirer. "I was fairly close to Mike Spence. He was becoming better and better. He was a slow developer, he wasn't that quick in Formula 1 when he was at Lotus, but when he went to BRM he suddenly found his speed."

Another British driver who showed brief flashes of promise before an untimely death was Piers Courage, heir to the Courage brewing fortune. Mike Young, who came to know him while working for Frank Williams, feels he could have gone far. "I'm sure he would have gone on to be a lot better. Many drivers in those days were moneyed, but he had a natural ability. He was a very quiet, unassuming guy. It's very difficult to say [how far he would have gone] because the equipment was never there. He and Frank had two second places in the 1969 Grand Prix season, which wasn't too bad for a privateer with no money, working from a telephone box."

The Belgian driver Jacky Ickx burst onto the international scene in 1966, when he drove in Formula 2 for Ken Tyrrell. The following year, he set third fastest lap in practice for the German Grand Prix at the wheel of a 1600cc Formula 2 Matra, and was running fourth, ahead of many Formula 1 cars, before forced to retire. The 1968 season brought him a debut victory, by now with Ferrari but a switch to Brabham for 1969 seemed well-timed, and he scored two wins. Although he came close to winning the title, back with Ferrari in 1970, he never seemed quite as competitive. Peter Hennessy feels he would have benefited from staying longer at Brabham. "Jacky could have done better. I think he regretted leaving Brabham at the end of 1969; he should have stayed."

Mexican driver Pedro Rodriguez had been on the periphery of Grand Prix racing for several years, having sporadic outings for Ferrari and Lotus before his breakthrough victory in the works Cooper-Maserati at the 1967 South African Grand Prix. Denis Daviss has fond memories, not only of the race but the party thrown afterwards. "Pedro came to join us and, after various problems in the race at Kyalami, won. Considering he was only drafted in because we didn't have another driver, that was quite good. After the race, a little impromptu pool party was thrown for him. Pedro insisted that the mechanics came too and my big memory of that is of Ron Dennis swimming up and down the pool, fully dressed in his formal suit."

Alan Challis, who worked with the little Mexican driver at BRM, recalls him having a characteristically Latin approach to racing. "Pedro was a typical South American. Some places he was unbelievably quick but, circuits he didn't like, we might as well have left the car at home. You'd go to Spa and 'whoosh' but Zandvoort he hated, I don't know why. You'd have thought Zandvoort and Spa, okay, they're different, but they were both 'big-balls' circuits. He was a quick driver and it was very sad when he was killed. He didn't need to race; he wasn't a poor man, by any means. With the car, he liked it how he liked it. He knew how he wanted it to go. If you could make it right for him, you knew damn well he wouldn't be beaten."

Former BRM gearbox man Ben Casey also had a soft spot for Rodriguez, although he also admired his Swiss team-mate, Jo Siffert. "Pedro was my favourite driver, he was a racer. In Mexico in 1968, he came to me the night before the race and said 'Casey, is my gearbox alright?' I said 'Yes, Pedro.' 'It'd better be,' he said, 'if not I'll have the bandits take you off out into the hills and hang you.' So I had another look at it, just to make sure. I hoped he was joking. I liked Jo Siffert, as well. Pedro was a bit of a playboy, whereas Jo was more of a down-to-earth family man."

Rob Walker mechanic Tony Cleverley came to know Jo Siffert extremely well during the five seasons that the team ran the determined Swiss driver. "We got on well, we used to go out to Switzerland and use his workshop, stay out there for hillclimbs

Marvellous Mexican: Pedro Rodriguez was drafted into the works Cooper team for the 1967 South African Grand Prix to fill a void in the driver line-up, and promptly won the race. Shown here with team mechanic Denis Daviss, he invited all of the mechanics to the after-race party, at which Ron Dennis could be found swimming up and down the pool in his formal suit ... (Denis Daviss)

Siffert, shown here with Cleverley (right) at the 1969 Spanish Grand Prix, 'started off with no money, and had to really dedicate himself to motor racing.' (Ford Motor Company)

Calm before the storm: Ronnie Peterson chats to a journalist alongside his March 701 in the paddock after practice for the 1970 Belgian Grand Prix at Spa-Francorchamps. Later in the weekend he would be arrested and spend a night in the cells, almost missing the race in the process. (Peter Bracewell)

and things like that. He was great and could think of nothing else but motor racing. He started off with no money and had to really dedicate himself to it."

The 1971 season was a tumultuous one for BRM because it lost its two best drivers – a mortal blow from which the team never recovered. Alan Challis noticed a real difference in Jo Siffert's approach to racing immediately after Rodriguez's death. "The day after Pedro was killed, it was as though somebody had flicked a switch in Jo's brain. The next weekend was Silverstone, the British Grand Prix, but he was a different man. He'd suddenly realised that the team was on his back now and he became more professional, more switched on. He was always quick but from then on, he was as quick as anyone else out there."

Siffert and the mercurial Swede Ronnie Peterson both drove March Formula 1 cars in the 1970 season. In the case of the former, it nearly finished his career as he had a very poor season, failing to score a single point. In fact, neither did Peterson, a seventh place being the best finish both drivers achieved, but his performances in the uncompetitive Antique Automobiles March 701 suggested he was a driver with a great future. As well as racing in the premier class, Peterson drove a March 702 in Formula 2 that year. Peter Bracewell, who built and worked on Ronnie's Formula 1 car, remembers it well. "At the time that Tony Reeson and I were at Bicester building the car, Ronnie was racing

Formula 2. He was doing quite well, although he was having lots of accidents. Keith Leighton was his Formula 2 mechanic, and every weekend he'd be out racing with Ronnie. We'd go back to work on a Monday morning and he'd be ripping this Formula 2 to pieces, building up another chassis because Ronnie had crashed it."

Leighton remembers that period vividly. "I first met Ronnie in 1969; he was in Formula 3 at the time. He was quiet, learning English, and waiting for a car to drive. We did some Formula 2 with the Malcolm Guthrie-entered 702, which was a complete s**tbox. We had it going fairly well in the end, mainly by telling Ronnie it was a good

---

Track record   Peter Bracewell

❝I was working for Colin Crabbe, who was the boss of Antique Automobiles. He was also a racing driver and used to race historic cars, Maseratis and Ferraris and all sorts of things. In 1969, he bought a Cooper-Maserati and we went Grand Prix racing with Vic Elford driving. The first race we went to with it was Monte Carlo. Although it was an old car, he finished seventh. Colin and Vic got on quite well that year and we did a deal with McLaren – they had a sidepod M7A that was lying redundant at the factory. Tony Reeson and I went down and built this car, put it all together and then we ran Vic in that, for two or three races that year until he had an accident at the Nurburgring, which finished us off for that season."

Peter stayed with Crabbe into 1970, when his team ran Swede Ronnie Peterson in his debut Formula 1 season, driving a March 701. In 1972 he joined BRM, where he worked with the likes of Jean-Pierre Beltoise, Peter Gethin, Reine Wisell and François Migault until its demise at the end of 1977.

Bracewell became involved in racing through his boss, Colin Crabbe. (Peter Bracewell)

---

car, saying that there was nothing wrong with it, it was him. The car was a complete piece of s**t but he carried it on his shoulders. The Formula 2 car was a spaceframe [a tubular chassis] in 1970. I guess March wasn't paying Arch Motors, which was making the chassis frames, because we had an abundance of damaged frames. By mid-year, it was a case of 'We've damaged the left front, there's one with right front damage up there, if I take all that off there and weld it on here, I've made myself a chassis. I was actually making frames from old frames. At the Nürburgring, where Ronnie hadn't been before, we had three crashes. When he arrived back at the pits on foot after one accident in practice, I asked him how the car was: 'I don't know, I can't see it,' he replied.

Apparently, it had ended up in a tree. The funny thing was, we kept on plugging away so that, by the end of the year we were competitive. Nowadays, they have computers and God knows what, but then it was simply rule of thumb and a case of 'Let's try this.'"

Tony Reeson remembers the Swede as a very personable young man. "He was a terrific guy. One of the nicest young lads you could meet. He would sit and talk to you and try and discuss things. Colin Crabbe had a little garage in a village outside Bourne, and he used to come and sit out the front and have a cup of tea. My Auntie would come walking up the village and he'd stop and talk to her. He was the unluckiest one, because he never won a World Championship."

Despite his shy, gentle nature, the young Swede managed to get himself arrested that year, during the weekend of the Belgian Grand Prix, and nearly missed the race as a result, as Peter Bracewell explains. "Ronnie was rushing into the circuit on race day; it was chaos with people everywhere, and he actually clipped a policeman with the wing of his hire car. They immediately arrested him but Louis Stanley persuaded the police to bring him back for the race. We prepared the car and popped it onto the grid to wait for its driver. The police turned up with Ronnie in their car, and he stepped straight out of the police car and into the race car, so he could do the race. Then, as soon as the race was over, the police were there again. He was out of the race car, back into the police car and down to the police station. They kept him in overnight and Louis negotiated for his release on the Monday morning. It was unfair because he was a nice guy: not an aggressive type of person at all."

Ray Wardell built the very first March Formula 3 car that Peterson drove towards the end of 1969, and worked with him when he ran in the works March Formula 2 team in 1971 and 1972. He recalls it was evident right from the first time he saw the Swede race that he was something special. "I presume it was Alan Rees who recognised it and brought Ronnie into March. He was very spectacular, there was lots of talent there, though he was not very technically sound."

Leighton concurs, saying: "He wasn't much of a test driver. He drove a car to its maximum. Whatever you gave him, he drove it as fast as he could, so he would mask a problem. That was probably his downfall most of the way through his racing career because he took what he was given and went 10/10ths. You always want the guy behind the steering wheel to give it 10/10ths but we weren't really getting that technical feedback. Over the years, I worked with a lot of drivers who have been good at that. If Ronnie had been like that, he would have won a lot more races."

A vivid account of Peterson's all-out approach to driving is provided by Leighton's description of their visit to the Rouen-les-Essarts road circuit in France for a Formula 2 race in 1970. "After the pits, it was downhill. If you think Eau Rouge is bad at Spa, Rouen had four corners going downhill to a hairpin at the bottom, and Peterson took that old Malcolm Guthrie car down the hill flat out, without any wings on it. That's when you realised there was something special about the guy. The next year we went there knowing that it was going to be flat out down the hill, so we'd already made the car without any wings. In 1971 with the March, we put the front wings on the back. That was his first win in a Formula 2 car at that race. Once he started, he kept on and won the European Championship, the French Championship, and everything else, but the start of it was Rouen. I think before that he was trying too hard. At Pau, for instance, he

Peterson: His philosophy was 'win or bust.' (Ford Motor Company)

would have won the race by a lap but was trying so hard that he ended up whacking the kerb and knocking the bottom off the gearbox."

Peterson's hard driving style meant the teams he raced for often had to 'beef up' their machines to withstand a hammering from him. This was certainly the case with John Player Team Lotus in 1973. Had he been kinder to his car, he would have been right in the hunt for the Championship, as Leighton explains. "There were several races when he should have won but didn't. At Zandvoort, he hammered the gearbox and it broke. In Spain, he was probably 30 seconds ahead but was murdering the gearbox, whereas Emerson [Fittipaldi] was taking it easy, knowing it was a hard place on transmissions."

After three seasons at Lotus, Peterson had a spell back in a private March, then an ill-judged move to Tyrrell for 1977 put a further brake on his career, as Leighton recalls. "The six-wheeler had its heyday the first year because Goodyear made the tyres for it.

Peterson (shown here in the Italian Grand Prix) should have mounted a stronger championship challenge in 1973, but was too hard on his cars. (Ford Motor Company)

Track record   Keith Leighton

" *My father had a garage in Earls Barton near Northampton and he did stock car racing back in the early 50s right through to the early 60s. He ended up winning the World Championship a couple of times. So right from a very early age, I was a mechanic. Every day after school I'd be doing something in the garage. In 1964, I was leaving school and thinking of trying to get to Rolls-Royce, Jaguar or Coventry Climax when somebody told me about this new company that was just starting up in Northampton called Cosworth.*

"I called and asked if there were any vacancies and ended up having an interview. I was only 15 years old. They said 'We don't take trainees, we only take fully qualified people, we're a small company that specialises.' I told them I'd built engines, so they took me on to prove myself. Next thing I knew, I was working there and very quickly I was building engines. Because I was young and enthusiastic, I ended up in the Development Department, where they wanted somebody who would work long hours.

"The great thing was that both Mike Costin and Keith Duckworth wanted to play with their development engines, so I became the 'hands-on' guy, most of the time with Mike Costin. What a great opportunity. We did the FVA first, then the Formula 1 engine. Many nights I was there until 10 or 11 o'clock with Mike and Keith, fudging around, trying to make the thing work. That was a great foundation to get involved in racing. I didn't really enjoy just building engines, so when the engine went into production, I moved onto the Cosworth four-wheel-drive Formula 1 car. Robin Herd was commissioned to design it and I ended up being a mechanic, fabricator, you name it, along with John Thompson. The death of that was when they didn't ban wings and the aerodynamics made four-wheel-drive obsolete. There was really nothing left to do at Cosworth because the development department became redundant and all they had to offer me was building production engines. Robin started talking about this new venture, March and I joined them for the 1970 season."

Leighton struck up a firm friendship with Ronnie Peterson during his time running the Swede at March in Formula 2. In 1972, he joined Ron Dennis's Rondel Racing team, Peterson following him to do Formula 2 and then the pair moved to Team Lotus in 1973 to do Formula 1 with the Lotus 72 alongside Emerson Fittipaldi. He stayed there until the end of the 1975 season. After three years running his own fabrication company, he moved to the US, where he ran a variety of Indy and IMSA cars, including being the engineer on the 1996 Indy 500-winning car of Buddy Lazier. He is now involved part-time in historic Formula 1 and with Ferrari's F1 Clienti programme running modern Ferrari Formula 1 cars.

Leighton learned his trade building engines at Cosworth, but became known as Peterson's mechanic.
(Keith Leighton)

The following year when Ronnie was driving they weren't interested in developing the tyres any more so that was a one year wonder."

Frustratingly, the one occasion later in his career that Peterson drove a car clearly capable of winning the World Championship, he was the number two driver in the team and had to give way to team leader Mario Andretti. At the wheel of the Lotus 78 and, later in the year, a Type 79, he would finish second in the title race. Bob Dance recalls that the Swede was a very dutiful and loyal team-mate. "Ronnie was very respectful and kept the pressure on, and also won races if Mario fell by the wayside. But if there had been another year after that, there would have been a different status in the team and he would have become an equal number one. He was pleasant enough to get on with. I met up with him when he was at March in 1971: he was no trouble and very quick. Having Mario as the 'technical' driver, as it were, the one who set up the cars and discussed it all with the Old Man, Ronnie would be happy to set up his car the same, and would certainly go as quickly. It probably did irk Mario a bit." Tragically, Peterson perished as a result of injuries sustained in a first lap crash in the 1978 Italian Grand Prix, so the question of what would happen in 1979 never arose ...

Another promising young driver who found himself at the wheel of a March 701 in 1970 was François Cevert. He was drafted into the Tyrrell team, which was running Marches at the time, following Johnny Servoz-Gavin's abrupt decision to retire after the Monaco Grand Prix. He fitted in well at Tyrrell; the perfect pupil for the master, Jackie Stewart, to pass his knowledge and experience onto. He won his first race in the US Grand Prix in Watkins Glen in 1971 but, sadly, this would be his only victory. Success eluded him in 1972 and in 1973 when, much as Peterson would do for Andretti five years later, he played the loyal, respectful number two to Jackie Stewart, following him home to 1-2 finishes in Belgium, Holland and Germany. Then, in practice for the last race of the season at the Watkins Glen track, the scene of his triumph two years previously, he died in an accident which left the Tyrrell team – indeed, the whole of the paddock – devastated.

Former Tyrrell mechanic Neil Davis still remembers the Frenchman with tremendous fondness. "François was a superb guy. He loved life and lived it to the full, and was a really great driver, too. We'll never know what really happened that day but it was driver error. What can I say; he was simply a good guy. If you speak to Jackie now, he would say that François was probably quicker than him towards the end of Jackie's career. Because of who Jackie was, I am sure that François – not that he was instructed to, I don't think Ken would ever do that – followed Jackie and learnt a hell of a lot from him. Drivers these days appear not to talk to each other or give each other any advantage, but we were a team and Jackie was fantastic with François, he taught him everything. How to set up the car, which gear to use at a certain corner, and things like that. And François was a good learner as well as a very quick and very good driver. As far as I'm concerned, he was just unfortunate. He was the only one we lost through the whole of our Formula 1 time, which was a pretty impressive record in those days."

Roy Topp, who worked on Stewart's car at the time, was also in no doubt that Cevert had what it took to make it right to the top, and would have been a strong contender for the World Championship title in 1974, had he lived. "He had 'it,' without a doubt. Francois would have beaten everyone, he was something else, a man with a lot of talent.

Tyrrell twins: Jackie Stewart, François Cevert and Elf Team Tyrrell were the dominant force in 1973, the Scot leading his young French team-mate home to a 1-2 finish no fewer than three times. They are shown here jinking through the chicane at Monaco, where Stewart won and Cevert finished fourth. (Roy Topp)

Had François been there with Jody [Scheckter] driving the other car, we'd have had quite a formidable team, and I think François would have outshone Jody."

With Jackie Stewart announcing his retirement at the end of the 1973 season, and the death of his intended replacement Cevert, Tyrrell was forced to recruit two new drivers for 1974. While Jody Scheckter won three races and took third in the Championship title race, his team-mate, Frenchman Patrick Depailler, took longer to settle in, winning no races and finishing ninth in the title chase. In five seasons with the team, he won only one race before switching to Ligier in 1979 and Alfa Romeo in 1980. It was at the wheel of the Alfa that he died in a testing accident at the Hockenheim circuit in Germany. Roy Topp remembers Lady Luck didn't always smile on him at Tyrrell. "Depailler was a little bit unlucky at times, things didn't quite go his way. But he was a driver with a lot of talent, a very smooth driver, good on the car, very similar to Jackie. I thought he deserved to have done better than he did."

Another Frenchman to make a limited impact on Formula 1 was Jean-Pierre Beltoise. Probably best remembered for a tremendous victory driving for BRM at Monaco in 1972 in treacherous rainy conditions, he was a multiple French motorcycle

Depailler: 'A very smooth driver, good on the car' but 'a bit unlucky at times.' (Roy Topp)

racing champion in the early 1960s, before making the switch to four wheels. But in 1964 he experienced a terrible crash at Reims, which nearly ended his career and left him with a permanently weakened left arm with limited movement. Former BRM chief mechanic Alan Challis reckons that, but for this, Beltoise would have gone a lot further. "One driver I always think was super skilful was Jean-Pierre Beltoise. At Monaco, it was his finesse that won that race."

Tony Reeson agrees, also identifying the Frenchman's lack of strength as the reason for his failure to make more of an impact. "After that accident, he wasn't strong enough physically. One time at Monaco we had to lift him out of the cockpit." Nonetheless, as Roger Barsby pointed out, his 1972 victory breathed much-needed new life into a flagging BRM team. "Beltoise, even with his disability, was good. When he won in

Final hurrah: The BRM team celebrates Jean-Pierre Beltoise's win at Monaco in 1972, little knowing it would be its last victory. Back row, left to right: Vern Schuppan, Rob Fowler, Tony Southgate, Alan Challis, Louis Stanley, Jean Stanley, Gerry van der Weyden, Peter Bracewell, Tony Reeson, Jimmy Collins, Franz Pucker, David Stubley. Front row, left to right: Sue Southgate, Neil Johnson, Pat Carvath, Alec Stokes at front, unknown behind him, unknown, Willy Southgate, Roger Barsby. (Pat Carvath)

Monte Carlo in the rain, it really pulled us round a bit, because we were becoming very despondent at the time."

Young British driver Tony Brise enjoyed a meteoric rise through the ranks, and was virtually unbeatable in many of the formulae he competed in. It was therefore inevitable that, sooner or later, he would find himself in Formula 1, under the wing of Graham Hill at Embassy Racing. Mike Young remembers him as a likeable, technically competent driver. "I liked him. He was a friendly guy and wanted to get on with the programme. He certainly had all the attributes that most of the best drivers had. He didn't make a lot of fuss, he jumped into the car and seemed to drive around a lot of problems, but knew what the problems were." Sadly, Brise's potential was never fulfilled, because, in November 1975, he died in a plane crash, along with the plane's pilot, Graham Hill, and most of the key members of the Embassy Racing team.

Another talented driver to perish in a plane crash was the Brazilian Carlos Pace, who started in Formula 1 with Frank Williams, spent his formative years at Team Surtees, and then switched to Bernie Ecclestone's Brabham team, for whom he won his home Grand Prix in 1975. He had endured a difficult first season with the flat-12, Alfa Romeo-engined BT45 in 1976, but the car was much improved for 1977 and, with John Watson as the other driver, this strong pairing seemed destined to challenge for wins on a regular basis. A second place in the opening race of the season in Argentina seemed to confirm this, while another second on the grid in South Africa also boded well, before problems intervened in the race. However, prior to the start of the European season came the shocking news of his fatal accident.

Bob Dance, who was Brabham's chief mechanic at the time, remembers Pace with great affection. "He was an ideal chap to have in a team. I had the greatest respect for him as a person. He was really a team driver. He got on well with the mechanics and with Bernie, and would have fun with the lads in the evening. He could be a bit fiery and temperamental but really a very nice bloke. And he had ability, too. He would make the effort in testing to try and extract the best out of a car and explain what was happening to it. He was a good chap in my book and I would have liked to have seen him come to the top."

Former Brabham team manager Herbie Blash also held the Brazilian in high esteem. "He was very close to Bernie – someone quite special as a person – who obviously had talent as a driver. He had the ability to become a World Champion, though wouldn't have been a Michael Schumacher-type champion. He took his racing seriously, but not that seriously."

Although he came close to winning the World Championship title on several occasions, most notably in 1981 for Williams, the Argentinian driver Carlos Reutemann never truly fulfilled his potential. Bob Dance remembers Reutemann as slightly enigmatic and unpredictable. "Reutemann on his day, when his temperament was right, was spectacularly quick. He was a bit moody but quite a kind person. Bernie used to say to him 'You have filmstar looks but you don't present yourself.' He would shrug his shoulders and that was it, he climbed in and drove. If everything was fine, it was fine and if it wasn't, he didn't go well at all."

One driver still remembered in almost reverential terms by the mechanics who worked with him, and also race fans, is French-Canadian Gilles Villeneuve, father of

Carlos Pace: 'An ideal chap to have in the team who would have fun with the lads in the evening' according to former Brabham chief mechanic Bob Dance, shown here with the Brazilian discussing set-up on the BT44 Formula 1 car, shortly after Pace had switched to the team during the 1974 season. (Eamon Fullalove)

1997 World Champion Jacques. After a stunning debut with McLaren at the 1977 British Grand Prix, he was quickly signed up by Ferrari; the only other marque of Formula 1 car he would drive in his career. Often struggling with an uncompetitive car, Villeneuve's final season of 1982 started badly with two retirements and a disqualification, and then his team-mate, Didier Pironi, 'did the dirty' on him at the San Marino Grand Prix, passing him on the final lap to take victory, in defiance of team orders to hold position. For the next race, Villeneuve was riled and fired up, and it was in this frame of mind that he collided with another car in practice, and died as a result.

Ray Wardell remembers Villeneuve as a more technical driver than most. "Gilles had a much better understanding of the car itself. It was a pleasure to work with him. I hadn't realised that he had been World Champion on snowmobiles. He had worked for a snowmobile manufacturer and developed and raced them. He wasn't a qualified engineer or anything, but had a very good understanding of the mechanical side of things. When I joined him, he'd already done one or two years of Formula Atlantic in Canada but hadn't grasped what it actually took to make the car work. Between the two of us it was very successful. He was probably the best of the young drivers I worked with.

"There was no question that Villeneuve really had talent. He only wanted to do one thing and that was be the quickest, every time he climbed into the car. There were no half measures. Even if you were testing, he still had to take the car to the limit every single time, there was no holding him back at all. In some cases, in the Formula Atlantic programme, we were very dominant. If I called him in during practice and said 'That's quick enough,' as long as he felt he'd done his best, he was quite happy."

Wardell also confirms that the French-Canadian would work out where the limit was on corners by going faster and faster until he spun. "If you had a conversation

Track record   Herbie Blash

"I'd always had an interest in mechanics. I was driving and pulling cars and tractors apart when I was 12 years old, so mechanical blood was inside me. I worked in the main garage at Rob Walker's, doing an apprenticeship but sometimes worked for the race team as well.

"After Rob Walker, I moved to Lotus. Because Rob was running a 49, I was often taking bits and pieces up to them, so got to know the Lotus people quite well. I was still going to college at that time but when I finished, I really wanted to see if I could work for a team that actually built cars. Lo and behold, I was very fortunate to go directly on to the Formula 1 team at Lotus, which was almost unheard of in those days. You'd give your right arm to work for them because Lotus then was as Ferrari is today. Money never came into it, you wanted to do it because you loved racing. That was at the end of 1968.

"My going-away card from Rob Walker said 'I hope you are going to enjoy your all-nighters!' I started work there on the Monday morning and in the Team Lotus building at that particular time there was no daylight whatsoever, even from the canteen down to the toilets, you never saw the light of day. I didn't leave there until Wednesday. That really was an extremely rude and hard welcome to the world of Lotus and Formula 1."

Herbie remained at Lotus until the end of the 1970 season, the death of the driver of the car he worked on – Jochen Rindt – at Monza that year profoundly affected him. After a spell working for Frank Williams, Herbie joined forces with Rindt's former manager Bernie Ecclestone, who had just bought the Brabham team, becoming his team manager. The relationship blossomed, the two bringing on a host of talented drivers, including Carlos Reutemann, Carlos Pace, Niki Lauda, John Watson and Nelson Piquet, who finally delivered them a much-deserved World Championship title in 1981 and followed it up with another in 1983. After Brabham folded in the early 1990s, Herbie moved on to work for Yamaha Motor Company, Japan, co-ordinating their Formula 1 programmes with Jordan and Tyrrell and he continues to be employed by the manufacturer, working on automotive projects.

Herbie is still involved in Formula 1, working as FIA Observer alongside Race Director Charlie Whiting. His role is still very hands-on: conducting a safety inspection of the track with Whiting before each meeting commences, co-ordinating the safety and medical cars, briefing drivers, team managers and marshals, monitoring teams' radio communications during the race and his most public role, shepherding Formula 1 drivers to be weighed and to the podium after the race.

A youthful Herbie Blash helps Tony Cleverley fuel Jo Siffert's Lotus 49 at the 1968 British Grand Prix, which it won, first time out. (Tony Cleverley)

with him about that, asking if it was really necessary, he would reply 'How else do I know where the limit is? If I haven't gone past it, I don't know where it is.' He chose his corners, he wouldn't do it in stupid places. Very rarely did he come unstuck. In the Atlantic programme during official practice, he wrote off one car in the very first race and another testing at St Jovite in Quebec. That was the only damage he ever did."

Under-achievers and 'might have beens'

In Formula 1 there's a whole panoply of drivers who, if they had the right lucky breaks at the right time in their career, might have progressed further. Therefore, it is interesting to hear mechanics' opinions about the 'might have beens' and those they felt should have achieved more than they actually did.

Ex-Tyrrell man Neil Davis identified the French-born Johnny Servoz-Gavin as a talented driver who, perhaps, didn't apply himself. "He was a bit of a playboy, old Johnny but a hell of a nice bloke. He smoked and drank and liked girls, all the things that normal people do. He was very quick. At Monaco in 1968, when Stewart couldn't drive, he took over and put it on the front row and led the race for ten laps until he clobbered the barrier."

Servoz-Gavin departed the scene abruptly after the 1970 Monaco Grand Prix. Apparently concerned that a problem with his vision was affecting his driving, he had hit the barriers in practice and failed to qualify. Davis remembers that they were never told about this, simply that he was stopping. "The next race we were going to was Spa, and Ken [Tyrrell] came to see us and said 'I've had a conversation with Johnny and he doesn't want to drive any more' and that was the end of it, he never did drive again."

Former Lotus mechanic Bill Cowe felt that John Miles was a driver who should have progressed further. "He was a very pleasant chap but I don't think his heart was really in it. He was far too intelligent and had a vivid imagination. To be a quick driver, you didn't need an imagination."

Mike Young also felt Miles could have gone further. "John was always there or thereabouts, but not quite. He was a number two at Lotus; perhaps that counted against him, or maybe he didn't have that last little bit that you need."

Although he won one Grand Prix, Peter Gethin also, perhaps, under-achieved in Formula 1 compared to his success in other racing categories. He was another who used to enjoy his racing driver status a little too much, perhaps, as former BRM mechanic Peter Bracewell observes. "We used to think that Gethin was a bit of a playboy. He was always chasing the women. He could have done with concentrating more on driving than larking about. Also, although he did well in his career in sports cars, [Henri] Pescarolo never really shone in Formula 1, never seemed to have that extra bit of flair."

Bob Sparshott, who worked with Pescarolo in 1976, found him to be nice enough – but perhaps being nice doesn't make a driver hungry enough to be a Grand Prix winner. "We ran a Surtees for Pescarolo. He had done a deal with John to run a third car but the works team didn't want the hassle, so I was given the job of running it in a few races. He was a very nice man and quite good in single-seaters early on in his career. He used to like to go fishing. Whenever you went anywhere he would say 'I have my fishing rod, if there's a river, I'm going to try to catch some fish.' A very peaceful man."

Sparshott also ran the DuPont family heir, Brett Lunger, in Formula 1 in 1977 and

1978. A decent enough Formula 5000 pilot, Lunger never seemed to make an impact at the top level, something Sparshott attributes to his failure to learn the right lines for circuits quickly enough. "He was good. I am sure his problem was that, on some of the more 'Mickey Mouse' circuits, he couldn't work out the lines. On the fast tracks with fewer corners like the Österreichring or Silverstone, he was really quick. But at Long Beach, he couldn't sort it out at all because there were so many bits of the track where you didn't take the right line because, if you did, you screwed up the next two corners. It took him a whole practice session to work it out."

There is a theory that, if from a wealthy background, the hunger to succeed – and to take risks in order to do so – is not quite as strong as with those who start with little or nothing. Sparshott feels that Lunger was slightly lacking in commitment, an assessment he supports with an example from one race in 1978. "At the Italian Grand Prix when Peterson died, Lunger did actually shunt himself and damaged the M23 quite badly. He wasn't hurt and we had a spare car there, which needed a bit doing. We were going to give it a go but he said 'No, I don't want to. I'm not going to race. I don't want to go back in.' He had a girlfriend who was always telling him 'Please, Brett, don't drive too fast,' all that sort of stuff, which is not very helpful. If you are a racing driver, it is part of the job, isn't it? You drive fast."

Sparshott also highlights a couple of British drivers who might have progressed further up the motor racing career ladder. "A guy I thought had a very wasted career was Mike Wilds. I thought Mike deserved better, he was a bit unlucky. Tony Trimmer, who I didn't actually work with but knew very well because he was at Frank Williams, was another very quick guy but ever so quiet, he never pushed himself forward and missed his opportunity. He used to win everything in Formula 3.

"Bill Ivy would have gone a long way, too; he was a quick driver. Bill was becoming involved with Frank Williams and learning all about four wheels, he was such a lovely little guy, he was hilarious: all 'Cor blimey' Cockney. He saw me in there one night, I was setting up the Formula 1 car as we used to with parallel bars and all that, doing the bump steer, and he stood there watching for ages. Then he asked 'Ere, Bob, what the f**k are you doing? I said 'That's bump steer, Bill.' He said 'What's that?' and I said 'When the wheels go up and down, you have to make sure they keep pointing straight ahead, you don't want all this toe-in and toe-out because if you are going over the bumps, you won't be able to control the car, it will make it unstable.' 'Do I have to do that on my Formula 2 then?' he asked, and I replied 'You have to.' 'F*****g Williams never told me anything about that,' he exclaimed, 'show me how to do it.' I explained and he went and did his own. He was a real little toughie. It was a tragedy that he was killed on a bike because that was to be his last season on two wheels."

10
The highs, lows, risks and responsibilities

Not a bad way to earn a living

It's fascinating to discover what aspects of their job mechanics liked best. Travelling was a large proportion of the work and, as many racing mechanics came from a background in the motor trade, it's unlikely they would have had the opportunity of regular trips abroad. Joining the forces could have been the only other way many of these mechanics would have seen the world. Going racing was for them, above all, a pretty big adventure, as Tony Robinson explains. "For somebody like myself, who comes from a very basic background, and had never been abroad, in those days it was rather exciting. The roads were not like they are now, they still had post-war surfaces which had endured a bit of a bashing. Plus, there was no euro, just lots of different currencies, so it was quite interesting from that point of view as well.

"It gave you a chance to see the world while doing something you were interested in. I liked the things that went with it. You worked very hard but when you are young that doesn't matter; you're not thinking about the hours you have to work because you are physically capable of doing them. The majority of people, when they are young, are not commercially-minded, they are not counting their pennies. In retrospect, you could say had we put the same amount of effort into working in a garage or some commercial venture, we would have ended up making a fortune, we couldn't fail. It was basically the excitement, I suppose. I'm still into it now and I'm nearly 80."

Not only was the work and travel stimulating but, despite the long hours and poor pay, it was in the main very enjoyable. Robinson found his early years, when he was much more hands-on as a mechanic rather than a manager, extremely rewarding, although his later time with BRP was also fun. "Working with Stirling Moss Ltd was my first taste of professional racing. I was learning the ropes. Certainly that was enjoyable, because I was young and, motor racing being what it was then, there was always a party after the race and a bit of free time before.

"Living out in Italy was good fun. When Stirling had the Maserati [250F], we were based in Modena for a couple of years. Afterwards, when I went with Bruce [Halford], also with a Maserati, the same applied for another couple of years. I suppose there are two types of enjoyment – one where you relaxed a little bit, did plenty of work but still enjoyed yourself, and another one gained through satisfaction with what you are doing. The four years with Stirling were quite enjoyable. The two years with Bruce, where I was more or less on my own all the time, were enjoyable, too, because it gave me

Track record   Bill Cowe

"I was doing some Formula Junior work in my spare time when I saw an advertisement from Team Lotus in the London Evening Standard, looking for race mechanics. I had an interview with Jim Endruweit and started there around February 1964, just after Jimmy [Clark] had won his World Championship."

Bill was involved on the Formula 1 section with drivers such as Clark, Mike Spence, Pete Arundell, Graham Hill, Jochen Rindt, John Miles and Mario Andretti before leaving the team at the end of the 1969 season. After a fifteen year layoff from motor sport, during which he worked for an agricultural engineering firm, he went to work for his former colleague Bob Sparshott and Alan Jakeman's BS Automotive Formula 3000 team. Spells with sports car and Formula 3 manufacturer Argo, Formula 3000 team Pacific, Tom's Toyota (touring and sports cars) and Nordic Racing (Formula 3000) followed, after which he moved to Prodrive, working on the Ferrari and Aston Martin GT1 programmes before retiring in 2006.

Bill Cowe, shown here on the left with fellow Team Lotus mechanic Leo Wybrott, worked with World Champion drivers like Jim Clark, Graham Hill, Jochen Rindt and Mario Andretti on both Formula 1 and Indy sections of the team. (Bill Cowe)

the opportunity of being more than just a mechanic. I was driving the truck, maintaining the car, living in Modena – when I wasn't at the races – and there was the opportunity to negotiate a starting price or an entry with the various race track owners. That was satisfactory *and* enjoyable.

"I suppose the best part of it was the period from 1958 to 1965 with BRP [British Racing Partnership], where I started with one car and a young apprentice mechanic, and ended up with a workshop and a fairly decent-sized outfit that was capable of not only working on, but building racing cars – where the engineering side of it was more satisfactory."

Stan Collier, who worked as a mechanic for the likes of BRP, Reg Parnell Racing, Rob Walker and Brabham between 1959 and 1981, highlighted the travel as the best part of the job from his point of view, but also pointed out that, in that era, mechanics were so much more in terms of their role within a team. "The travelling was not like it is now. When we started, we did everything; drove the trucks, built the cars and looked after them, and it was quite interesting."

Looking back, former Team Lotus mechanic Dick Scammell concedes that it was quite gruelling but a lot of fun: he has no regrets. "It was hard work but I'm not saying it wasn't enjoyable. At the time I thought 'Oh dear' but it was much better than working for Barclaycard or someone, wasn't it? Every day was different. All I remember is being out of bed a long time and working quite hard. They were different days because there wasn't the money. The entire Formula 1 team, although it had back-up with a panel-beating shop and things, was six people with three cars.

"I never thought about a pension. In those days, we lived the life we did and if you didn't like it, you could go and do something else. In fact, I enjoyed driving trucks across the continent, it was a way of life which had a lot going for it. You got to know the people you worked with pretty well, it was quite a good little group. We had a lot more fun in some ways than they do today, and were given a lot more freedom to do things than they are now. But motor racing moves on, doesn't it? Today is today and I'm still quite interested in the cars and racing now."

Pride in the job, with the focus on absolute quality, was another aspect which appealed to Peter Hennessy. "The class of work you were doing was very satisfying. The emphasis was on quality of work, rather than quantity. Coming from the motor trade that was a big difference. But you had time constraints which meant long hours, so that was a downside. Then again, I saw the world and I wouldn't have if I hadn't done this job."

'Work hard, play hard' is a moniker which suited well the Team Lotus mechanics. Bill Cowe has fond memories of the close relationships formed with his colleagues, particularly the after-race celebrations, although he recalls wryly that often they were too tired to appreciate them. "The best thing about the work was the camaraderie. In those days there used to be a prize-giving after the race, and that was always good because it was all over by then, the pressure was off and you could let your hair down a bit. But more often than not, you were so tired you went back to the hotel and bed because you'd worked solidly through the weekend, or before you arrived there."

A measure of how incredibly fulfilling it was being a racing mechanic in the 1950s, 60s and 70s is given by the simple assessment of former Rob Walker spannerman, Tony Cleverley. "When I think about that life now, there's nothing I would change."

The highs ...

In the immediate aftermath of World War Two, feelings of patriotism ran high, added to which, British teams were still trying to establish themselves as major forces within motor sport, even in the late 1950s, and breach the supremacy of top Italian marques like Ferrari and Maserati. Therefore, 'socking it to' the top Italian teams on home ground ranked pretty high on any mechanic's list of achievements. Derek Wootton, a mechanic on the British Vanwall team in the 1950s, had no hesitation in naming his personal high point. "Occupying the front row of the grid at Monza. Especially as it was in Italy ..." This refers to the fact that, in 1957, the front row of the Italian Grand Prix consisted of three British Racing Green-coloured Vanwalls, driven by three British drivers – Stuart Lewis-Evans, Stirling Moss and Tony Brooks – with only the Maserati of Fangio on the outside upholding Italian honour. Moss went on to complete the humiliation by winning the race. This event was symbolic of how the tide turned in the 1957 season, with British constructors breaking the Italian stranglehold on Grand Prix racing, never to look back.

Ask any mechanic and he will say that nothing beats the thrill of one of their drivers putting together a championship-winning run of performances. For Hughie Absalom, Jack Brabham's victory in the first year of the new 3-litre Formula was a real achievement. "The 1966 season was quite something, for Jack to turn up with his own car, his own engine, and do what he did ... We helped along the way and that was very rewarding. His success was down to a combination of factors. The engine was a fairly medium-safe package; it wasn't a high powered combination. He hit it just right. The car was quite good, Jack was in the right place at the right time and Denny was quite good as well. It was perfect timing on his part and the tyres had a lot to do with it. In those days, Firestones were quite strong and we came in with Goodyear."

"In terms of race wins, my high point would have been Reims 1966, the first race that Jack won. Bandini's Ferrari was leading but he broke a throttle cable and Jack took over. The same weekend we also won the Formula 2 race, taking first and second with the Brabham-Hondas, so that was probably the top one. Outside Formula 1, with the Chaparral team, in a Lola T500, we won the three American 500-mile races in 1978 with Al Unser Senior, and it's never been done since. There's only one 500-mile race now but in those days it was quite an amazing feat."

Ray Wardell recalls an unusual high point, significant more from the point of view of the manner of the victory than the importance of the race itself. "Probably the best race we won was the 1967 Las Vegas Can-Am event, when the McLarens were totally dominant. I was taken out there with John Surtees, one other mechanic, and a new Lola that turned out to be rubbish. Vegas was the last race of the Can-Am series and John decided to dig out the previous year's car from storage in LA, as he felt it was better. We spent about two weeks rebuilding it, took it to Vegas and won the race.

"The two McLarens failed and Donohue, driving the Penske car, was leading with one lap to go and we were second, quite a way behind. Donohue ran out of fuel about 300 or 400 yards from the chequered flag. We didn't know whether he was going to roll to a stop or manage to coast over the line ahead of John, and we were jumping up on the pitwall and waving John on, trying to make him understand that he had to keep going, which he did and won. That was probably the most satisfying one because of all that work. It was probably the most profitable race to win, too. It certainly was at that stage of my career, anyway."

Former Tyrrell mechanic Neil Davis has no doubt about his personal highlight. "The 1968 German Grand Prix at the Nürburgring, when Jackie [Stewart] won by four minutes. They should never have started the race. Normal people would not have run a race in those conditions. How the drivers drove, I don't know. You couldn't see a hundred yards down the road, it was absolutely amazing. It took around 10 minutes to do a lap in those days; he came past and Ken [Tyrrell] looked at me and said 'There must have been a big shunt,' because it seemed a long time before anybody else came round. After that, his lead extended every lap until it was four minutes. Really incredible."

His former colleague, Roger Hill, who was Tyrrell chief mechanic, says that nothing beats the feeling of winning, particularly taking the world title. "Winning the championship, I used to like that, being involved in winning any race."

For BRM mechanic Peter Bracewell, wins did not come along often, particularly in the latter days of the company, so for him it was easy to pick his favourite. "Winning Monte Carlo in 1972 with Beltoise. It was very wet. I was working on Peter Gethin's car and he crashed. The previous Grand Prix was at Jarama, and afterwards we did a bit of testing, stayed in the garages and rebuilt the cars ready for Monte Carlo. Then we drove round from Jarama to Monte Carlo. I did quite a lot of work on the car that Beltoise was driving, which won the race."

... and the lows

Not surprisingly, the lows recalled by mechanics mainly concern drivers being killed in accidents, because they tended to get to know them very well, so it affected them personally, as Tony Robinson relates. "The downside was when you became very friendly with the drivers and they were killed. That was not very pleasant, a bad downside."

The death of François Cevert was particularly shocking, because the Frenchman was universally loved and admired throughout the racing world. For Neil Davis, Cevert's death was the lowest point in his career. "Losing François at Watkins Glen: you don't know what to say, what to do, you are in a trance, really. We had to pack up the car in a box and bring it home; it was pretty awful. We didn't race because Ken withdrew the cars, and it was a pretty miserable time for everybody. It was Jackie's last race, too. That was terrible, very sad."

Roy Topp also identifies that day as the nadir of his career. "That was so sad, you

couldn't describe it, unbelievable, definitely the lowest point, one of the worst moments I can remember. Two years before when he won the Grand Prix, he gave us all a little gold medal because his family had a jewellery business. It had a picture of him in the Tyrrell with his hands in the air."

For Hughie Absalom, his darkest day came with Team Lotus at Indy in 1968, when Mike Spence hit the wall at Turn 1 during unofficial testing, and died. "I was with Mike that day. We were looking after his car. He went out and drove the Granatelli

Cevert: His death came as a terrible shock to everyone in the paddock, and was a low point for everyone involved in the team. He is shown here at the wheel of Tyrrell 002, at the 1972 Belgian Grand Prix, with Roger Hill (kneeling) and Roy Topp in attendance. (Roy Topp)

car [another Lotus 56 turbine], and that was what he was killed in. We were all there when it happened, so that was not very nice. I think if Spence hadn't been killed he would probably have won that race because he was flying."

Alan Challis, former chief mechanic at BRM, remembers the non-Championship Victory Race at Brands Hatch in 1971, when Jo Siffert lost his life, as a particular low point, which led to at least one of his mechanics quitting. "The day Seppi died. There's no doubt that it affected the mechanics concerned. I didn't think of stopping but the lad who was number one on that car actually did quit."

Second to the impact of loss of life was the tremendous toll on mechanics' personal lives due to the long, irregular hours they worked, as Tony Robinson explains. "Eventually, most people in motor racing end up divorced because of the unsociable hours you work. Certainly amongst racing drivers, most of the friends I know, are on their third wives. I divorced, partly because of the lack of time that I was at home, I was forever living out of a suitcase. In 1960, I was married in May, went to Monte Carlo for the race, took the new wife with me and worked every night."

Stan Collier recalls that the hours were particularly savage for teams which built their own cars, rather than running customer chassis. "When we were building cars, you would go there in the morning and return home at 11 o'clock at night; it was like that for a couple of years, non-stop, we didn't have holidays or anything. Even when you returned from a race meeting, if there was any damage, that had to be repaired. We used to do our own engines and gearboxes, too, so it was a lot of work."

As Ray Wardell explains, it seems nothing could prepare wives for the experience of being a 'mechanic's widow.' "It was very difficult. I tried to demonstrate to my wife-to-be what it was going to be like by taking her to a few races, including going out to the States for two or three Can-Am races. I thought she understood what that life was all about but our marriage didn't survive."

For a close-knit team like BRM, which was based in the town of Bourne in Lincolnshire, the impact of absent husbands was reduced by the wives socialising together, according to Ben Casey. "My wife used to moan a bit because I was never at home. But as we all lived in or around Bourne, all the ladies used to gather together, so at least they didn't get lonely."

Dick Scammell agrees racing does mean that home life takes something of a back seat. "After 12 years with Lotus, I was at the stage where I was living out of a suitcase. By that time I was doing Formula 1 and Formula 2, and anything else that was going on because I was in charge of the team. I needed a month or so off but you can't do that in racing, so I had to leave. It put a big strain on the family, that's for sure. My wife was very understanding, I have to say. But racing makes you pretty selfish, really. I'm afraid unless you are a bit selfish, you aren't going to survive in it."

One way the impact of long hours away from home could be reduced was to fly mechanics to races, rather than making them drive the transporter there. Roger Hill remembers Ken Tyrrell as an early pioneer of this approach. "Ken's was one of the first teams to fly us to races, otherwise you never had any time at home. Ken used to try and make sure that you did, because a lot of guys had problems, a lot of broken marriages and all that crap."

In terms of races as low points, Dick Scammell is quite definite on the worst moment for him, although one other does run it close. "My lowest point was the Lotus turbines at Indy in 1968. We had it completely and utterly sewn up and the two lead cars failed within a lap of each other. The 1964 Mexican Grand Prix also took me a long time to get over, when Jimmy was going to win the Championship and it broke on the last lap. I was thinking 'I am going to wake up in a minute, this is not really happening.' I remember Colin [Chapman] saying to me, as we were walking down the pit lane after the race 'This is really character-building isn't it?' Actually, in a way he was pretty good at that. He could become very excitable when you made an error but if something happened that he thought was not particularly anybody's fault, then he was fairly reasonable; he was as disappointed as we were."

Their lives in our hands

Mechanics literally held the safety and lives of the drivers in their hands, and were often the very last people to talk to them before they went out onto the track.

Tony Robinson encapsulates the attitude of many who lived through an era when a shockingly large number of drivers lost their lives in racing accidents. "Quite honestly,

First time out: Nattily-dressed Lotus boss Colin Chapman looks on while Dick Scammell (kneeling) helps Graham Hill start the turbine engine on his 1968 four-wheel-drive Lotus 56 Indy car. He is being assisted by Pratt & Whitney engineer 'Flameout' Fred Cowley, while designer Maurice Phillippe (in suit and tie) looks on with the rest of the Team Lotus staff in the background. Scammell describes the failure of these cars in the closing laps of the Indy 500 as the lowest point of his career. (Dick Scammell)

I never thought about it at the time, although I did afterwards. When these accidents happen, you have things to do, so you have a sad moment but are so busy that you move on to the next race. It tends to affect you for a few weeks but, once they are buried, you tend to put it out of your mind, though you never truly forget. I remember them today, all of them, and it is sad. All the time it would run through your mind, wondering whether it was something you had or hadn't done. At the end of the day I have never really come across an incident where I've thought that it was a mechanic's fault. Maybe that's good in a way.

"With most of the accidents there has been a logical reason, other than a mechanical failure. There's only one mystery still outstanding and that is Stirling's accident in 1962 at Goodwood, which has never been fathomed out. Certainly we had no evidence at all on any of the deaths or injuries that they had been caused by a mechanical failure. If there had been one and it was proved, then it's a reason to be upset. As you grow older, you do wonder. But at least I can sit here now and say, thank goodness that none of them was down to me."

A consequence of being involved with a car or team where one of its drivers is killed is that mechanics can become more detached afterwards, as a defence against being hurt in the same way again, as Alan Challis explains. "The first person who died that I was personally involved with was Jo Siffert, and after that I tried to step back a bit. We'd had Pedro, who we were heavily involved with, killed in a Ferrari sports car, and Jo, and before that Mike Spence. All of a sudden you are thinking 'I shouldn't be too close to these guys' because it's there: every time you do the seat belts up and wave them down the pit lane, they might not come back. Before that, even though I was seeing other people being killed, it never really sank properly into my brain that it could happen."

Former BRM man Pat Carvath found the responsibility weighed heavily on him. "The worst thing about any motor race was the first ten laps. You thought 'If it's gone ten laps, we've done things right.' But you put a car on the starting line and think 'Christ, I hope I've done this and I hope I've done that.' Particularly when you are the mechanic in charge of the car – you used to have one on the engine and one on the gearbox but the chassis was a single mechanic's responsibility. It put years on me ..."

Some mechanics took a rather more pragmatic, detached view of drivers being killed, along the lines of 'It happens – but life goes on.' Tony Cleverley explains this attitude. "Whenever we lost a driver it was always a sad moment, but you had to get on with it. I was young enough to let it drift over my head and think 'Well, we've done our best and that's all I can think about.' Stan Collier, who worked with Cleverley later in his career at Rob Walkers, had a similar outlook. "It does upset you but you have to carry on. You have to say 'They knew what they were doing. No-one put a gun to their head to make them drive."

Dick Scammell was another to distance himself slightly from the drivers, and he also held the view that nobody made the drivers do what they did. "Firstly, I don't think I was as close to the drivers as some people. Secondly, I took a fairly hard view. Yes, it was very bad that they died but they knew what they were doing. I used to cope with it by carrying on with the job. There were several occasions when the only thing I could think of doing was what I considered to be the most sensible at the time. It happened at Monza in 1970 [when Jochen Rindt had a fatal accident in practice]. We knew that the first time round [Jim Clark's collision with von Trips in 1961] it had been very difficult so I said to the lads 'Right, let's pack up now and leave Italy as quickly as we can.

"It sounds very cold-hearted but that was the way it was. I was very sad about it, obviously, I was quite close to Jochen but I also thought that he knew what he was doing and we had to do the best we could in the circumstances. You do feel responsible, too, because, on occasions, it's not their fault, it is something you are associated with. With Jochen's accident I don't know what happened – maybe a front brake shaft did break, I don't think it was ever totally proven but it looked a bit that way – and although I didn't design the shaft, it was on a car I was associated with, therefore I did feel responsible. It is something that you try not to think about."

Arthur Birchall recalls that the way in which he and his fellow mechanics dealt with the death of Mike Spence at Indy in 1968 was to pay their respects and then go straight back to work. "I was out testing at Indy with Jimmy [Clark] a week before he died. Then I went back out to Indy in May and Mike Spence was killed on May 7th. That came as a hell of a shock. The way we dealt with it was that Jim Endruweit went out and bought four black ties, we went to a memorial service for him at the funeral parlour in Indiana, and then carried on with our work the following day. I believed I was fairly good at my job and that if I quit and they let some nutter work on the cars, there could be more of these accidents. I was very methodical. I don't think I had any failures or breakages that were down to me.

"The only time anything like that happened to me was when a wheel came off a Lotus Elan at Crystal Palace. The Old Man gave me a hell of a bollocking, but it was a common fault, the front wheel nuts coming undone on the Lotus Elan. He said 'I can fire you on the spot, or keep you, realising that you'll never leave a wheel nut loose again.' I don't believe that I ever did leave a wheel nut loose. Afterwards, we had quite a long investigation into why the wheel nut actually came off. It was a reverse taper, the Elan wheel nut locked up differently to a conventional knock-on wheel and the angles were slightly different. It only had to move very, very slightly and all of a sudden it became loose. They were modified after that."

The fact that mechanics were usually tremendously overworked could actually operate as a coping/insurance mechanism against the dangers of racing, as former March and Lotus mechanic Keith Leighton relates. "You never had time to think of the dangers. We had so much work to do. Nowadays, you have 12 guys to work on a car and it's a completely different atmosphere. In those days you had two people and probably two cars, so that when you'd finished your primary race car, you then had to go and change the ratios and do some other things on your spare car. To get everything done was all you could possibly do, and then you wouldn't even have time to clean your hands before practice started." Hughie Absalom is thankful that he never actually worked on a car someone died in, but believes that a mechanic can only do his best and that is all that can be expected of them. "You have to keep it at arm's length and get on with it. I can't imagine what it must be like for some of these guys that would have been working on the car that a guy was killed in. Fortunately, that never happened to me. You do the best you can and hope that everything is okay. You knew that you had a guy's life in your hands, but that's just how it was."

Gerry Hones agrees that the responsibility used to weigh on him but felt that it was important to speak out and make a nuisance of himself if there was something he was unhappy about. "I used to think about it all the time. All you can do is your best. If there is something that you don't like, you say you don't like it, and argue and make yourself unpopular, keep on. I never lost a driver." Neil Davis was another who felt the pressure to always do the right thing. "You were so conscious that, if you did something, it had to be done right, you had to be happy with it."

For some mechanics, the pressure proved too much and they either moved on to other positions within a team, or left the sport completely. Ray Wardell is one who found accidents involving his drivers profoundly distressing. "It is a bit of a sensitive subject for me. As a mechanic, I realised that I was responsible for every nut and bolt on the car, and accepted that responsibility; that part never really bothered me. I was fairly reluctant to become too close to drivers, because you were aware of what might happen.

"It did actually almost happen one day, when we were running Ronnie [Peterson] in the Formula 3 March in 1969. It was quite horrendous. The Montlhéry circuit had this banking and they tried to slow down all the cars by putting straw bale chicanes in. It was the very first lap and the field came down off the banking and braked into the chicane, right in front of the pits. It was late in the day and Ronnie went into that chicane in probably about sixth or seventh place, couldn't see the exit, and clipped the straw bales. The car somersaulted about five or six times, landed upside down and started to burn.

"I've always been amazed at my own reaction. I remember running to the car. There was no pit wall or anything and I was running flat out and absolutely no-one else was moving. I couldn't understand; why didn't somebody do something? There didn't seem to be any fire marshals, nothing. When I reached the car, I vaguely remember it being upside down and I think I pulled him out. What was strange was that the only thing that was burning on him was his shoelaces and he was out cold. After that, everyone else took over and I had a bit of a breakdown, I suppose. It was a strange feeling. Sadly, that affected the rest of my work. Because then the Formula 1 programme started and the next thing I knew we were at Zandvoort [for the 1970 Dutch Grand Prix].

"A car had gone off and all you could see out of the back of the pits was this incredible cloud of black smoke. I didn't know who it was at the time but, as it turned out, my car – with Jo Siffert – had stopped on the same lap with a blown engine. I didn't know it was the engine, I thought it was our car out there and that was it, that was the last time I ever worked on a car and I've dreaded fire ever since. Say what you like about [Jackie] Stewart and the pressure that was applied, but he did a hell of a good job in getting things changed."

Mike Lowman is another person who found, and still finds, that drivers being killed really affected him. "I used to think about it all the time, absolutely. I lost a lot of friends in motor racing in that period of time. I don't mind telling you I've sat in a paddock and cried. It still affects me. Hell, they were guys that I knew, who I'd had breakfast or lunch or had fun with, and then something goes wrong and it's all over. It grieves me. I become very emotional, I'm not one of those people who can bottle up all that stuff. The responsibility used to weigh very heavily on me."

For others, like former Team Lotus mechanic Steve May, superstitions and rituals were a way of managing their fears. "I was very superstitious. Emerson [Fittipaldi] has exactly the same birth date as me, although he is a year older. I used to have a ritual that I went through, before any of my drivers ever went out. I did the same thing every time and, 'touch wood,' not one of my drivers came to serious harm. The only time any of my drivers went to hospital was when Ronnie [Peterson] crashed at Zandvoort, in testing, with the Lotus 76."

Some mechanics never doubted their abilities, so did not think about the risks of things going wrong. Former Lotus mechanic Jim Pickles was very much in that camp. "I don't recall ever having doubted my own work. Maybe that is complacency but I didn't see it that way." The confidence of youth also sustained Bill Cowe, another ex-

Lotus man. "We were pretty young in those days, and I suppose with youth comes unbelievable confidence. I was far surer of myself then than I am now."

Former Tyrrell chief mechanic Roger Hill feels the most important thing was to learn from mistakes. "In motor racing, there are a lot of ups and downs, but it pretty well evens itself out. You mustn't let the downs affect you too much, otherwise you can't perform. If it is a problem with something that was done, or the way you prepared the cars, then you needed to learn that it wasn't what you should do, as quickly as possible. We all knew it was dangerous. They [the drivers] all knew what the score was, that's motor racing. Looking back it was crazy. It's still dangerous but it's nothing like it used to be. We lost more than one driver a year in those days, it was ridiculous."

Hill also feels that remaining calm, level-headed. and doing things in a consistent way is the key to avoiding mistakes. "You have to make sure that things are done how they should be. You can't send somebody out in a car that is not correct, not done properly, or not in a fit condition. We always tried to do everything exactly as it should be and if we were in any doubt about it, we spoke up to try and make sure that it was. We said to all the mechanics that worked for us 'What we want you to do, is to do what we want, not what you think you should do. If you have a problem with that, come and talk to us because we need to know.' Otherwise you have five different blokes all doing different things. We did a good job and it had to be right."

Bob Dance feels that good communication and teamwork and trust in your colleagues are paramount. "You have to have faith in the lads who are working with you and you have to have faith in yourself. The main dramas are when people are rushed and they panic. Mario [Andretti] was always extremely calm, and if he saw any panic developing he would want to tone it down a bit. The main objective was keeping cool, calm and collected, and then you are in charge of a situation. If somebody is trying to rush a driver out of the pits whilst others are battling to try and do up the wheels, you have to make sure that your job is done before you let them out. It is important to remain composed in all situations."

Alan Challis likens the burden of responsibility on mechanics to do a good job to that felt by the technicians who assemble large passenger jets – their work is vital but not always given the recognition it deserves. "I don't think any books I've read show how meticulous mechanics have to be, whether it is now or twenty-five years ago. The whole thing relies on the guys that put them together and the drivers rely on those guys. It is like putting an aeroplane together. We all happily jump on an aircraft and I wouldn't think one person out of the 400 on a jumbo jet thinks about the fact that somebody's bolted the thing together. By the time you are a Grand Prix mechanic, it is not as if you've just left school and not gone through the business. Nowadays, it is so engineer-orientated, but still down to the same type of people to hold the thing together."

11
Nuts and bolts

The life of a racing mechanic was rarely predictable, their place and conditions of work changing on an almost daily basis. Added to which teams like Cooper, Lotus, Brabham and McLaren operated in many different disciplines of the sport (Formula 1, Indy, sports cars, Can-Am, etc), so there was the opportunity to work on a tremendous variety of racing car types. During the 1950s, 60s and 70s, mechanics also moved between teams, often following a favourite driver or manager, and their experiences have produced a wealth of diverse recollections.

Cottage industry Cooper

Although Cooper benefited during the 1950s from pioneering the rear-engined format, firstly in 500cc Formula 3 cars, then later Formula 2 and Formula 1 versions, it was not a sophisticated set-up and, in later years, undoubtedly suffered from a lack of investment in facilities, as mechanic Mike Barney explains. "There was no equipment at Cooper at all. It wasn't until I moved to McLaren in the late 1960s that we were kitted out with any sort of decent equipment, machines or hand tools. We had nothing like that at Cooper. If you couldn't file it by hand in a vice, you couldn't make it, that's how it was. The Formula 1 team at Cooper used to make the whole car, build the chassis, father and son team Peter and Fred Bedding made the aluminium bodies in the corner, and it all came together. Climax supplied the engines and Jack Knight did the gearboxes. We made all the suspension and the frames, that sort of thing, so it was a lot of work. In those days, we used to start after the last race of the season, and work flat out until the following March, when we'd test the cars at Goodwood. It was incredibly hard."

A fairly consistent theme running through the Cooper years was of the

Cottage industry Cooper: The Formula 1 team at Cooper was based in this mezzanine level built into the rafters of its Surbiton factory, and reached via a precarious-looking walkway. (Ray Rowe)

innovative son, John, battling with his father, Charlie, to obtain approval for spending on projects. Barney feels that, left to their own devices, they probably wouldn't have been as successful as they were had it not been for the influence of Jack Brabham and competitor unreliability. "Charlie always used to stick his nose in and try and stop John spending. There were tremendous rows in the office upstairs because John had embarked on some expensive programme that it turned out Charlie hadn't approved. Their saviour was Jack Brabham. The Coopers weren't terribly good at communicating with the people that mattered, whereas they probably listened to Brabham because he knew what he was talking about. At the risk of being unfair to Cooper, the thing about the firm was it happened to be in the right place at the right time."

Fuji failure

In 1966 a group of Indy racers was invited to take part in a race at the Fuji Speedway

John Cooper (standing) and Jack Brabham proudly display Cooper's 1961 Indy car prior to departure to the fabled 'Brickyard.' (Mike Barney)

in Japan. The entry included 1965 Indy 500 winner Jim Clark in a works-entered Lotus 38 with a quad-cam Ford engine. Unfortunately, an incident on the last practice day before the race meant that Clark was unable to start. Lotus boss Colin Chapman, used to starting up the BRM H16 engines which the team had used in Formula 1 that year, forgot which engine was in the car and began revving the Ford, which needed much gentler treatment, with the result that the engine blew.

Arthur Birchall, one of only two Lotus mechanics who travelled to the event, recounts their epic efforts to try and salvage the situation. "Indy engines were very different. It took a long time to warm them up. He opened the throttle and that was it, it was all over. Mike Underwood was with me and we dismantled the engine in the paddock, and somebody went off to Tokyo to try and find the bearings for it. If we couldn't obtain those, we intended to try and run it as a six-cylinder instead of a V8, to try and earn the start money. But we were overtaken by time and lack of facilities. We had the engine three-quarters back together but couldn't fit it in the car before the race started, so that was the end of it. A formidable task but we gave it a go nevertheless."

Marvellous Matra

In the mid-1960s, the Matra aerospace concern entered motor racing with its acquisition of fellow French company Automobiles René Bonnet. Initially successful in sports cars, the marque expanded into Formula 3 and Formula 2, and really began to make headway when it linked up with Ken Tyrrell and Jackie Stewart. With its background in aerospace, Matra brought new levels of professionalism to the construction of racing cars, as former Tyrrell mechanic Neil Davis recounts. "Matra was fantastic. Its engineering was second

An early test of the Matra Formula 1 car, showing (left to right) Roger Hill, Neil Davis, Jackie Stewart in car, Ken Tyrrell and two unidentified Matra personnel. Hill feels this may be an interim car using a Matra MS7 Formula 2 chassis, and that the photo was taken at the Montlhéry circuit in France. (Roger Hill)

to none and everybody was in awe of the cars because they were so well made.

"I went to where the monocoques were built on many occasions, and there were rockets being manufactured alongside them, it was an incredible place. Brabham and even Lotus were not making cars to anywhere near the standard of Matra at that time."

Later, the Matra-Tyrrell-Stewart combination moved into Formula 1 and, in its second full season, secured the World Championship title in 1969. However, the determination to make an all-French Formula 1 contender compromised its efforts and lost Stewart's great talents, after which the team never really challenged for the Championship on a consistent basis again.

Lotus fragility

Looking back, former Lotus chief mechanic Dick Scammell is struck by the relative frailty of many of the cars he worked on in the 1960s. "I look at these cars and there is nothing of them. If you look at a Lotus 18, it is a tiny little car with a few tubes. We used to work night and day on it. You have to remember that there was only a lead mechanic and a helper on each car, and there was a lot of crack-testing to do in those days – everything was crack-tested the night before the race.

"Colin was forward-looking and the cars were built down to weight. Therefore, they needed a lot more checking than a well over-designed car. Some of the things we checked, the other teams didn't because they hadn't the need to. But the way the Lotus was at that stage, it was skinned down in places, which meant you needed to check things quite often."

When asked if he finds it hurtful that people often refer to Lotus racing cars as

Lotus racing cars were built down to weight and needed a lot of checking, according to Dick Scammell. Here, he works on Jim Clark's race-winning Lotus 25 in the tech shed at Watkins Glen in 1962, with Trevor Taylor's sister car just visible behind. Jim Hall's privately-entered white Lotus 21, number 25 – which blew its engine in practice and did not start – is in the background. (Dick Scammell)

always breaking, Scammell agrees he does. "Yes, it does hurt. It is people being wise after the event. My reply to them is, well, they may have been like that but, goodness me, they won a lot of Grands Prix didn't they? Some of the cars that didn't fall apart, didn't win anything. Sometimes the price of making progress is to push the frontiers a bit hard and Lotus was doing that with car design. The consequence is that you have more failures. It happens in all walks of life, it is not common to racing. I would say, look at the record."

The Eagle fails to fly

The 1968 season witnessed the evolution of wings on Formula 1 cars, led by Ferrari and Brabham. Grand Prix designers had been surprisingly slow to adopt this new technology, successfully used by Jim Hall's Chaparral team in the North American Can-Am series, and on the world stage with the 2F sports car that had won a round of the World Sports Car Championship in 1967 with a high, suspension-mounted rear wing.

Perhaps even more surprising, given he had raced against the Chaparrals in the Can-Am series, was Dan Gurney's failure to adopt any such structure on his Eagle Formula 1 car. When he belatedly did, as team mechanic Mike Lowman recalls, it was with a particularly unsophisticated device. "The Formula 1 car had a very rudimentary wing on the back. No-one ever went to wind tunnels to my knowledge, it was more a case of 'We'll make a section that looks something like this …' and we attached it to the exhaust mounting brackets.

"It couldn't have been developing too much downforce, or the brackets would have buckled. At the front we had little guide plates on the side of the nose." This failure to keep up technologically was symptomatic of the Eagle team's 1968 season and, at the end of the year, it withdrew from Formula 1. As Lowman explains, much of the poor performance was down to finance, or rather the lack of it. "Dan was trying to run three programmes with a very limited budget. One of them had to go and, unfortunately, it was Formula 1. After that, he concentrated more on the Indy cars and the tin-tops that he ran for Chrysler."

Sandbagging at Indy

Lotus came to Indy in 1968 with a revolutionary design in three different areas. Firstly, body shape was that of a door-stop in an attempt to harness the airflow over the car more effectively than the traditional cigar-shaped chassis. Secondly, it used a Pratt & Whitney turbine engine rather than the more conventional, naturally aspirated V8s or turbocharged Fords and Offenhausers. Thirdly, it adopted the Ferguson four-wheel-drive system proven by the previous year's STP-Paxton turbine car. The first public appearance of the 56 at Indy was in spring testing in March, where Jim Clark drove it, his last appearance at the Brickyard before his death.

Arthur Birchall recalls that, because of a court case taking place at the time, Clark was told by STP boss (and team sponsor) Andy Granatelli to take it easy. "I went out there when Jimmy tested that. He thought it was absolutely fantastic. Andy Granatelli told him to sandbag, it would have been banned had they realised how quickly it went." Birchall explains that the troubles they had in March would be the same as the ones that surfaced in the race itself. "We had the same problems with that car, with the fuel

What might have been: Less than two weeks before his death, Jim Clark poses at the wheel of the 1968 Lotus 56 turbine Indy car during initial testing in March. He was told to 'sandbag' due to a court case taking place at the time which could have seen turbines banned from the Brickyard, but even so reported that the car was 'fantastic.' (Indianapolis Motor Speedway)

pump, when it was testing with Jimmy as we did in the race. Granatelli wanted his STP gasoline treatment in the car, so we ran unleaded petrol with some additive, which didn't work. The JP4/JP5 jet fuel [as used in aircraft turbine engines] is self-lubricating, whereas petrol tends to wash away the lubricant.

Old versus new: The two doorstop Lotus 56 wedges pose alongside the more traditional Eagle-Offy. This is the front row for the 1968 Indy 500, and shows the pole-winning car of Joe Leonard (60), second-fastest car of Graham Hill (70), and third-placed qualifier Bobby Unser (3). (Arthur Birchall)

"We had the fuel pump pick-up break and I dismantled and repaired it. Then we had a quill shaft break. I actually made up one to do the job, which was a good strong one. The only car that had my quill shaft in for the race was Graham's, which he crashed. The other two had the Pratt & Whitney-modified quill shafts and they broke, both within a lap of each other." Leading with nine of the 200 laps remaining, initially Joe Leonard's first-placed car, then Art Pollard's seventh-placed machine, dropped out with the same problem. In order to accommodate the rear axle, the team had been forced to add a spacer between the engine and the fuel pump, and it was the extra shaft added to connect the two which broke on both cars, costing the team certain victory.

It was a particularly bitter pill to swallow after the tragic death of team driver Mike Spence in practice, as Jim Pickles recalls. "It was difficult to deal with, but there was a little bit of a feeling of 'We have to get on with it.' It affects people differently, of course. At that time it hit the Old Man [Colin Chapman] hard, and he virtually pulled out. It was [Team Lotus Competitions Manager] Andrew Ferguson really who virtually held us together and said 'Come on, we have to do something' and we did. We were in better shape than in 1967. I was a little more experienced, the cars were better, we were having proper sleep because the cars were behaving properly, and, of course, that doesn't half make a difference. Regardless of the retirement of the cars in the race, it was a bloody good year, even though it didn't come up trumps at the end."

Honda does Indy ... in 1968

Whilst Honda is, at the time of writing, the dominant – indeed, the only – engine supplier in the Indy Racing League, it is a little-known fact that a Honda engine first ran at Indianapolis as long ago as 1968. Denis Daviss, one of the mechanics for the team that year, describes the background to this clandestine visit. "I had a reasonably good time at Honda because the engineer who designed the Formula 2 engines used to travel with me by road, which was quite good because we'd stop and have a little party most nights. That was Mr Kawamoto, who became President of Honda. After the last race in Mexico, Mr Nakamura [the team manager], unbeknown to anybody within Honda, had decided he wanted to go to Indianapolis, to see how his Formula 1 car would run there. We used the car that had done the least work – which Jo Bonnier drove in Mexico – and it was sent down to Indianapolis on the back of a car transporter. Meanwhile, I nipped down there and waited for everyone to appear.

"When Mr Nakamura arrived, we altered the fuel settings. It was running petrol, and had come from Mexico, which is a high-altitude circuit, so we had to change all that. We tested for three days, round and round and round. John Surtees was there but he didn't come to the race track because he wouldn't have been able to drive the car, he'd have had to do a rookie test so they used [former Honda Formula 1 driver] Ronnie Bucknum." Bucknum ran laps, according to Nakamura's test report, of just over 158mph, but was restricted by strong winds and felt that, in better conditions, a lap of over 160mph would have been within reach. Additionally, if they had run methanol, it was estimated that laps of 162-164mph were realistic. This compares with Joe Leonard's 1968 pole qualifying speed of almost 172mph in the turbine four-wheel-drive Lotus 56, while the fastest 4.2-litre, normally aspirated engine (of A J Foyt) lapped at just under 167mph. When one considers that the Honda was just a 3-litre engine, its performance was quite impressive. The test would also have been one of the few times when a car with a high wing ran at the Brickyard. An intriguing technical exercise, and a case of 'what might have been;' ultimately, however, Honda would never compete at the Brickyard as a constructor.

Honda at Indy: Driver Ronnie Bucknum (left, with foot on rear wheel), George Moore (centre), a journalist with the Indianapolis Star newspaper, and Honda mechanic Denis Daviss (right) 'chew the fat' during the November 1968 Indy test. (Denis Daviss)

A rare photo: If you look carefully between Denis Daviss (left) and Goodyear tyre technician Chuck Randall (centre), you can just see the Honda RA301 flashing down the start/finish straight at Indy. Art Lamey from Champion Spark Plugs (right) looks on. (Denis Daviss)

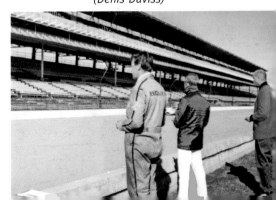

Life in the fast lane ...

Mechanics were never the best-paid employees of racing teams. Denis Daviss remembers two men who went on to be very successful in their own right but who literally lived on the breadline in the early years. "Jo Ramirez and Ermanno Cuoghi [who were working at Ford Advanced Vehicles in Slough at the time] used to share a house and come to work on a little scooter. One day, I saw Jo eating his lunch: two slices of white bread with a slice of brown bread in the middle."

The origins of Team Chamaco-Collect

During the 1966 season, a curiously-named privateer team, running a 2-litre BRM P261, entered Formula 1. Team Chamaco-Collect was owned by a wealthy individual called Bernard White, and ran his cousin, Vic Wilson, Bob Bondurant and Innes Ireland in the car at different times of the year. Roland Moate was a mechanic for the team and gives an insight to the source of the unusual name. "It was after a bullfighter friend of Bernard's from Marbella called Chamaco. Chamaco was the team name and Collect represented the prizes.

"We became mixed up with the *Grand Prix* film – that made us a lot of money. It paid for the car and another Ferrari as well. At each circuit, we sprayed it a different colour and put various bits on it to make it look like something else."

Crabbe's Cooper clincher

After the Cooper team, which the family sold to the Chipstead Motor Group in April 1965, finally closed its doors at the end of the 1969 season, the team's assets – including its Formula 1 cars – were sold off at auction. Peter Bracewell, who was with Colin Crabbe's Antique Automobiles concern at the time, remembers one particularly amusing incident involving his burly boss. "He went down and bought a Cooper-Maserati. He came in early the following morning to have a look at it before anybody else arrived. This was probably about 7.30am and we didn't start until 8.30am. It was still on the trailer, tied on, and he decided to sit in it, but then he couldn't get out again. He had to sit there until we arrived at 8.30, when we proceeded to take off all the bodywork to help him out."

How Mario finally won Indy ...

Eamon Fullalove was a mechanic on the works Lotus team at Indianapolis in 1969. However, when the team was forced to withdraw its cars following a machining failure that caused Mario Andretti to crash heavily in practice, Fullalove had the chance to switch teams with the American, who decided instead to drive a Brawner Hawk. It turned out to be a good move, as he recounts. "When Mario crashed the four-wheel-drive car, the Lotus 64, Andretti's team boss, Jim Magee, asked Colin if I could come onboard and help them just for the race, and he agreed. At the time, it was running a turbocharged Ford engine. After qualifying, we realised that it was running too hot for the race, so we put a radiator up by his head.

"We ran that radiator on Carburetion Day [a final practice session after qualifying has taken place, where the cars run in 'race day' trim] and everything was perfect. Then the organisers said we couldn't change the configuration of the car, it had to run exactly as it had qualified, and told us to take it off. That was on the Thursday before the race. We were in big trouble, because we knew there was no way it would run 500 miles. The Brawner Hawk had big side tanks on it for the fuel, and the seat tank was basically an

Mario's moment: With TV and press cameras following his every move, Mario Andretti rolls out to qualify for the 1969 Indy 500 at the wheel of the Brawner Hawk he switched to following his practice crash in – and the subsequent withdrawal of – his Lotus 64. He would qualify second behind A J Foyt and go on to win the race. Note the single nose fin for the 'left-turn only' Brickyard. (Eamon Fullalove)

empty cavity. Maurice [Phillippe, designer] decided to put a radiator in the seat back, a scoop on the bottom of the car, and let it exhaust out the back. We worked all night. Maurice drew up a few sketches and I made all the brackets, mounted it and plumbed it in. We started Friday morning and finished the night before the race, probably about nine o'clock. We didn't know if it was going to help or not, but it was the only option we had. It worked out fine and he won. Mario always credits me for that, he always remembers. The day after the race, we took the gearbox apart and it had about four or five teeth left on top gear. She was a 500-mile car and wouldn't have done two more laps."

Do it yourself

Another aspect of life as a mechanic in the 1950s, 60s and 70s was the amount of fabrication work they were required to do, as Neil Davis explains. "We did have spares, but sometimes you had to go down to the local blacksmith, find a bit of metal and make it yourself. Mechanics today are good guys but only do one area of the car, whereas we had two mechanics on each car and they did absolutely everything. If something was broken, they had to fix it. We used to carry a welding kit but if we wanted something a bit special done, we had to go and find it."

Track record   Eamon Fullalove

❝I applied to Team Lotus through an advertisement in Autosport and they took me on. I was 17 when I came over from Belfast and had been in London only about six months. My first job was looking after the truck but I also helped Allan [McCall] on the build of Jimmy [Clark's] car for the 1966 Indy 500, the one where Jimmy finished 2nd to Graham Hill, because there was no-one else to do it. While the race team were away, I'd learn to weld and machine things on lathes."

Eamon went to Brabham in 1968 to do Indy, then returned to Lotus briefly in 1969 when they ran the four-wheel-drive Type 64s, before switching teams to work on Mario Andretti's Brawner Hawk, which promptly won that year's race. He settled in Indianapolis, where he spent many years building race cars and doing general fabrication work. He is now back in the UK building monocoques and wings for historic racing cars.

Eamon Fullalove was just 17 when he joined Team Lotus. He is seen here (far right) a year later, at the 1967 Indy 500 with (from left) Arthur Birchall, Lotus boss Colin Chapman and Mike Underwood, with Jim Clark in the car. (Indianapolis Motor Speedway)

The mad March hares

The Bicester-based March concern arrived on the motor racing scene in a flurry of publicity, and with bold plans to service the Formula 1, Formula 2, Formula 3, Formula Ford and Formula B markets in its first year. However, behind the glossy exterior, Bob Sparshott remembers that, in the works, things were a little less organised. "All I remember is that it was a mass of airlines, wires and pipes all over the floor, and the stores in the corner. I say stores but, in fact, there were just loads of open boxes, nuts, bolts, jubilee clips, a sea of stuff, all over the place, because they were trying to build all their other types of cars as well [as the Formula 1 cars]. It was a hell of an undertaking."

The race after the race

Tony Reeson, who worked with the Antique Automobiles team in 1970 when it ran Ronnie Peterson in a March 701, remembers that, incredibly, they went through the whole year with one engine. "We ran a complete season, until the Austrian GP, with only one engine, which was on loan from March because Cosworth couldn't supply us with an engine. We were struggling all the way through."

His colleague, Peter Bracewell, explains that, after every race, for Cosworth customers there was another race that was as important as the one on the track: to return to the Cosworth works in Northampton to have the engines rebuilt. "After every race the engine was taken out and driven smartly to Northampton, because they used to be rebuilt in the order they arrived. It didn't matter whether you had one engine or two; if you were there first, you had your engine rebuilt and back before anyone else. Often it was a race after the race to travel back to base, pull out the engines and drive overnight to Northampton to be there for eight o'clock on the Monday morning, or, sometimes, as we only had one engine, we'd take it out at the circuit, put in a frame so that the car was still moveable, load it up and somebody nipped off with the engine, straight to Northampton."

Getting by, with perks

Given the long hours and often quite difficult working conditions, it is probably fair to say that money wasn't the main motivation for mechanics. However, when asked, most wouldn't have had it any other way. Gerry Hones is one. "Considering the hours you worked, the pay wasn't brilliant. You were away from home so much, but I worked at McLaren until I was 78 and it gave me a good living. When we won the World Sports Car Championship at Aston Martin, my bonus from that at the end of the year – we used to work for 10 per cent of the prize money – was £70. My wages at the time were £12 a week, so it was the equivalent of six weeks' wages."

Peter Hennessy reckons that, compared to what he would have expected to earn as a mechanic in a regular garage, the money wasn't too bad. "I'd say the pay was always above average. When I started in motor racing, my pay was on a par with the miners, and miners were always considered to earn good wages."

Dick Scammell remembers not having much to spend while 'in the field,' and the uncertainty of the somewhat ad hoc arrangements of Team Lotus. "We had a daily allowance but it wasn't generous, so any meal you could scrounge, you did. Sometimes you went to race meetings not knowing where you were going to keep the cars or where you were going to stay, which is not quite like today. But we survived."

When Tony Reeson was taken on by BRM in 1972, his wage was still relatively low but, as he pointed out, there were always other ways of increasing your income as a mechanic. "I was offered a weekly wage of £29, plus my share of the B team 10 per cent racing bonus. So it wasn't great money but, like politicians, we made money on expenses."

Tell it like it really is ...

There were obviously many occasions when mechanics' jobs were made considerably more difficult by driver error, but, more often than not, even if they thought that the driver could have done better, they rarely expressed their feelings to the drivers. However, former Lotus mechanic Jim Pickles remembers one occasion when the patience of one of his fellow workers snapped. "It was the 1971 British Grand Prix at Silverstone. The trucks for the supporting races, for saloon cars and Formula 3, were all parked on the Hangar Straight, while we were in the main paddock. We had done all our work during the morning and were quite well sorted. I said to Peter [Warr] that I was popping over to see how Ian [Campbell] was doing with the Formula 3 cars, because I did a couple of years on that team with him.

"Dave Walker [Team Lotus works driver] had been about to go out to start his race but, on the way out for the parade lap, somehow or other he'd pranged it. He had to turn around and go back, and Ian had to rush back to the truck. When I arrived there, he was frantically trying to do something because both right-hand rear radius arms were bent. I did what I could to help and we banged on a couple of new radius arms, screwing them out and in until we thought it looked right by eye. We had no time to do proper set-ups and sent him out like that. While we were doing that, Walker appeared rather apologetic and sheepish and said to Ian 'I'm sorry about that, is there anything I can do to help?' Ian was furious; he turned to him and said 'Bloody drive. You couldn't drive a greasy stick up a dog's a**e, now p**s off.'" Fortunately, Walker redeemed himself by winning the race ...

Tifosi troubles ...

The fervent patriotism of Italian racing fans is legendary. However, sometimes their efforts to ensure a home win went a little over the top, as Roy Topp recalls. "When we were at Monza with Tyrrell, in those days you all worked from the awnings in your trucks because the pits were only little boxes where you stored your fuel. They had all these buildings with tiled roofs all the way round which, somehow, a lot of Italians had climbed up onto and were tearing the tiles off and throwing them down, it was unbelievable. I don't think anyone was hurt. This was after one of the practice sessions. Jackie [Stewart] said to me 'Come with me and protect me' so I grabbed a jack handle. I thought 'What am I going to do against 50,000 Italians?' At Monza with the crowd, it was a bit like coaches or cars going through Longleat with the monkeys tearing bits off; they'd take anything they could. We made it through okay, which was good because I don't know what I thought I was going to do with that jack handle."

Driver psychology

Some drivers liked to make tiny changes to their car set-up, and this irked the mechanics who tired of their drivers' constant fiddling. Tony Reeson remembers how they would deal with it at BRM. "They'd come in at night and tell us which ratios they wanted changing, and [BRM gearbox man] Ben Casey would say 'Yeah, okay, we'll change that for you.' But the final decision was made by the team manager, Tim Parnell, and the bloke who was doing the changing. We'd say 'Look, it's okay but if the wind changes direction, or if it becomes windier, he's going to want to go back to these as soon as he starts.'

"So in the morning, they'd come in and ask 'Did you do it?' and we'd say 'Yeah, everything's done.' They'd come in to the pits and say 'That's a lot better,' whereas in fact, all these things were in the drivers' minds."

Bernie's blasting

Former BRM mechanic Roger Barsby was on the team when it won in the early 1970s, so the gradual decline of fortunes, culminating in its final embarrassing year as Stanley-BRM in 1977, was particularly frustrating for him. Fortunately, he did manage to find an unwitting victim on whom he could vent some of his pent-up anger. "My biggest claim to fame is telling Bernie Ecclestone to f**k off. It was when we were running the P207 that Len Terry designed. We were going to take it to Argentina in 1977, but when we reached Gatwick the crate wouldn't go in the hold of the aeroplane. We went back to Bourne and they said we'd do a little more testing and then go to Interlagos for the Brazilian Grand Prix. When we arrived and built up the car, we knew it was no good because we went testing in England in the winter and the bloody thing still boiled, so we had no chance in a hot climate.

"But Big Lou [team boss Louis Stanley] said 'Take it, it'll be alright.' We did a bit of practice but it was absolutely hopeless. In the race, the car did one lap before it came in to retire – due to overheating. There was nothing else we could do but begin taking it apart to put it back in the boxes again. Ecclestone [owner of the Brabham team at the time] came looking round the back of where we were working and asked 'What are you doing?' and I said 'Why don't you f**k off?' He went rushing off to Tim Parnell and said 'Tim, one of your mechanics told me to f**k off,' to which Tim responded 'Well, did you go?' And that was that."

Fan car flap

Stan Collier fondly remembers the Brabham-Alfa BT46B, the so-called 'fan car,' which won its one and only race in Sweden in 1978. "We took them to Sweden, did the race, which we won, and then it was agreed that we wouldn't run it any more. It wasn't actually banned. Bernie [Ecclestone, Brabham owner] had a gentleman's agreement that they wouldn't run it any more. I believe Chapman already had one on the way. They were no different to work on than the standard car. The fan was on the back of the gearbox, that's all, and it had skirts round the outside to achieve the suction effect. It worked well. But the trouble was that it picked up all the grit and stones which would wear out the blades on the fan. By the time the race was ended, they were virtually gone."

Bob goes flying

Although it is usually the drivers who bear the lion's share of risk in motor racing, occasionally, mechanics find themselves in danger, most often in the melee of the pitlane. Bob Dance was the victim of a freak accident one day, whilst testing with Ayrton Senna early in 1987, fortunately emerging relatively unscathed. "We had finished with Renault, and it was the first run for the Honda engine in a Lotus. This was at Donington, working out of the old collecting area garage at the end of the pits. We had exclusive use of the track, and Gerard Ducarouge [Lotus chief designer] was there with his Mercedes, parked in front of the pit area. I was on the phone to the works when the car went out on its first lap and caught fire in the engine compartment at the first corner. Gerard said 'Quick, quick, grab an extinguisher, let's go after it.' We went off in his Mercedes with an extinguisher but Ayrton didn't stop, he was still going round. He knew it was on fire but he was looking for a marshal's point and a fire extinguisher. He went three-quarters of the way round the circuit and stopped, more or less in the middle of the track, with the back end fairly well alight.

"I jumped out with my fire extinguisher and ran round the front of Gerard's Mercedes. The next thing I had taken off and was up the bonnet of this Rover fire tender car, which had come the wrong way round the circuit and driven through the thick smoke, not expecting to see anybody on the other side. They knocked me down and the impact cracked the windscreen. I took a bit of a whack though, fortunately, didn't break anything. Ayrton and Gerard sort of forgot about the fire and wanted to hit the marshals. Once the fire was out, that was the end of the day anyway, I was taken off to the Derby Royal Infirmary for a check-up and then PEW [Team Lotus Team Manager Peter Warr] sent an aeroplane to pick me up because he said I couldn't drive back after that. I was lucky, really ..."

How the job has changed

Alan Challis, who started with BRM in 1958 and retired from Williams F1 only relatively recently, is uniquely positioned to comment on how the job of a Formula 1 mechanic has changed during that time. "At BRM, once you became number one mechanic on the car, you and the driver virtually did it between you. The driver knew what he wanted – or you hoped he did – and you did it. As the years have gone on, it has become more engineer-orientated. The mechanic's job is to do more what the engineers tell him. The mechanics really don't deal with the drivers any more, certainly as far as set-up is concerned, although they'll work with the driver on cockpit comfort, and that sort of thing. But the engineering side of the car is not done by mechanics any more, not by the chief mechanic, even. Every driver has his own engineer, plus a couple of computer guys and his electronics people working with him.

"When I first started, the BRM race team had two cars, a bloke on each car, an engine man, a gearbox man, a chief mechanic and a truckie. That was the race team. Today, there are four mechanics per car; at least two electricians, at least one hydraulics man, and a sub-assembly man who looks after the gearboxes, the uprights and the brakes. I don't know how many truckies there are – probably ten. Truckies is the wrong word these days; they deal with all the pit equipment and refuelling gear, and that side of things. Plus a chief mechanic. All told, there will not be one team with fewer than 50 people at a race. It is a different beast, a multi-million pound exercise these days."

Multi-million pound certainly – even after budgets have been reduced – but whether it is more fun for the mechanics these days is questionable. Those who lived through the period 1950 to the end of the 70s will probably say not, and, after reading their stories in this book, I feel confident you will agree with them ...

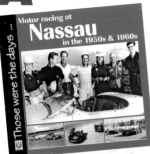

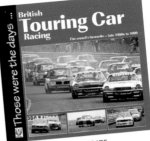

Index